chamomile

ginkgo

garlic

black cohosh

myrrh

rosemary

plantain

dill

EveryWoman's® Guide to
Ageless Natural Beauty

EveryWoman's®
Guide to Ageless
Natural Beauty

SALLY FREEMAN

BOOKSPAN
Garden City, New York

Published by GuildAmerica® Books,
an imprint of BOOKSPAN
401 Franklin Avenue, Garden City, New York 11530

EveryWoman's® and GuildAmerica® Books are registered
trademarks of BOOKSPAN.

The following recipes appeared in "The Housewife's Rich Cabinet"
exhibition catalog and are reprinted by permission of the Folger
Shakespeare Library: "For the Bath," "A Perfume for a Chamber,"
"A Sweet Bag To Scent Clothes," "How To Keep Hair Clean and Preserve
It," "To Take Away Sunburn," "To Kill Warts," and "Remedies for the
Hair When it Splits."

ISBN: 0-7394-1144-6

Although the information and guidance in this book are appropriate in
most cases, it is recommended that you consult your own dermatologist
or physician concerning your personal skin and hair care.

Jacket and book design by Vertigo Design, NYC

To my sons, Toby and Eben Freeman; my daughters-in-law, Celia Freeman and Rekha Menon; and my grandson, Kiran Menon Freeman; this book is dedicated with much love and great thanks for blessing my life.

Acknowledgments

NO BOOK EVER GETS WRITTEN AND PUBLISHED WITHOUT THE HELP of a number of people, including the professionals who make it happen and the patient friends and family who put up with writerly quirks and preoccupations.

Once again, I am fortunate to have GuildAmerica® Books as my publisher, Karen Murgolo as my editor, and Barbara Greenman as Executive Editor. I have never felt so pampered by a publisher or blessed with such exacting and creative editing. Thanks to Vertigo Design, and illustrator Chris Duke for another beautiful book, to Nora Reichard for a painstaking copyedit, and to editor Ruth Kogan for bringing it all together. As always, my thanks to literary agent Rita Rosenkranz for her warm support and wise handling of the business details.

The recipes in this book were tested on friends, not animals. None was more willing and encouraging than Linda Buck, who found time in her busy schedule to try out beauty products, undergo experiments that did not always turn out to be beauty treatments, and help me keep my spirits up. Thanks to Elizabeth Stewart for faithfully testing a range of cosmetic experiments and giving constructive feedback. My old friend Sharon Wolf, bless her, was my unofficial marketing consultant and my official and unfailingly supportive friend. Thanks to kindred spirit Judith St. Croix for her warmth, patient ear, wise counsel, and for surrounding me with art and beauty. I am grateful to Susan Cakars for years of seeing me through difficult projects, to Chris Erickson for her friendship and product testing, to Olga Melbardis for research leads, and to Jayshree Menon for Indian recipes. This book literally could not have been written by a cyberdummy such as myself without the advice, help, and expertise of my good friends and computer experts Patrick Yanez, Eric Herman, and Marcelo. Thanks also to Phyllis Giobbi, proprietor of The Herb Garden in Portland, Maine, for supplying me with high-quality herbs and helping me track down ones that were hard to find.

The New York Botanical Garden and the main branch of the New York Public Library were major research sources for this project. My thanks to the library staffs, especially to Stephen Sinon, head research librarian at the Botanical Garden, for invaluable help and suggestions. Thanks also to the Folger Shakespeare Library for cooperating.

Several people shared with me their considerable knowledge of cosmetics and skin care. I am grateful to Catherine Corkery, Ettia Tal, Carl Halpert, Trygve Harris, Martha Sanchez, Sydney Briscese, and Dr. Benjamin Kligler, and to Linda Buck for the gardening interview.

As with my earlier book, *Everywoman's® Guide to Natural Home Remedies,* New York City Technical College was an enormously helpful resource. Thanks to ESL instructors Kemala Karmen and Elaine Sohn for their cooperation, and the following participants in English as a Second Language classes for contributing a wonderful international array of recipes and home remedies for various skin and hair problems: Marie Lenine Dorlus, Elsa Sandoval, Barbara Henriquez, Candida Foster, America Hernandez, Marie Benoit, Wesner Moseaci, Lissa Exil, Mercy Espinoza, Francoise St. Louis, Zanellyz Parajon, Rosa and Vinicio Bermeo, Myriam Sanchez, Adel Almathil, Nidia Ceas, Jose O Pena, Jerry Celestin, Sonia Marte, Win Yee, Maria Trevino, Rosa Howard, Bessy Zelaya, Gilberte Jean Jacques, and Miguelina Mata Diaz.

CONTENTS

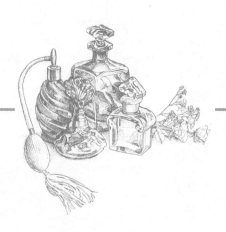

EveryWoman's® Guide to
Ageless Natural Beauty

CHAPTER 1

BEAUTY

A BRIEF HISTORY, INGREDIENTS
AND TECHNIQUES

W hat, exactly, is ageless natural beauty? The answer
depends on where in the world and when—which
century—you ask the question. Leaf through a
history of world art, or spend some time in one of the great
museums. What do Rubens's voluptuous nudes and Modigliani's

long-necked sylphs have in common? In many parts of the world, including our own not so long ago, the more flesh there was to clothe a woman's bones, the more desirable she was. Broad hips, an expansive girth, and generous breasts suggested ease of child bearing and suckling—a utilitarian beauty, you might say.

In other times and cultures, the ideal woman might be slender and childlike, gaunt and perhaps decadent, or trim with shapely muscles and a self-reliant gait. It depends on who is doing the looking. Men and women often have different standards of beauty, broadly generalized by Rubens's and Modigliani's femmes.

As you will note from the brief history below, "ageless" and "natural" have been part of the beauty equation only from time to time.

During the eighteenth century, when a smallpox epidemic swept Europe, few escaped its ravages. As a class, dairymaids were most likely to be exempt, many having been immunized by a bout with cowpox, a milder form of the disease.

Upper-class women, lucky enough to survive but not so lucky to avoid the pox completely, concealed their scars with silk, taffeta, or leather patches shaped like stars or crescent moons; whitened their complexions with powdered lead; and rouged their cheeks by rubbing them with Spanish leather. Eyebrows fashioned of moleskin replaced natural ones; massive hairdos, held together with lard, provided nests for lice and mice.

"In no other period has beauty been so artificially created," writes Fenja Gunn in her fascinating history of cosmetics, *The Artificial Face*. Much of the artifice, she reminds us, was a strategy that had evolved to cope with ill health and consequent loss of beauty resulting from unsanitary living conditions and personal hygiene that was, at best, casual. The early Christian missionaries had declared baths an evil vanity. As a result, people of both genders doused themselves with strong perfume and kept their hair short to discourage lice, then concealed their shorn tresses under powdered wigs.

This period ended with the French Revolution. By the nineteenth century, artifice was out and the natural look was in. The ideal woman was pretty, slim, and feminine. She wore her hair in a simple coil and applied rouge and powder sparingly. Daily baths became the fashion; so did delicate perfumes. Cosmetics, now formulated to correct skin faults rather than conceal them, were often made at home of natural ingredients.

By midcentury, postrevolutionary simplicity had become rigid and formulaic. The ideal Victorian beauty, Gunn reminds us, had the childlike beauty of a china doll—all dimples, blushes, and ringlets. Her makeup was subtle and intended to leave her face looking natural. Painted women were regarded as vulgar, even morally questionable— an attitude that, at least as early as ancient Greece, had served to keep married women firmly in their place.

All that changed by the end of the nineteenth century when the great actress Sarah Bernhardt ushered in Edwardian sensuality by the shocking act of freshening her elaborate makeup in public. Women in the performing arts would continue to shape the concept of beauty throughout the twentieth century.

The ideal Edwardian face was voluptuous and rosy, framed by a mountain of frizzed curls, and crowned by a plumed hat. Pale skin, rigorously protected from the sun, would be the standard until after World War II, as it had been since the Middle Ages.

Aside from their pallor, however, about all that links the medieval woman with the Edwardian beauty is her gender. Married off to serve her family's business or political aspirations, the medieval woman was regarded as little more than a vessel for breeding offspring. Accordingly, all hair was plucked from her eyebrows and forehead to eliminate as much of her individuality as possible. The ideal medieval female, Gunn tells us, had small features, gray eyes, and red lips and cheeks accentuated by white face powder made of lead. This masklike visage remained the standard for several hundred years.

By the 1920s, makeup was used by women of all social classes to proclaim their liberation from Victorian conventions. Brows were plucked and shaped with an eyebrow pencil; the mouth was brightened with lipstick, a new French product that was eagerly embraced by the flappers. Men strenuously objected to this shocking embellishment, which made wearing it all the more fun. The older generation of women soon joined in.

Throughout the twentieth century, the American female face has, at various times, been plucked, powdered, and painted; or unadorned—frequently in direct opposition to the prevailing conventions of femininity. In the Victorian age, the freshly scrubbed, natural look indicated innocence and submission to the rigid conventions of the era. In the counterculture of the 1960s and '70s, the same fresh-scrubbed cheek, innocent of makeup, proclaimed rebellion: a reaction to all the June Cleavers wearing spike heels, pearls, and lipstick while vacuuming the living-room carpet.

Contemporary women are rediscovering the importance of healthy skin and the natural products that help keep it that way. Some of the chemicals that are added to face creams, shampoos, and body lotions are irritants; a few, particularly deodorants and hair dyes, are suspected carcinogens. Buying "natural" beauty preparations is safer, but there are no guarantees. The herbs so proudly advertised on the labels may be present in such tiny amounts that they might as well not be there at all. Smaller companies, especially cottage industries, may indeed deliver what they promise, but at a high price to the consumer.

The best way to make sure that what you are putting on your skin is pure and natural is to make your own cosmetics. And that, gentle reader, connects you to a tradition that started before recorded time.

Concocting your own face creams, shampoos, and fragrances is a magical and joyous process—a pinch of this, a stir of that, and you end up with something unexpected that feels and smells better than anything you could buy in a store. The process is neither lengthy nor difficult. The longest you will spend on any recipe in this book is an hour, and about half of that time is spent waiting for an infusion to be ready or a wax mixture to melt or cool. As for special skills required . . . if you have ever melted a square of chocolate, you know how to melt beeswax. If you know how to make a hollandaise sauce, you can make a face cream—like the delicious sauce, face cream is essentially an emulsion. As with cooking, your cosmetic-making skills improve the more often you use them. And—again like cooking—depending on the time you have available and your inclination, you can whip up something easy, quick, and simple, or try a more challenging recipe.

The recipes in this book were created in rural Maine from ingredients gathered from the pantry, home-grown or foraged, or ordered over the Internet. See the appendix for details.

As for ingredients, some recipes are based on supplies you probably already have in your pantry. You might want to start with those recipes and then expand your repertoire as you build your stock of ingredients. Some, such as rosewater and certain vegetable oils, can be found in supermarkets. Beeswax, herbs, herbal extracts and essential oils are sold in health food stores or herbal outlets. When your herb shop doesn't carry a particular item, they will probably order it for you, especially if you are a regular customer. More recently, the Internet has proven to be a great source for finding natural ingredients. There are lots of sites from which you can order; some have been in business for years as brick-and-mortar stores and have already earned excellent reputations.

Below you will find information on some of the techniques and ingredients used in making cosmetics. If you are an old hand at cosmetics making, you may want to skip this section.

SHELF LIFE OF HOMEMADE COSMETICS

HOW LONG A PREPARATION WILL LAST DEPENDS MAINLY ON WHAT IT is and what it contains, how you produced it, and how you store it. How clean is your kitchen? Did you scrub, then sterilize your containers? For best results, scald everything you use, including countertops, cutting boards, blender, and other appliances and utensils. Perishable ingredients must be refrigerated until you are ready to use them. A hot, steamy kitchen, a humid summer day, or prolonged rain are not the best conditions for making products such as face creams and body lotions.

Preparations made with fresh fruits or vegetables can last from a day or so to a week if they are refrigerated. In general, products that do not contain water can last for several months. These include lip balms, hand salves, and solid deodorants. This is also true of products containing alcohol, such as spray deodorants, floral waters, colognes, and perfumes. Of the face creams, the orange aloe moisturizer lasts the longest—up to a year if unopened and refrigerated. Aloe is antibacterial and antifungal, so it discourages mold as well as bacterial contamination. Olive oil, as you probably know if you use it for cooking, keeps a long time without refrigeration. If the orange water you use contains alcohol, that, too, extends shelf life. The cream deodorant has a comparable shelf life due to the presence of aloe and also the clay, which absorbs moisture and impurities.

Most shampoos won't last longer than a week. Emulsions are, essentially, food; they're vulnerable to bacteria and mold. Face creams and body lotions that do not contain aloe are similar to edible products in their vulnerability to fungi and bacteria. Keep them cool and dry, preferably refrigerated, and they should last three or four weeks. Some, if refrigerated, can last for months.

Sunscreens, which contain antioxidant green tea and antibacterial aloe, can last a couple of months or more. Powders for the bath and face and other dry products can last for several months.

Storage conditions also determine shelf life. Dip into a jar of face cream with a dirty finger and keep the jar on a shelf in your steamy bathroom in the summertime, and you won't get more than a few days' use out of it.

Face masks are the most perishable cosmetic. Make enough for only one application and throw any leftovers away.

Natural preservatives extend shelf life. Gum benzoin, beloved of the Elizabethans, who called it benjamin, is widely available and excellent. Some contemporary natural cosmetics manufacturers use and recommend grapefruit extract.

TIPS FROM TRYGVE ON PREPARING TO MAKE YOUR OWN COSMETICS

TRYGVE HARRIS IS PRESIDENT OF ENFLEURAGE, AN AROMATHERAPY SHOP IN Manhattan's Greenwich Village. She creates sumptuous face masks, macerated oils, and body lotions, and sells them in her shop or through the mail, along with essential oils she imports from all over the world.

No matter how much fun you think you're going to have making your own cosmetics, when you shop for materials, don't overbuy. It's better to determine what you will use for one recipe and purchase only what you need.

Have everything ready before you begin, especially if you are melting beeswax, which can harden before you assemble your ingredients. Know which essential oils you will use and how much. If you are using more than one, make up your blend beforehand. Always add these last.

Make sure that you have enough—actually, you should have more than enough—sterile, or at least very clean, containers. Ones made of amber or blue glass, which shut out light, are best. Aluminum is okay for some things, but the metal may interact with certain substances such as acids. Use wide-mouthed glass or double-walled plastic jars—not narrow-mouthed bottles—for your creams and salves.

When adding vegetable oil to any mixture, pour it in slowly. If you are heating two or more oils together, the order in which you add them depends on how well they accept heat. For example, olive oil does well over high heat; hemp oil does not. Figure out which of your oils are least affected by heat and add them first. Olive, safflower, or almond oil can go in first; hemp, avocado, or comfrey oil last.

TECHNIQUES AND PROCEDURES FOR MAKING COSMETICS

Grinding Herbs

A blender or food processor may be adequate for grinding dried-flower petals and leaves. A spice mill or coffee grinder is best for pulverizing roots, seeds, and resins. Certain ingredients, such as frankincense, have a lingering aroma, and they can flavor the next batch of coffee beans you grind. The most practical way to avoid this is to use a separate grinder for your herbs and flowers. Otherwise, clean your grinder with a small brush—the ones sold for applying makeup work well—then wipe the bowl with a damp cloth and wash the lid. Manufacturers' directions don't usually cover herbs and flowers, so you will have to guess how long to grind them. If fourteen seconds of grinding does not reduce the plant to a powder, try again.

Infusions

To make an infusion, steep fresh or dried plant leaves in hot liquid. Most often the liquid is water. For cosmetics, distilled water is preferable because chlorine or minerals in tap water can affect your final product. Let the water boil for a minute or so to kill any bacteria, then let it cool for a few seconds before pouring it over the plants. Most cosmetics recipes call for a strong infusion—one to three tablespoons fresh or dried plant parts steeped for thirty minutes in a cup of water. To avoid spoilage, it is important to strain all solid particles from the infusion. The filter paper you use in your coffeemaker will do the job.

Seeds and roots need to be boiled to release their properties. Simmer them gently in a glass or enamel pan for ten to thirty minutes, depending on the recipe.

Many recipes call for an infused oil. The best results come from using the slow method: place fresh or dried plants in a clear glass jar with a tight-fitting lid. Cover the plant with oil. To avoid moldering, be sure the plant is completely submerged in the oil. Place the mixture on a sunny windowsill for a couple of weeks, and shake daily. You might want to make several infusions at one time so you will have a variety of infused oils on hand when you need them.

If you need an infused oil right away, place the herbs and oil in the top of a glass or enamel double boiler. Bring the water to a boil, then lower the heat so the water is simmering. The oil should be warm enough to draw the active ingredients from the plant, but not so hot that it cooks them. Consult the recipe for how long to infuse the oil.

Emulsions

Most face creams, cream deodorants, and body lotions contain oil and water in one form or another. The trick is to get them to emulsify. First you add lecithin, a vegetable gum, or resin to help bind these two incompatible substances together; then you employ a mechanical process to reduce the fat or oil to minute particles that will remain suspended in the watery liquid without sinking to the bottom. In days of yore, the latter was accomplished by prolonged stirring, preferably in a chilly room—not an occupation for the faint of wrist. This procedure could take hours, and the marriage of water and oil, unlike the miracle at Cana, might turn out to be no more enduring than a one-night stand. Indeed, if Galen's cold cream were truly produced by the great doctor himself, it's a wonder that he managed to get anything else done. Nowadays we can make an emulsion in seconds with a ten-speed electric blender.

The secret to an emulsion is to have all of your ingredients at room temperature (see Trygve's advice on pages 6–7). Oils should be heated very carefully so they won't burn. If you are infusing herbs in hot oil, you want the herbs to steep, not cook! A double boiler does the job very nicely. Most herbalists prefer glass because it is nonporous and nontoxic, and it allows you to see what's going on at all times. The ideal surface for heating waxes and oils is one that gets very warm but not superhot, such as an old-fashioned woodstove or a modern burner-less range.

If you are working with beeswax, add the cooled oil and wax mixture when it becomes thick and opaque but is still a liquid. If a skin of wax forms over the mixture before you get to use it, simply stir it back in. If the wax hardens, remelt it.

Pour the water (e.g., aloe, infusion, etc.) into the blender, then operate the machine at its highest speed. A high speed is crucial; for this reason, a food processor won't work. Add the thickened oil steadily. It will be too thick to flow in a stream, so you will have to guide it into the blender jar with a rubber spatula. You will know that your cream or lotion has emulsified when the motor slows down and sputters. At this point, with the motor still on, carefully scrape down the sides of the blender jar with the spatula. Some blends—a cream deodorant containing clay, for example—may take a bit of prodding and coaxing with the spatula before the ingredients unite. Once they emulsify, leave the blender on for another thirty to sixty seconds until your emulsion is smooth, glossy, and the consistency of thick dairy cream.

Pour immediately into sterilized glass jars. Face creams and body lotions, because they contain water, are vulnerable to bacterial contamination, so your hands, utensils, kitchen, and ingredients must be scrupulously clean. A cool, dry room is your best working environment. Allow the cream to cool thoroughly before you screw on the lid; otherwise, the condensation from a warm mixture may collect on the inside of the lid and degrade your product.

Your cream will last longer if you store it in the refrigerator. Heat, moisture, and bacteria can cause your emulsion to separate and/or turn rancid. A steamy bathroom provides an ideal climate for microbes to proliferate, so don't keep any homemade cosmetics there. When you scoop cream from a jar, wash your hands first or use a cosmetic spatula so you won't introduce bacteria.

Unlike lip balms and solid deodorants, which can be made in small quantities, you need at least a cup of emulsifying material in a thirty-two-ounce blender jar to mix properly. It is possible to work with half that amount, but to get it to emulsify you must repeatedly stop the blender, scrape down the sides of the jar, and mix it with the other ingredients. After repeating the process for a few minutes, you can coax the ingredients into mingling, but it takes a lot of work and time, and it's hard on the blender.

Supplies and Ingredients

You don't need fancy equipment to make cosmetics. People have been making excellent ones for centuries with nothing more high tech than a pot or kettle, an open fire, plants that grow in the local countryside, and perhaps some beeswax and animal fat.

All the equipment you need is probably already in your kitchen: a double boiler; a saucepan or two, preferably made of glass or enamel; a wooden spoon; a whisk; a grater; a good knife or two; a chopping block; a coffee or spice grinder; a high-speed electric blender; perhaps a mortar and pestle; and lots of clean glass containers with screw-tops or tight-fitting lids.

As for ingredients, an annotated list appears below. Some of the basics—culinary herbs and spices, honey, olive and other salad oils, cornstarch, baking soda, salt, oatmeal, rice, cornmeal, possibly bran and barley, and certainly fresh fruits and vegetables, you most likely have on hand.

Some things that you will need to buy include beeswax, an essential oil or two—lavender and rose are good for starters—castile soap, rosewater, and orange-flower water. Your basic herb collection might include rosemary, rose, lavender, chamomile, orris root, stinging nettles, alkanet root, peppermint, calendula, gum benzoin, aloe vera, green tea, and witch hazel. If you garden, you probably have much more.

Below is a list of the ingredients used to make recipes in this book. All of the unusual ones can be ordered over the Internet. See the appendix for suppliers. (The exception is orange water. If you find an Internet source, please let me know.)

ALKANET ROOT (*Alkanna tinctoria*) A blue flower native to the Mediterranean. Since antiquity the root has been used to redden the lips and cheeks. It contains a beautiful red dye. It is one of the few roots that gives up its color in oil—from rose to deep red and reddish brown, depending on how much you add and what other ingredients you use.

ALLSPICE (*Pimento dioica*) So-called because the scent is a combination of clove, juniper, black pepper, and cinnamon, allspice is a member of the pimento family. It gives beige to brown tone and spiciness to face powder and lasting scent to dusting powder and after-shave lotion. The essential oil is used in Eastern perfumes.

ALMOND (*Prunus dulcis*) The pulverized nuts make a gentle exfoliant. Almond oil is light; stays fresh for a long time; and soothes, softens, conditions, and nourishes the skin. It does cost a lot, however, and other oils are equally effective. Use it to remove eye makeup and add to face creams. Massage therapists like it because it is light and allows for an easy glide.

ALOE (*Aloe vera, Aloe barbadensis*) The gel of this plant, native to the desert and tropics, is astringent, demulcent, antiseptic, and antifungal. It heals burns, smoothes wrinkles, deodorizes, and treats athlete's foot and other fungal infections. Use in face cream, body lotion, and shampoo. You can buy it dried or bottled, but fresh is best.

ANGELICA (*Angelica archangelica*) The distilled root is used to make a fragrant toilet water; it is also added to soaps and perfumes as a fixative.

ANNATO (*Bixa orellana*) A carotenoid in the seed of this South American shrub gives orange color to body paint, cheese, margarine, chocolate, soaps, and lipstick. One of the few plants that gives up its color in oil. Look for it in supermarkets and Hispanic grocery stores as well as herb outlets.

APPLE (*Malus* spp.) Good for oily skin. Use in a face mask combined with oats and barley. Apple juice and malt vinegar in a hair rinse are said to give golden highlights.

APRICOT (*Prunus armeniaca*) The ground seeds can be used as an exfoliant, the crushed fruit in a face mask for dry skin. The oil, used in face creams, is expensive.

ARNICA (*Arnica montana*) The small yellow flower of this mountain plant is used in Europe for sports injuries. Excellent with rosemary, makes a soothing massage oil for aches and pains.

ARROWROOT (*Maranta arundinacea*) The powdered root of this Caribbean plant is used in tooth powder and dusting powder. It helps moisturizers penetrate the skin.

AVOCADO (*Persea americana*) Rich in lecithin, vitamins A and E, and protein, the buttery green flesh of this tropical fruit tones and moisturizes dry and mature skin. The oil is antioxidant, nourishing, and penetrating. It heals scaly skin and scalp, softens tissue, and regenerates cells. Add last to a blend that is to be heated; does not do well over high heat. (Don't throw the peel away—rub the pulpy side over your face for a quick moisturizer.)

BALSAM OF PERU (*Myroxylon balsamum*) Aromatic tree that grows in El Salvador. A resin with a vanilla-like scent is collected from the trunk, used in shampoo to moisturize hair and give it body. The essential oil is used as perfume fixative and added to soap for creamy lather.

BALSAM OF TOLU (*Myroxylon balsamum* var. *pereiae*) From a tree related to balsam of Peru. The uses are similar, but the scent is more subtle.

BANANA (*Musa paradisiaca*) Mashed green banana applied to a wound helps stop bleeding. Ripe banana in a face mask moisturizes dry skin almost as well as avocado. For blemished skin, mix near-ripe fruit with yogurt and apply as a face mask.

BARLEY (*Hordeum vulgare*) This cereal grain has little gluten, so it is not sticky. Use in face masks, dusting powder, and as dry shampoo. Heals blemishes, soothes irritation, and softens roughness.

BEE POLLEN Rich in protein, vitamins, calcium, and other minerals, bee pollen is available dry or fresh. The latter is preferable. Mash it in a mortar and add to face cream, body lotion. Renews skin. Excellent in antiaging cream. May cause an allergic reaction in sensitive people.

BEESWAX Beige to white, extracted from honeycomb, beeswax has the fragrance of honey. Used as an emulsifier and thickener, it provides creamy to solid texture to face cream, body lotion, salve, lip balm, solid deodorant, and other cosmetics. You can buy it granulated or in a solid block. May cause an allergic reaction in sensitive people.

BENZOIN (*Styrax benzoin*) Sometimes called ben or benjamin, the resin comes from a tropical tree or shrub. A perfume fixative, both the essential oil and resin emulsify and preserve. Use in creams, lotions, dusting powder, and other fragrance items.

BERGAMOT (*Citrus bergamia*) The oil from the peel of this citrus fruit is antiseptic, astringent, and deodorant. Add to face mask for acne, to shampoo and rinse for oily hair, to deodorant. Frequently used in perfumery. Can make skin sensitive to sunlight.

BORAX (*Sodium borate*) A white mineral found in South America and the American Southwest, borax is used in soaps, cold cream, and bath salts. Science writer Ruth Winter warns of possible toxicity.

BOXWOOD (*Buxus sempervirens*) A shrub that grows in Europe and America. Contains buxine, which stimulates hair follicles. A decoction of the evergreen leaves and wood shavings, rubbed regularly into the scalp, supposedly restores hair. Use with care and only on healthy, unbroken skin.

CALENDULA (*Calendula officinalis*) Also known as common or pot marigold, this sunny orange flower soothes and heals. Good in baby oil, baby lotion, and baby powder, and in creams and lotions for sensitive skin. Contains salicylic acid. Apply the fresh juice to banish warts.

CARAWAY (*Carum carvi*) The aromatic seeds can be used in soaps, sachets, and sunscreen.

CARROT (*Daucus carota*) Rich in beta carotene, grated carrot in a face mask soothes, softens, and clarifies skin.

CASTILE SOAP Formerly made of pure olive, now a blend of olive and coconut or jojoba oils, castile soap is sold as a bar or liquid. Mild and gentle, use as a base for shampoo, face, and body cleansers. It lathers even in hard water.

CASTOR OIL (*Ricinus communis*) The only oil that will dissolve in alcohol, this oil from a tropical or desert shrub constitutes up to 65 percent of most lipsticks. Extracts color from alkanet root so it stains lips. Add to soap to moisturize and harden.

CHAMOMILE, WILD OR GERMAN (*Matricaria chamomilla*), Roman chamomile (*Anthemis nobilis*) Use in shampoo and hair rinse to bring out blond highlights; in skin freshener, face cream, and body lotion to soothe irritated skin. Possible allergen.

CITRONELLA (*Cymbopogon nardus*) An Indian grass with a scent similar to lemon grass, citronella is often used in perfumery. It is also a very effective insect repellent.

CLAY Powdered rock containing silica, aluminum, iron, calcium, magnesium, zinc, and potassium. In a face mask it draws out oils, cellular debris, dirt, and toxins as it dries. For dry skin add oil or honey to the mask to moisturize. Use white clay for sensitive skin, green clay for oily. Clay is also used in masks and deodorants. Fuller's earth, or bentonite, is a brown clay—the fossil remains of tiny organisms on the ocean floor.

CLOVE (*Eugenia aromatica*) Essential oil from the clove bud or leaf adds spice and richness to perfumes. Blended with lavender oil, it gives a new and different scent. Clove is a skin irritant, so use with caution and very diluted.

CLOVER, RED (*Trifolium pratense*) Red clover infusion soothes chapped skin and softens and brightens oily hair. Use in shampoo, face cream, and body lotion. May cause sensitivity to sunlight.

COCONUT OIL (*Cocos nucifera*) Solid at cool room temperatures, liquid in hot climates, this oil comes from the fruit of the coconut palm. In the tropics where coconuts grow, the oil is rubbed into the scalp and hair as a hot-oil treatment to make the hair strong and glossy. A moisturizer, coconut oil is added to skin cream and lipstick. For increased lather, it is also added to shampoo. Use sparingly—too much coconut oil is actually drying.

COMFREY (*Symphytum officinale*) The stout leaves and root of this wild plant contain allantoin. This chemical has remarkable healing and regenerative properties. Excellent in antiaging cream. However, comfrey is also toxic to the liver and not for internal use.

CORIANDER (*Coriandrum sativum*) The essential oil smells sweet and spicy and is used in spice blends. The powdered seed mixed with honey is said to heal boils. Nice in after-shave lotion.

CORNFLOWER (*Centaura cyanus*) Also called bachelor's button, the lovely blue flower of this old-fashioned garden plant yields a blue dye.

CORN SILK (*Zea mays*) In bath or face powder, it makes the skin feel silky. You can buy the dried silk or save and dry your own.

CUCUMBER (*Cucumis sativus*) Cooling and astringent, sliced cucumber is a traditional remedy for puffy or irritated eyes. Blend a chunk of cucumber with yogurt for an instant antiwrinkle cream.

EGG A face mask of beaten egg whites is astringent, corrects oily skin, and heals acne. Applied to the hands, beaten egg white is said to heal chapping. The yolk is a moisturizer and rich in lecithin. Use in a face mask for dry skin, add to shampoo to make the hair strong and glossy.

ELDER (*Sambucus nigra*) Elder blossoms have been used for centuries to heal, soften, and whiten skin, and to smooth wrinkles. Used in a face mask, elder flowers are said to dissolve accumulated sebum and clean out clogged pores. Repeated applications of elderberry juice is said to kill warts. Use in face cream, shaving cream, and after-shave lotion.

FRANKINCENSE (*Boswellia sacra*) Since antiquity this resin, gathered from the trunk of an African tree, has been burned as incense in religious ceremonies. The scent is earthy, heavy, sharp, and penetrating. The essential oil is recommended for aging skin. Perfumer Edith G. Bailes writes that frankincense and myrrh, "when melted together in sweet oil and painted on the skin, would remove unwanted hair when the dried mixture was peeled off." The resin works well in face masks, especially the paraffin mask; when added to creams and lotions, it causes the mixture to spoil.

GARLIC (*Allium sativum*) Antiseptic. Rub a cut clove over the skin to heal acne.

GERANIUM (*Pelargonium* spp.) The scent of the essential oil is similar to rose, and like that flower, blends with almost all other scents.

GINKGO (*Ginkgo biloba*) The herb known as ginkgo is composed of the leaves of the maidenhair tree. Native to China, ginkgo is an antioxidant, scavenging free radicals that cause cell and tissue damage. Ginkgo also stimulates circulation. Use it in antioxidant and antiaging creams and lotions.

GLYCERIN A sweet, heavy liquid obtained by distilling animal fat, glycerin has a range of cosmetic and industrial uses. It is soluble in alcohol and prevents water from freezing. It is used to extract aromatic and medicinal substances from plants and to preserve fats. Glycerin is antiseptic. It softens the skin and helps it to hold water. Paradoxically, it also draws moisture from the skin, so don't use glycerin products if you have dry skin. Add to soaps, including shaving soaps, and freshener for oily skin.

GRAPEFRUIT (*Citrus paradisi*) The essential oil, pressed from the peel, blends well with spicy scents, patchouli, and sandalwood. Grapefruit seed extract is used to preserve natural cosmetics.

GUM TRAGACANTH (*Astragalus gummifera*), also known as "gum dragon," is a resin extracted from the root and stem of a spiny shrub. It is slightly acidic, and makes a soft paste that softens, emulsifies, and keeps cake makeup and eye shadow together.

HAZELNUT OIL (*Corylus* spp.) A slightly astringent oil that can be added to deodorants and preparations for oily skin.

HENNA (*Lawsonia inermis*) The powdered leaves of this African and Middle Eastern shrub are used to dye the skin and hair. Neutral henna gives hair reddish highlights. The addition of other plants creates a range of colors, blond through black. The color lasts for about six weeks.

HIBISCUS (*Hibiscus rosa-sinensis*) A deep red tropical flower. Applied as a hair pack, hibiscus brightens and softens dark hair, and stimulates hair growth.

HONEY Moisturizer, skin softener, antibacterial, emulsifier. Added to face and body lotions, honey soothes, heals, and nourishes. Use in a face mask to moisturize dry skin; add a small amount to soaps and shampoos.

HORSERADISH (*Armoracia rusticana*) Slice the root, boil it in milk, and apply to blemishes. Horseradish stimulates circulation and is antiseptic and healing.

HORSETAIL (*Equisetum arvense*), also called shavegrass, is a primitive, jointed plant that somewhat resembles asparagus. An infusion strengthens and nourishes the skin, hair, nails, and bones. Add horsetail to shampoo to repair damaged hair, to fingernail soaks to strengthen nails. It soothes irritated skin and heals blemishes.

INDIGO (*Indigofera tinctoria*) The powdered leaves of this tropical shrub make a black hair dye that was popular before chemical and more toxic ones replaced it.

JASMINE (*Jasminum officinale*) Native to Iran, the white blossoms have a very sweet fragrance. They yield an essential oil used in most great perfumes. Good in face creams and body lotions for dry, sensitive, or mature skin.

JOJOBA OIL (*Simmondsia chinensis*) A small California tree or shrub that yields a soft wax which is similar to spermaceti—a waxy substance from the head of a sperm whale—and sometimes used as a substitute. Recommended for all types of skin, especially mature and dry, jojoba oil also resembles sebum. It softens and moisturizes, helps prevent oil buildup on the scalp.

KIWIFRUIT (*Actinidia deliciosa*) Rich in vitamin C, magnesium, and a meat-tenderizing enzyme, this emerald tropical fruit softens skin, helps dissolve dead skin cells, and banishes cellulite. Added to a shampoo or hair pack, the mashed or juiced fruit softens and conditions dry or damaged hair.

LADY'S MANTLE (*Alchemilla vulgaris*) Native to both tropic and temperate zones, this wild plant of the uplands has scalloped leaves that make an infusion recommended for troubled skin. Applied to the face, it is said to keep the skin young-looking; rubbed on the breasts, it supposedly firms them.

LANOLIN Oil from sheep's wool, similar to human sebum, lanolin is readily absorbed and moisturizing. Available in cream and liquid form, it is an excellent addition to hand and body lotions. May cause allergic reaction.

LAVENDER (*Lavendula officinalis*) Fragrant lavender was originally used to scent soap. English lavender is preferable to the French variety. It blends well with clove, rose, and patchouli. Steep the dried blossoms in vodka to make a fragrant water. Use lavishly in dusting powder and sachets. Sew into sleep pillows, and add the oil or the blossom to bath salts to relieve insomnia. The oil is antiseptic, helpful in acne, wonderful in perfume. Use in skin lotion and face cream.

LECITHIN Antioxidant, emollient, emulsifying, lecithin is extracted from soybeans and other plants. Sold as a liquid and a powder, lecithin helps skin hold water, and is good in face creams and body lotion.

LEMON (*Citrus limon*) The juice of this sour tropical fruit is deodorant, a bleach, antiseptic, and astringent. In a hair rinse, lemon juice lightens and restores normal acidity. Regular applications to the skin are said to prevent wrinkles. Do not go in the sun with lemon juice on your skin—it increases the skin's sensitivity to sunlight.

LEMON BALM (*Melissa officinalis*) These lemon-scented leaves soothe sensitive skin. Use in face cream, body lotion, shaving lotion, and facial steams. Lemon balm is sedative and tranquillizing. Use it in bath salts and herbal baths to relieve tension and insomnia.

LEMONGRASS (*Cymbopogon citratus*) Native to India and Sri Lanka, this grass cools and refreshes, and has a strong lemon-peel scent. Use it in dusting powder and shampoo.

LOOSESTRIFE (*Lythrum salicaria*) An infusion of this heatherlike plant in a hair rinse is said to give a golden tint to hair and leave it soft and silky.

LOVAGE (*Levisticum officinale*) The leaves are deodorant. Use them in bath salts and deodorant.

MARJORAM (*Origanum majorana*) The lasting scent, reminiscent of pine, makes this familiar culinary herb a traditional favorite for perfume and dusting powder. You can make a delightful scented oil by laying fresh blossoms over absorbent cotton saturated with oil. Use in a hair rinse to brighten dull hair.

MARSHMALLOW (*Althea officinalis*) The soothing and softening qualities of marshmallow root are valuable in body lotion and shaving cream. Use as a poultice to draw out toxins and heal skin eruptions.

MILK A classic beauty treatment in many cultures, milk contains lactic acid, an alpha hydroxy that exfoliates, reduces the appearance of wrinkles and fine lines, and renews the skin. Milk protein hydrates the skin, and repairs damaged hair and split ends. Milk solids (whey) soften the skin. Mixing milk with essential oil before adding to the bath helps disperse the oil.

MINT (*Mentha piperita*) Antibacterial and stimulating, peppermint is good for dry skin, encouraging it to produce more oil. It stimulates circulation and gives a fresh tingle to face creams, body lotion, toothpaste, face masks, and shampoo. A drop in carrier oil provides a zing to your lovemaking.

MYRRH (*Commiphora myrrha*) Myrrh "tears" are scraped off trees that grow in hot, dry climates. This resin is distilled and often blended with frankincense oil. The powdered resin is antiseptic and remarkably healing. Use it in cuticle creams, body lotion, and perfume.

NEROLI OIL (*Citrus aurantium*) One of the world's most costly oils, neroli is named after an Italian princess who used it to scent her gloves. It is distilled from the blossoms of the bitter orange tree. Besides its use in perfumery, neroli moisturizes and rejuvenates the skin. Use it in skin fresheners, face cream, and body lotion when you really feel like treating yourself.

NETTLE, OR STINGING NETTLE (*Urtica dioica*) The prickly leaves of this wild plant must be harvested with leather gloves. Nettle is excellent for the hair, stimulating growth, softening, adding shine, and darkening gray hair. Use in shampoo and hair rinses.

OAT (*Avena sativa*) Powdered oat exfoliates, cleanses, absorbs dirt and oil and ultraviolet radiation. Use in face masks, dusting powder, soap, face cream, body lotion, and sunscreen.

OLIVE OIL (*Olea europaea*) Oil from the fruit of this Mediterranean tree is used in several kinds of commercial cosmetics. It heals, moisturizes, and stays fresh for a long time. Add it to face cream, body lotion, and hot-oil hair treatments.

ORANGE-FLOWER WATER (*Citrus aurantium*) Sold in Greek and Middle Eastern grocery stores, this fragrant water has uses similar to neroli oil. If you can't find it, substitute orange-blossom infusion.

ORRISROOT (*Iridaceae florentina*) The dried and powdered root of the Florentine iris is used as a perfume fixative. Absorbent and aromatic, it makes a good addition to dusting powder, perfume, bath salts, and dry shampoo. It was once used in tooth powders. Orrisroot can cause an allergic reaction in sensitive people.

PAPAYA (*Carica papaya*) This orange tropical fruit is rich in antioxidants beta carotene and vitamin C. The green fruit contains papain, a meat-tenderizing enzyme that dissolves dead skin cells. Use in a face mask as an exfoliant.

PATCHOULI (*Pogostemon cablin*) The fragrant leaves of this East Indian shrub were once packed with Indian shawls to attest to their authenticity. The fragrance brings back the sixties to anyone who lived through that decade. The essential oil is antiseptic, aphrodisiac, deodorant, and antifungal; it rejuvenates cells and treats acne and eczema. Use in shampoo, face cream, body lotion, deodorant, and perfume.

PEACH (*Prunus persica*) Use in face masks for dry skin. The ground seeds are exfoliative.

PETROLEUM JELLY In perfumery this clear, oily substance is used like fat or oil in making pomades. It can be used as a base for face and body creams or straight up as a moisturizer.

PINEAPPLE (*Ananas comosus*) This tropical fruit has a range of medicinal and cosmetic uses. The fresh fruit contains bromelain, a protein-digesting enzyme that various writers recommend for dissolving corns and warts, including plantar's warts. The alpha hydroxy acids in pineapple dissolve the "glue" that holds dead skin cells together and banish wrinkles. Pineapple is astringent. Regular applications are said to thicken the epidermis and help it hold water.

PLANTAIN (*Plantago major*) The ribbed, spade-shaped leaves of this common backyard wildling contain allantoin, a chemical that rejuvenates skin cells. Plantain is astringent and traditionally used to heal cuts and wounds and arrest bleeding. It can replace comfrey in antiaging cream.

ROSE (*Rosa* spp.) Astringent, antiseptic, soothing, healing, rejuvenating, and fragrant, dried rose petals or their essential oil are good for all skin types and make a wonderful addition to just about any cosmetic you care to make. Add to soap, deodorant, perfume, dusting powder, and face and body lotions. Rosewater cools and freshens. Use it in skin freshener and face cream. Rosewater and glycerin hand lotion is a classic.

ROSEMARY (*Rosmarinus officinalis*) The narrow leaves of this wild and cultivated herb stimulate circulation. Infused, they give hair strength and gloss and stimulate growth. Distilled, the leaves yield a fragrant essential oil that is a strong antioxidant and antiseptic, and important in perfumery. Use in shampoo, hair rinse, massage oil, and perfumes.

SAGE (*Salvia officinalis*) Use this antiseptic and astringent herb in toners for oily skin and shampoos for oily hair, and in deodorants. It heals acne and reduces perspiration. Used in a rinse, sage restores color to graying hair.

SANDALWOOD (*Santalum album*) The beige or red-orange chips of sandalwood come from a tree native to India and Australia. It is one of the oldest perfume materials known. The heavy, woody scent is suitable in cosmetics for both genders. It is good for all skin types, and helpful in treating dry, chapped, or inflamed skin. When the reddish chips are simmered, they produce a lovely rose liquid. Use sandalwood chips or powder or the essential oil in shampoo, skin cream, body lotions, soaps, and, of course, perfume. Goes well with patchouli and vetiver.

SEAWEED Bladder wrack and kelp are the most commonly used. The latter is readily available and inexpensive. If you live near an unpolluted seashore, gather your own and dry it. Seaweed is mucilaginous. It softens and revitalizes the skin and helps it to hold water. Use it in antiaging creams and lotions.

SESAME OIL (*Sesamum orientale*) Oil pressed from the seeds of this tropical and African plant is antioxidant and retards spoiling. It is an excellent sunscreen, blocking 30 percent of ultraviolet (UV) radiation.

SHEA BUTTER (*Vitallaria paradoxa*) Known in Africa as karite butter, it is extracted from the tiny, almond-shaped fruit of a tree native to West Africa. The oil solidifies at 70 degrees, but in the African heat it is liquid. Herbalists there recommend it for internal and external purification. It is a great moisturizer and has a variety of uses ranging from dry skin to eczema and psoriasis, stretch marks, and arthritis. Use it in soap, sunscreen, face cream, and body lotion. As it ages, color ranges from ivory to beige to gray. Smells a bit like ski wax.

SOAPWORT (*Saponaria officinalis*) Also known as bouncing bet, soapwort has pink blossoms that resemble phlox, but with ragged edges. All parts of the plant have saponins, or soaping agents, but the strongest concentration is in the root. It was used in medieval times as a laundry soap; now it is sometimes used to clean fine silks and tapestry. A decoction, used alone or added to shampoo softens the hair and brings out lovely highlights.

SOUTHERNWOOD (*Artemisia abrotanum*) Native to southern Europe, southernwood has been used for centuries as a cure for baldness. Mix it with olive oil and use in a hot-oil treatment for dry hair. A southernwood infusion is said to brighten dull hair.

STRAWBERRY (*Fragaria ananassa*) To soften and nourish oily skin, apply crushed fresh berries in a face pack. Cut a berry and swipe it over your face for quick cleansing. The Seneca Indians brushed their teeth with crushed berries. They are said to remove tartar.

TEA TREE OIL (*Melaleuca alternifolia*) Antiseptic, antifungal, antiviral, this Australian import smells like mint and eucalyptus. It will banish athlete's foot and heal acne. Use it in soap, dandruff shampoo, deodorant, and mouthwash.

THYME (*Thymus vulgaris*) Antibacterial, deodorant, and astringent, thyme is good in oily-skin toners and deodorants. Use white thyme oil in bath salts to ease muscle aches and strains.

TOMATO (*Lycopersicon esculentum*) Use in face packs for oily skin. Raw tomato is a folk remedy for burns.

TONKA, OR TONQUIN BEAN (*Dipteryx odorata*) is the black seed of a Brazilian tree. It has wrinkled skin and a strong vanilla scent. Not for internal use, the seed contains coumarin, a blood thinner. Use in sachets and extracts.

TURMERIC (*Curcuma longa*) The powdered root of this plant, native to India, is a powerful antioxidant and anti-inflammatory. For beautiful skin, take it internally and use it in face masks. In a salve, it helps heal eczema and psoriasis. Be careful, though—it does stain. Add a teaspoonful to ¼ cup of hot water and mix in shampoo to brighten and highlight blond to light-brown hair.

VANILLA (*Vanilla planifolia*) Use in toilet water, perfume, sachets, and dusting powder. Combines well with rose.

VETIVER (*Vetiveria zizanoides*) The root of this Indian and Sri Lankan grass has an earthy fragrance somewhat like sandalwood. In India the grass is woven into fragrant mats. In perfumery vetiver is a catalyst and fixative. Use in perfume and sachets; it combines well with sandalwood.

VITAMIN C (ascorbic acid) An antioxidant, add to antiaging cream as a preservative and to prevent cellular damage caused by free radicals.

VITAMIN E (tocopherol) An antioxidant, vitamin E preserves oils and fats. External applications help prevent scarring, and may protect skin from free radical damage caused by sunlight and air pollution.

WALNUT, BLACK (*Juglans nigra*) The dried, powdered shells are chocolate brown and excellent for coloring hair. Use alone or mixed with neutral henna. The powder is also good for eyebrow color or eyeshadow when mixed with gum tragacanth. Apply with a small brush.

WITCH HAZEL (*Hamamelis virginiana*) Astringent and deodorant, an infusion of witch hazel leaves can be used as a mouthwash, oily-skin toner, or deodorant.

YARROW (*Achillea millefolium*) A wild plant that grows on lawns and in fields, yarrow is astringent, anti-inflammatory, antibacterial, and antifungal. Use it in deodorant and freshener for oily skin. May cause an allergic reaction.

YLANG-YLANG (*Cananga odorata*) This fragrant tropical flower grows wild in the Philippines. Oil distilled from the blossoms is very sweet and used in woody perfume blends. The scent is considered an aphrodisiac. Add to face cream, body lotion, soap, and perfume.

YUCCA (*Yucca glauca*) This desert plant is also known as Spanish bayonet because of its sword-shaped leaves. Southwest Native American tribes used it for food, medicine, and shampoo. The root contains saponins, which make suds when the plant is swished in water. Simmered in water for fifteen minutes, the root produces a reddish decoction that makes no lather to speak of but softens the hair and brings out highlights.

CHAPTER 2

YOUR FACE

DEEPER THAN SKIN DEEP

Close your eyes. Can you conjure up the scent and texture of your loved one's skin? Your child's? Of all of our bodily organs, this flexible web of fat, blood vessels, oil glands, and nerve endings is the most visible, sensitive, and extensive. If all the skin in your body were unfolded like a bolt of fabric, stitched together, and spread out, it would extend for several miles. Naked of fur or feather, richly and variously hued, this sensuous garment is your body's first line of defense against microbes, solar radiation, environmental pollution, and temperature extremes. Sweat and oil glands flush out waste and toxins, immune cells guard your health, blood vessels regulate your temperature, a cushion of fat keeps you warm.

By its degree of suppleness, tone, and texture, and, to some extent, its hue, your skin is the ultimate indication of your emotional weathers and state of health. In some cultures and certain medical systems, the initial diagnosis is often based on observing the skin and how efficiently it performs its functions. Whether we are aware of it or not, the first thing we are likely to notice about other people is their skin; it tells us their approximate age and how well they care for themselves. As a result, the condition of our skin is likely to factor into how attractive we are to other people.

Our epidermis and underlying dermis are made up mostly of collagen and elastin, protein fibers that provide tone, structure, and elasticity. As we age, our bodies produce less of these proteins, and less of the pigment that protects them from sun damage. Our sebaceous glands function less vigorously. Our skin tends to be lighter in color, less resilient, drier, and increasingly vulnerable to damage from sun, harsh weather, and injury.

The cells of the top epidermal layer (*stratum corneum*) are scaly, filled with the protein keratin, and covered with an oily, waterproofing film. This layer is constantly being shed and replaced by the granular

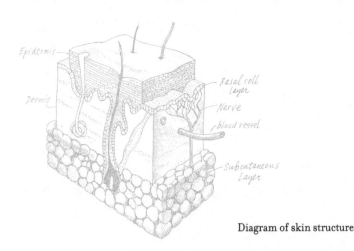

Diagram of skin structure

cells from an underlying skin layer (*stratum granulosum*), a renewal that slows down as we age.

Underneath these two layers and the transparent layer of skin that separates them (*stratum lucidum*), in the thicker germinating layer (*stratum germinativum*), new cells of various shapes are born. Here we find melanin, the dark pigment that protects our skin from ultraviolet rays. UV radiation can wreak havoc on the protein fibers elastin and collagen, drying out the skin and causing premature aging and skin cancer.

The two layers of the underlying dermis contain lymph and blood vessels, oil and sweat glands, nerves, hair follicles and the tiny muscles that move them, as well as some pigment. Supporting it all is a layer of fat that thins as we age, causing our skin to loosen and wrinkle.

Dr. Benjamin Kligler, director of the Beth Israel Center for Health and Healing in New York City, and assistant professor of family medicine at Albert Einstein College of Medicine, observes that maintaining healthy skin is a lifelong proposition.

"You need to start when you are very young," Dr. Kligler says. "Sun damage is the number one problem we have with our skin. Rather than indicating health, a suntan represents skin damage. Shielding your skin from the sun with protective clothing and sunblock is critical. By the time you reach your sixties and seventies, there isn't much you can do to repair sun damage. On the other hand, if you have taken good care of your skin, by now you have lifelong protection."

Acquiring a light tan is possible for some skin types, Dr. Kligler says—notably those with a Mediterranean or dark complexion, but very difficult for Scandinavians and other fair-skinned people. It should be done very slowly, he says, for brief intervals when the sun is not intense, over a long period of time (See Basic Skin Care section, page 29 for specifics).

Adequate fluid intake is also critical, Dr. Kligler says. Eight daily six- to eight-ounce servings of filtered water, fruit juice, or herbal tea hydrate and support the underlying structure of our skin and promote its healthy aging. Keeping hydrated doesn't cure dry skin, he says, but it can maintain the interstitial fluid between the cells that helps form the flexible matrix that supports it. Without that support, the skin can sag and shrivel. This happens when dehydration occurs.

Kligler points out that to avoid dehydration, we not only have to take in fluids, but the right kind of fluids. Coffee, tea, and soft drinks are diuretics. By a process of osmosis, they draw moisture from our tissues. The result is that we urinate more frequently. Salt also draws moisture from our tissues.

A diet based on organically grown food is another cornerstone of Dr. Kligler's program for healthy, youthful skin. "There is no good research to prove this," Kligler says, "but it does make sense that breaking down chemical pesticides and fertilizers places an enormous workload on our bodies, particularly our kidneys and liver. This process diverts energy from our vital bodily functions. I feel particularly strongly about dairy products, because cows suck up everything, and that goes into the milk. Meat, too, unless it is organically grown, is full of antibiotics used to treat the animal and chemical fertilizers and pesticides from the animal feed."

Another key element in Dr. Kligler's skin regime is eating the right kind of fat. He says, "Currently we have a lot of information based on studies of how eating certain fats affect our cell membranes. Saturated fats and hydrogenated oils (trans fats) do not contribute to the health of our skin cells. Omega 6 fatty acids, found in polyunsaturated vegetable oils and trans fats, can stimulate the inflammatory process. We need some inflammatory activity because that's how our bodies fight infection. The answer is to reduce our intake of omega 6 oils—such as soy, corn, and peanut oils—and replace them with olive oil."

Flaxseed, borage, and evening primrose oils provide the omega 3 fatty acids, which Dr. Kligler and many other skin-care experts believe are essential for lustrous skin.

"For overall skin health," Dr. Kligler concludes, "I would also recommend supplements containing 400 international units (IUs) of vitamin E. Thirty to fifty daily milligrams of zinc help balance hormone production, and this is especially important for people with acne."

BASIC SKIN CARE

MOST DERMATOLOGISTS, AESTHETICIANS, AND OTHER SKIN-CARE experts agree that following the guidelines below help you maintain youthful, healthy skin.

AVOID THE SUN BETWEEN 10 A.M. AND 4 P.M.
SUNTAN VS. PALE SKIN AS FASHION STATEMENT

At least as far back as medieval times, a pale complexion distinguished gentry and nobility from peasants who were suntanned from outdoor labor. A woman of that era achieved a pale complexion by applying lead- or flour-based powder to her face. A wimple headdress partially shielded her face from the sun. Later, in Elizabethan England, people of both genders wore masks as a sun shield when they went outdoors—a practice that continued into the eighteenth century. It was not until after World War II that suntans became chic. A bronze face was no longer assumed to be the result of field work; instead, it implied that the bronzed one had nothing better to do than loll around on a beach, or perhaps was wealthy enough to travel to a resort. The result of that revised attitude is visible in wrinkles, sun damage, and premature aging.

Before suntans became fashionable, a woman venturing forth in the daytime protected her face with a hat or parasol and the rest of her body with wrist-length sleeves, ankle-length skirts, and gloves. Head-to-toe coverage still makes sense. Most skin damage is caused by free radicals produced when skin interacts with the sun's ultraviolet rays. (Tanning booths and unshielded halogen lightbulbs, which also emit UVA radiation, should be avoided, too.)

Sunscreen (SPF 15 or higher) is a must. Apply it generously year-round. In times and seasons when sunlight is the most intense, be sure to renew it frequently, especially when you sweat or swim. The SPF number indicates how long you can stay in the sun without burning. Theoretically, if you get burned after a five-minute sunbath, with SPF 15 sunscreen you could safely remain in the sun for an hour and a quarter. In practice, this is not always the case.

Not all sun damage is visible. The majority of sunscreens block the ultraviolet-B radiation that causes sunburn, but not the ultraviolet-A rays that cause melanoma, the most deadly type of skin cancer. Overexposure to sunlight, even when protected by a sunscreen, can depress your immune system and damage the underlying structure of your skin.

Certain foods and drugs increase your sensitivity to sunlight. These include citrus fruits, deodorant soaps, retin A, antibiotics, diuretics, tranquilizers, antidepressants, and some herbs, including yarrow, bergamot, and Saint John's wort.

As Dr. Kligler emphasizes, what you eat affects how your skin looks. The American Cancer Society recommends five to nine servings of fruits and vegetables every day. The antioxidants they contain are your first line of defense against free-radical damage. Vitamins A, C, and E, beta-carotene, and the mineral selenium help keep your skin healthy. The highest concentrations of beta-carotene, which your body converts to vitamin A, are found in deep-green and yellow fruits and vegetables such as cantaloupe, papaya, broccoli, and leafy greens. Vitamin C is plentiful in most fresh fruits and vegetables, especially citrus fruits, rose hips, peppers, and broccoli. The latter is a virtual antioxidant powerhouse, rich in carotene, vitamin C, and selenium. Selenium is also found in onions, garlic, mushrooms, brewer's yeast, and seafood. To get vitamin E, include wheat germ, nuts, whole grains, leafy greens, and safflower, soybean, or sunflower oil in your diet. Vegetables that are raw or have been lightly steamed retain the most vitamins.

Fruits, vegetables, and whole grains are also high in fiber. This indigestible cellulose material, which your grandmother may have called roughage, plays an important role in digestion and elimination, essential to overall health, including that of your skin.

Even the best diets, however, don't always deliver all the nutrients we need. The Center for Science in the Public Interest recommends a multivitamin and mineral supplement, noting that supplements need not be expensive—you can find good-quality vitamins at discount department stores. In addition, you may want to take extra antioxidant supplements. The RDA for vitamin C is 250 to 500 milligrams, for vitamin E 200 to 800 international units. The selenium RDA for nonpregnant women is 55 micrograms; for vitamin A it's 1,300 international units for pregnant women, 800 international units for the rest.

DON'T SMOKE.

Smoking produces free radicals that age and dry your skin. Inhaling tobacco smoke also constricts your blood vessels, impeding circulation that is responsible for your healthy color. The odor of tobacco smoke clings to your skin, hair and breath; nicotine stains your teeth and fingers.

AVOID EXTREMES OF HEAT AND COLD.

Rinsing your face in water that is too hot, or exposing it to an open fire or icy winds, can rupture small capillaries under the surface of your skin, etching a web of threadlike veins.

EXERCISE.

Studies indicate that regular exercise helps you maintain skin thickness and elasticity. It also increases circulation, brings oxygen to your cells, and imparts a healthy glow. The lactic acid released in sweat is one of the alpha hydroxy acids, a natural exfoliant that stimulates skin renewal.

GET YOUR BEAUTY SLEEP.

While you sleep, toxins are released through your skin, and all of your bodily tissue is renewed.

EXFOLIATE.

The top layer of your skin contains mostly dead skin cells. Removing them with complexion grains, a cleansing face mask, or even a rough washcloth allows new cells to surface, giving your skin a fresh, youthful appearance.

In the rest of this chapter you will find suggestions for coping with specific skin problems and recipes for ageless natural beauty.

FOR HEAT OR SCURF IN THE FACE

TAKE A PINT OF CREAM *as thick as can be scummed, then take of chamomile one handful, pick, wash, and shred it very small, then put it into the cream, and let it boil very softly, til it comes to an Oil, never stirring it after putting in the herbs at first, but scum it clean, when you see the oil come to the top, then boil a little faster, and strain it out through a thin linin cloth, and then anoint the face therewith.*

from *The Queen's Closet Opened,* by Queen Henrietta Maria

DRY SKIN

of the aging process. Overexposure to sun, wind, winter temperatures, central heating or air-conditioning are also drying. If your skin remains tight for hours after you wash it, and has an ashen, flaky appearance, you probably have dry skin. A protective layer of oil on the skin surface protects against water evaporation. If your oil glands do not produce enough sebum, skin cells lose water and you need to apply a moisturizing agent to help lock in the oil.

Ettia Tal, the oft-quoted, much-publicized proprietor of Ettia Holistic Day Spa in New York City, believes that moisturizers are unnecessary. "When you put them on, you don't give your skin the chance to develop its natural moisture, so the skin gets lazy. If you nourish your body properly, your natural moisture comes out."

Some of the strategies you read about in the previous section apply to dry skin as well: avoid tobacco, alcohol, and caffeine, which are dehydrating; protect your skin from the drying effects of the sun by wearing protective clothing and applying sunblock with a SPF of at least 15. You need to drink at least two quarts of fluid every day to hydrate bodily tissues and flush out wastes and toxins. Your diet should include omega 6 and omega 3 oils from olive oil, fatty fish, or flaxseed, and lots of deep-green or yellow fruits and vegetables, which are sources of vitamin A.

In addition, you should humidify your indoor environment, especially during the winter months when stoves or central heating dry the air. You can do this with a humidifier or vaporizer, or you can set containers filled with water on your stove or radiators. The moisture given off by house plants and their damp soil will raise humidity levels; so will a simmering teakettle or a bathtub partially filled with water.

Gentle massage improves circulation and helps to relieve dryness and wrinkles. Using gentle, upward strokes, work your fingers over your throat, chin, cheeks, and forehead. Massage these areas for one minute, stroking in tiny, clockwise circles: the outer edges of your eyes, where laugh lines appear; under your eyes just below the pupils, and on your chin below the incisors. Your hands will glide more easily

SOLUTION

MOISTURIZERS FROM AROUND THE WORLD

For centuries women in all climes and cultures have kept their skin moist and soft with a variety of simple strategies based on the materials that are readily available to them.

- Marshmallow root has great skin softening powers. To make a light day-time moisturizer, cover 3 tablespoons ground or shaved root with 1 cup boiling distilled water. Steep for thirty minutes and strain.

- Women of the British Isles are famous for their lovely complexions. Constant moisture from fog and rain preserves the softness and suppleness of youth. To simulate this effect, mist your face with an atomizer containing spring water, rosewater, orange water, or one of the toners listed on page 61.

- According to Catherine Corkery, a former Peace Corps volunteer who spent four years in Senegal, the Animas, an indigenous African people, use shea (karite) butter as an all-over moisturizer. This material is extracted from the almond-shaped seeds of the shea tree. In temperate climates shea butter is very thick, beige to grayish, and waxy, but in hot Senegal, it is usually a liquid. You can buy it in any city, Corkery says. (See the appendix for suppliers in the United States.) It makes the skin shine, and it smells good. During the dry season when people's feet crack and even bleed from going barefoot on the dry soil, they rub shea butter into their skin at night, and by the next morning their feet are healed.

- In Greece and other Mediterranean areas, olive oil is the chosen moisturizer. The pure oil heals abrasions, burns, bruises, and chapping. For this reason it is often used as the basis for homemade medicinal salves and ointments. Olive oil also provides sunscreen protection, absorbing about 20 percent of solar radiation.

- Sesame, sunflower, coconut, and corn oils are used in India. Ayurvedic physician Deepak Chopra recommends smoothing on sesame oil before bathing or showering for its invigorating effects. Sesame oil also gives excellent sun protection, screening out about 30 percent of harmful rays.

- In the Caribbean, coconut oil—also a sunscreen—and coco a butter are used. You have to be judicious about how much coconut oil you apply: Too much will dry out your skin. Cocoa butter is also used to prevent or remove scars. It is allergenic, though, so before you spread it on your face, test it on a small area of skin.

- A Caribbean recipe: Pour orange juice into an electric blender, add some honey and aloe vera, blend for about a minute, then drink the resulting mixture. The honey, applied externally, moisturizes and heals. Orange juice contains substantial amounts of vitamin C, a powerful antioxidant that protects against skin damage and premature aging. External applications of aloe are very healing; taken internally, fresh aloe is laxative and helps the body eliminate toxins. (The bottled juice is purgative.)

- Women in the Dominican Republic apply the starchy water used for rinsing rice and leave it on for thirty minutes.

- Women in Puerto Rico roll the seed of an avocado over their faces.

- Shepherds have an excellent moisturizer, said to be chemically similar to human sebum, in the lanolin they collect from sheep wool. You can buy liquid lanolin in health food stores. A little dab will certainly do you, because it is very thick and heavy. It is also allergenic, so apply to a small area first to make sure it doesn't irritate your skin.

- Some women, and their grandmothers, swear by petroleum jelly—in a pinch, it does do the job.

- A few dermatologists recommend hydrogenated vegetable shortening because it is very emollient and contains no preservatives.

- Most vegetable oils are slightly acidic, thus easily absorbed by the skin. The rich, green oil of the avocado is antioxidant and very nourishing. It contains substantial amounts of vitamins A, D, and E as well as lecithin. Wheat-germ oil, which is rich in vitamin E, is considered particularly good for aging skin. Among its many virtues it is said to prevent scarring. Peanut oil is penetrating. Essential fatty acids in borage, evening primrose, flaxseed, and other seed oils help keep your skin lustrous and healthy. Other oils that nourish and protect the skin include almond, jojoba, kukui nut, soybean, and white camellia oils.

- Trigve Harris, aromatherapist and owner of Enfleurage in Manhattan, considers facial oil blends the most enjoyable cosmetics to make. She likes to figure out the best oils to use and the best essential oils to add to that blend. She often uses apricot oil, which is rich in fatty acids, (GHLs). Hazelnut oil, which is astringent, is good for oily skin.

All of these vegetable oils will be even more effective if you add healing herbs. To ½ cup of oil, add 2 tablespoons dried marigold or chamomile petals, elder, jasmine, or orange blossoms, or comfrey leaves. Pour into a clear glass jar. Allow the mixture to steep on a sunny windowsill, radiator, or other warm place for two or three weeks, shaking daily. Strain and bottle.

if you first lubricate your skin with one of the moisturizers described in the following section.

Most soaps are alkaline and upset the pH balance of your skin, which is acidic. Whether or not people with dry skin should use soap is a matter of controversy among skin experts: Ettia and some other experts say never; others say that Dove or a similar mild, fatty soap is acceptable. Homemade soaps containing honey, vegetable oils, and moisturizing essential oils are an excellent alternative. After washing your face with soap, you can restore the acid mantle by adding a tablespoon of cider vinegar to a quart of warm water and rinsing your face with it.

It is also a good idea to cleanse, nourish, and moisturize your skin by applying a face mask once every week or two. For details, see pages 51 to 60.

Moisturizers

The best time to apply a lubricant is after a bath or shower when your skin is warm and slightly damp. Apply the moisturizer in upward strokes, give it ten minutes to sink in, then gently massage the remainder into your skin. Remove any excess with a tissue or absorbent cotton. For optimum absorption, apply to clean skin before you bathe. Steam from the bath water helps the oil penetrate the surface.

QUICK MOISTURIZING CREAM

You can whip up a moisturizing cream in no time by melting coconut oil, cocoa butter, shea butter, lanolin, palm oil, petroleum jelly, or other solid lubricant in the top of a double boiler. Melt the lubricant, add any of the herbs listed in the previous section, simmer gently for

EMULSIONS

Actually, these creams take less than fifty minutes to make. Prepared ingredients such as orange water, bottled aloe vera gel, or beeswax beads speed up the process.

◆ If you have made a hollandaise sauce, you know how to make an emulsion, the basis for a moisturizing cream. For more information about making an emulsion, please see pages 8 to 10 in chapter one.

a half hour, then strain out the herbs and allow the oil to solidify again.

ORANGE BLOSSOM ALOE CREAM

This moisturizer does wonders for dry or aging skin, but it's a favorite with all ages and both genders. Of all the facial creams described here, this one stays fresh the longest. Besides its cosmetic uses, the cream is very effective at treating sunburn, chapping, and other irritations. Orange blossoms moisturize, smooth wrinkles, and stimulate cell replacement. Both aloe and olive oil soothe and heal chapped and irritated skin, improve skin tone, and act as a mild sunscreen. Gum benzoin and aloe kill bacteria. The latter is antifungal as well.

2/3 cup olive oil

2 tablespoons chopped beeswax or beeswax beads

A pinch of boric acid

1/4 tsp. gum benzoin

1/3 cup fresh or bottled aloe vera gel

1/3 cup orange water or orange blossom infusion (steep 2
    tablespoons orange blossoms in one cup boiling distilled
    water for thirty minutes)

PLACE oil, beeswax, boric acid, and gum benzoin in top part of a glass or enamel double boiler, and heat gently until wax dissolves. Remove from heat and cool until the mixture is thick and opaque but not hardened. Pour aloe and orange water into blender jar, and run the machine at the highest speed. Add the oil mixture about a tablespoonful at a time. When the cream has emulsified and the texture is creamy, pour immediately into two- or four-ounce jars. If kept cool and clean, cream will last about six months.

VARIATION: ROSE CREAM Use the above recipe, replacing the orange water with rosewater. Add ten drops essential rose oil.

FOUR FLOWER BEAUTY CREAM

⅓ cup almond oil

⅓ cup olive oil

2 tablespoons chopped or granulated beeswax

¼ teaspoon powdered gum benzoin

A pinch of boric acid

2 drops essential oil of lavender

1 cup boiling water

1 tablespoon dried elder blossoms

1 tablespoon dried lavender flowers

1 tablespoon dried rose petals

1 tablespoon dried jasmine petals

1 tablespoon dried comfrey leaves

STEEP herbs in water for thirty minutes.

PLACE first five ingredients in top of double boiler and heat gently until wax melts. Remove from fire, cool slightly, add lavender oil. Meanwhile, strain the infusion, measure out ⅔ cup (discard the rest), and pour it into the jar of an electric blender. When wax mixture is thickened and opaque, but not hard, pour or spoon into blender with motor running at highest speed. When mixture is thick, glossy, and creamy, pour immediately into jars. Seal when cream is cool and re-frigerate.

ANTIOXIDANT CREAM

Free radicals released by sunlight can cause premature aging; so can air pollution. The antioxidant herbs in this cream counteract this effect by scavenging free radicals. The green tea is also a sunscreen. The benzoin and grapefruit seed extract prolong shelf life. The cream smells good, feels good, moisturizes, reduces wrinkles, and stays fresh for a long time.

¼ cup olive oil	1 tablespoon dried rosehips
2 tablespoons almond oil	1 tablespoon green tea
2 tablespoons canola oil	½ tablespoon dried echinacea
1 tablespoon plus 1½ teaspoons	root or leaves
beeswax	½ tablespoon dried rosemary
⅛ teaspoon benzoin	leaves
A pinch of boric acid	2 tablespoons aloe vera gel
⅔ cup distilled water	6 drops grapefruit seed extract

SIMMER rose hips in water for ten minutes, then strain and pour the hot broth over the green tea, echinacea and rosemary. Steep thirty minutes. Meanwhile, heat the oils, benzoin, boric acid, and beeswax until wax is melted, then cool until wax is opaque but not hard. Strain herb mixture and pour ⅓ cup into jar of electric blender, discarding remainder. Add aloe, set blender at highest speed, and slowly pour in wax mixture. When the cream is thoroughly emulsified, add the grapefruit seed extract and blend until thoroughly mixed. Bottle, cool, and refrigerate.

MATURE SKIN

WE ASSOCIATE WRINKLED, DRY, AND SAGGING SKIN WITH AGING. THE main culprit, though, is not time but exposure to the sun, which breaks down supporting elastin and collagen fibers, robs the epidermal layers of moisture, and causes the formation of the brown patches known as liver spots. Dehydration plays a part as well by undermining the supporting structure of the skin.

Strategies to avoid premature skin aging include adequate fluid intake—eight glasses a day—staying out of the sun, and, when that is not possible, wearing a broad-brimmed hat and sunscreen. It also helps to clear away dead skin cells by exfoliating regularly (see pages 44 to 50); and to treat the skin to a nourishing facial mask (see pages 51 to 60). Exercise increases collagen production, making the skin thicker and less prone to wrinkles. Not only does sweating flush out toxins, your perspiration contains lactic acid, one of those miraculous alpha hydroxies that renew and protect the skin.

FACE CREAM: BEST INGREDIENTS FOR YOUR SKIN TYPE

DRY SKIN: orange blossom, patchouli, ylang-ylang essential oil, lecithin, kelp and other seaweeds, coconut oil, jojoba, lanolin, shea butter

OILY SKIN: juniper, white oak bark, witch hazel, yarrow, peppermint, aloe vera, willow, apple, coconut, glycerine, sage, camphor, cypress

SENSITIVE SKIN: lavender, patchouli, geranium, rose, red clover, comfrey leaf or root, chamomile flowers, aloe vera, green tea, propolis, oatmeal, cypress, pine, lemon balm

ACNE: salicylic acid, cajeput oil, tea tree oil, juniper berry, fir, thyme, yarrow, lavender, garlic

MATURE SKIN: comfrey root or leaf; gingko, jojoba oil, shea butter, rosewater, rose oil, rose petals, brewer's yeast, bee pollen, avocado, frankincense essential oil

Puffiness, caused by bloating, is another unhappy consequence of the passage of time. Exercise is good for that, too. It steps up metabolism and encourages water loss through perspiration. A low-fat, low-sugar diet, with plenty of leafy greens and other fresh vegetables as well as vitamin B_6 supplements also help get rid of bloat.

Age Spots

Age spots, also known as liver spots or senile keratosis, consist of darkened skin patches that look like big freckles. Actually, that's what they are. In response to sun damage, skin cells clump together and are darkened with protective melatonin. Some dermatologists regard senile keratosis as a precursor to skin cancer. If you have them, seek medical advice.

The most common way of dealing with age spots is to peel them off with a strong concentration of alpha hydroxy acid. Don't try this at home. What you could do, however, is exfoliate all over once or twice a week, and work on the age spot daily with a mixture of cornmeal and sour milk, which contains lactic acid.

Jamaicans steep a leaf of fresh aloe vera in water for twenty-four hours and drink the juice to clear out the toxins they believe contribute to liver spots.

◆ Fresh pineapple, which contains the protein-digesting enzyme bromelain, helps fade and reduce age spots. Rub a piece over the age spot three times a day.

◆ Fresh lemon juice helps fade the age spot and speed skin renewal. Apply undiluted and rinse off thoroughly after ten minutes.

◆ Daily applications of shea butter are also said to lighten and soften age spots.

Wrinkles

As we grow older and sebaceous glands function less vigorously, our skin becomes dry. The layer of fat underneath our skin thins out, so the skin becomes loose. There is a dwindling supply of collagen and elastin, which give support. Dehydration may also contribute to the deterioration of the underlying structure of the skin. So we get wrinkles.

Some women cherish their laugh lines as the outward manifestations of wisdom and experience. However, to age gracefully, we must stay out of the sun, eat well, refrain from smoking, drink alcohol moderately, and nourish our skin with moisturizers and facials. The paraffin mask on pages 55 and 56 plumps up wrinkles and renews the skin. The avocado face mask on pages 56–57 also does wonders for mature skin, toning, firming, and moisturizing it. Myrhh and white wine, the astringents in the boxed quote, To Make Wrinkled Skin Smooth, would serve to tighten the skin and reduce the appearance of wrinkles.

Carlotta Karlson Jacobson and Catherine Ettlinger, in their book *How to Be Wrinkle-Free*, recommend these facial mask ingredients: a mixture of calcium powder, calcium carbonate, and plain yogurt; a peel-off mask made with 3 tablespoons water to 1 tablespoon plain gelatin. They also recommend these ingredients, alone or added to a mixture: caviar, fresh or rehydrated seaweed, clay, and bee pollen. To reduce the appearance of wrinkles, they recommend filling them in with egg white to make the skin appear smooth.

Leonard Stoller, in his magazine article "Beauty Recipes of Yesteryear," published in "The Givaudanian," gives this traditional face mask to ward off wrinkles: Boil four eggs in rosewater until they are firm. Add ½ ounce alum and ½ ounce almond oil. Beat the mixture until it forms a paste. Spread on the face.

TO MAKE A WRINKLED FACE SMOOTH

CAST POWDER OF MYRRH *on a heated plate of iron, then sprinkle it with white wine, that the fumes may better rise, and binding up your forehead, hold your face over it on some distance, and in doing so several times, the fume will fill the empty pores, and cause a smoothness in the skin.*

from *A Thousand Notable Things on Various Subjects,* by Thomas Lupton

This night cream is said to be famous since the time of the Crusades: Remove the yolks from 6 hard-boiled eggs, replace with myrrh and powdered sugar candy in equal parts. Fit the halves of the eggs together and set on a plate before a fire. Mix the resulting liquor with 32 grams of fat pork until it forms a pomatum. Apply in the morning, let it dry, and wipe off carefully. (NB: Those unfortunate readers without fireplaces or fat pork may prefer to bake their eggs in an oven set at low heat until the eggs release their store of melted sugar. The resulting liquid can be mixed with lard or coconut oil.)

ANTIAGING CREAM

If you are lucky enough to live near an unpolluted beach, you can gather and dry your own seaweed. Bladder wrack gathered on the Maine coast was used in this recipe, but you could add whatever seaweed is indigenous to your area, or buy kelp, bladder wrack, or wakami in a health food store. For more information on making face creams, see emulsions on page 8 to 10.

$1/2$ cup olive oil

1 tablespoon plus 2 teaspoons shaved beeswax

$1/8$ teaspoon powdered gum benzoin

A pinch of boric acid

2 tablespoons aloe vera gel

$2/3$ cup boiling water

1 tablespoon dried gingko leaves

1 tablespoon dried comfrey leaves

1 tablespoon dried, powdered seaweed

1 teaspoon pulverized bee pollen

6 drops essential oil of lavender

POUR the boiling water over gingko, comfrey and seaweed and steep for 30 minutes. About ten minutes before the infusion is ready, place oil, wax, benzoin, and boric acid in the top of a double boiler, and heat gently until wax is melted. When the wax mixture is thick and opaque, but still liquid, it is ready to use. Strain herbal mixture and pour ⅓ cup into electric blender jar discarding remainder. Add bee pollen, set blender at highest speed, and whirr briefly. Add lavender to wax mixture and slowly pour the mixture into the blender. When the emulsion is thoroughly mixed, scrape down the sides of the jar and beat for another minute. Pour immediately into sterile glass jars, cool and refrigerate.

OILY SKIN

YOUNG, HEALTHY SKIN PRODUCES A FAIR AMOUNT OF OIL. IF YOUR skin is excessively oily, it's important to keep it clean by washing at least twice a day and regularly using exfoliants and facial masks to remove dead skin and dirt and absorb oils. A plugged hair follicle can result in a blackhead, whitehead, or pimple; an inflammation or bacterial infection can bring on an acne attack.

A traditional strategy for correcting oily skin was to wash it in wine—white wine for fair skin, red wine for dark. When wine was not available, women used the juice of fresh cucumbers or the water in which spinach was boiled.

Applying a skin toner regularly helps refine, tone, and tighten your skin. See page 61 for suggestions.

OILY-SKIN FACE SPLASH

Use this astringent toner after a thorough cleansing with soap, exfoliants, mask, or all three.

- ½ tablespoon dried rosemary leaves
- ½ tablespoon dried witch hazel leaves and flowers
- ½ tablespoon dried thyme leaves
- ½ tablespoon fresh or dried, crushed juniper berries

1   cup boiling distilled water
1   tablespoon glycerin

STEEP the herbs in the water for thirty minutes. Strain and measure out ³/₄ cup of infusion. Add glycerin and pour into a bottle. Shake before using.

VARIATION: Substitute yarrow blossoms and leaves for the juniper. Yarrow can make your skin sensitive to sunlight, so if you apply this herb, do so at bedtime and wash your face thoroughly in the morning.

OILY-SKIN CREAM

Contrary to what you might think, a light face cream actually discourages your skin from producing excess oil and normalizes oil production. Grapeseed oil is slightly astringent. Hazelnut oil, used in commercially produced cosmetics, is more astringent but, alas, also harder to find, at least in the Northeast (see the appendix). All of the herbs in this recipe help tighten your skin and remove excess oil. Rosemary stimulates circulation; thyme and juniper are antiseptic and useful in treating acne, often the result of oily skin. If you have never made face cream before, please read instruction on making emulsions on pages 8 to 10.

²/₃ cup grapeseed or hazelnut oil		1¹/₃ cup boiling water	
1 tablespoon beeswax		2 tablespoons dried rosemary	
¹/₄ teaspoon powdered gum benzoin		2 tablespoons dried witch hazel	
A pinch of boric acid		2 tablespoons dried thyme	
¹/₄ teaspoon myrrh		2 tablespoons fresh or dried juniper	

MELT first five ingredients together in top of double boiler, then cool until the wax is opaque, but not hardened. Meanwhile, pour boiling water over the herbs and steep for thirty minutes. Measure out ²/₃ cup, discarding remainder, and place in the jar of an electric blender. Add the wax mixture, and blend at high speed until emulsified. Pour immediately into sterile glass jars, cool and refrigerate. Apply sparingly.

Egg white is a traditional beauty treatment, used for tightening and polishing the skin. Lemon juice is used for its astringent and bleaching action. Before applying the varnish, wash your face with the starchy water that has been used for rinsing rice.

Take equal parts lemon juice and the whites of fresh eggs; beat them well in a glazed earthen pan (glass or enamel would be fine). Put the mixture on a slow fire, and stir until it has the consistency of soft butter. Scent with essential oil. **Warning:** Citrus juice makes your skin sensitive to sunlight. Be sure to wash away all traces of the lemon juice before you venture outdoors.

Facial Cleansers

What we should use to clean our face is a matter of debate among skin-care experts, including women whose profession it is to be beautiful. Cold cream has been a traditional cleanser ever since the Greek physician Galen supposedly invented it back in the second century B.C. Science writer Deborah Chase is in the anti–cold cream camp. She maintains that oily cleansers cause the dead skin cells to clump together, and the oily residue attracts more dirt.

New York City aesthetician Ettia Tal recommends rubbing the face with a damp washcloth. Soap, she says, "contains a lot of alkaline; when you use it, it is like soap scum on the tub, like a pancake of cells gathering together." She recommends weekly exfoliation. In her spa she does this with papaya and pineapple enzymes and green tea to treat her clients.

Daily cleansing is a sensible routine for all types of skin. Once a day is enough for dry to normal skin; oily skin requires more frequent cleansing. A washcloth, which is slightly abrasive, acts as a mild exfoliant. The type of soap you should use—if any—depends on your skin type. Some people don't feel clean unless they have used soap. If you are one of them, stick to those without perfume or other allergenic ingredients. Glycerin in a soap softens your skin and leaves it squeaky clean, but it also draws oil from your skin. A pure, mild bar soap does the job for most people—see pages 124 to 129 for advice on making your own.

Thorough rinsing with tepid water is essential for washing away cellular debris and the traces of soap that can irritate and dry your face. The shower is an excellent place to rinse thoroughly. Afterward, to restore normal acidity, rinse your face with warm water to which cider vinegar has been added. A tablespoon of cider vinegar to a quart of warm water is about right. (See pages 113 to 114 for information on scented cosmetic vinegars.)

For more thorough cleansing, scrub with complexion grains to gently remove dead skin cells and allow new ones to work their way to the surface. Regular exfoliating can speed up skin renewal by as much as 30 percent.

Weekly or biweekly treatments are sufficient for dry or aging skin; two or three times a week may be appropriate for oily skin. Complexion grains can irritate acne and possibly instigate a flare-up, so if you have this problem, exfoliate with barley flour, finely ground rice, or oatmeal if you use anything at all. The same is true for very dark skin, which scars easily. Whatever your skin type, if you are in doubt about how often or how vigorously to use complexion grains, it is better to err on the side of restraint; there is some concern among skin-care professionals that exfoliating too often or too vigorously could thin the upper layer of the epidermis.

Complexion grains are easily made in a coffee grinder by reducing seeds, nuts, or grains to a meal or fine powder. Make a loose paste by adding water, milk, wine, or fruit juice in a ratio of 4 parts liquid to 3 parts grain or meal. Milk contains lactic acid, an alpha hydroxy—hence the famous milk baths that great beauties have used for centuries. Sour milk and buttermilk have even more lactic acid. Fruit juice contains glycolic acid and wine malic acid, both are alpha hydroxies. In a pinch, you could even use dry sugar to exfoliate. In addition to being slightly abrasive, sugar has been used for centuries to heal sores and scratches.

Smooth the paste over your throat and face, using your fingers. Avoid the lips and the area around the eyes. Gently stroke upward, using a circular motion, for a minute or two, rinse thoroughly in tepid water and pat dry. The shower is the most convenient place to use an exfoliant. If this is a weekly regime, you may want to use it on your body, too. A shower cap keeps the paste out of your hair and ears. Follow up with a moisturizer and/or skin toner, or apply a facial mask.

For your face, mix about 1 tablespoonful of complexion grains chosen from the list below with about 4 teaspoons sour milk, buttermilk, yogurt, regular milk, or apple juice, or enough to make a loose paste. For all-over exfoliation you will need about ¼ to ⅓ cup abrasive material.

OATMEAL cleanses, absorbs oil, and soothes. Finely ground oats are best for dry, mature, sensitive, and acned skin. A coarse grind is fine for normal and oily skin.

CORNMEAL AND SOUR MILK, unappetizing though the combination may sound, is a wonderful skin treatment that leaves your skin smooth and silky. You could substitute any of the liquids listed above, but sour milk has the most lactic acid.

RICE gives your skin a polished appearance.

BARLEY MEAL OR POWDER is mucilaginous and soothing, good for all skin types, but especially appreciated by those with dry, sensitive, or mature skin.

POWDERED KELP, like other ocean vegetation, is rich in minerals and good for mature skin. It can irritate sensitive skin.

BREWER'S YEAST stimulates circulation, perks up dull, sallow skin. **Bran** has been used for centuries by women to soothe irritation, smooth roughness, and whiten skin.

GROUND AVOCADO SEEDS cleanse your skin with mild abrasion and nourish it with monosaturated oils and antioxidant vitamins A, C, and E. To prepare the exfoliant, allow an avocado seed to dry, but not harden, chop coarsely, then pulverize in a seed or coffee grinder.

FRESH STRAWBERRIES are another traditional cleanser. Simply rub one over your face.

APRICOT SEEDS AND ALMONDS are frequently used in commercial preparations. See recipe on the following page.

SIMPLE ALMOND PASTE FOR WASHING FACE OR HANDS

FROM *PERFUMES AND COSMETICS, THEIR PREPARATION AND MANUFACTURE,* BY GEORGE WILLIAM ASKINSON

6 pounds almonds

2 quarts alcohol

4 quarts rosewater

10½ ounces oil of bergamot

3½ ounces oil of lemon

BLANCH and skin almonds, bruise them in a mortar, and set them in a glazed pot in boiling water. Pour over them 2 quarts rosewater heated to near boiling. Keep up the heat under it continually stirring until the almond meal and water form a uniform paste. Cool and add rosewater and oils dissolved in alcohol.

VARIATION: For the almonds substitute equal parts pistachios, blanched and reduced to meal, and powdered orrisroot. Add lemon, neroli, and orange peel oils.

AUTHOR'S NOTE: When Askinson wrote this recipe it had not been discovered that bergamot and citrus oils make skin sensitive to sunlight. Since all three are used in the recipe primarily for aroma, you could omit them.

PASTE

FROM *THE TOILET OF FLORA,* BY PIERRE-JOSEPH BUC'HOZ

All of the ingredients in this recipe were favored by the Elizabethans and Victorians, and continue to be used in natural skin care for the excellent reason that they really work. Beat some peeled and cored apples in a mortar with equal parts rosewater and white wine. Add some bread crumbs, blanched almonds, and a little white soap and simmer over a slow fire.

A FRENCH EXFOLIANT RECIPE

FROM "BEAUTY RECIPES OF YESTERYEAR" BY LEONARD STOLLER

Equal parts powdered pumpkin, gourd, and cucumber seeds
Enough cream to dilute, then enough milk to make a thin paste
1 grain musk
A few drops lemon oil

SPREAD this on the face, leave on for twenty minutes or overnight, then rinse with tepid water. Makes complexion bright and clear. **Warning:** Skin that has been treated with lemon oil is vulnerable to sun damage, so be sure to rinse thoroughly and apply sunscreen before going outdoors.

SEASHELL PASTE

THIS CHARMING RECIPE FROM EL SALVADOR COMES FROM AMERICA HERNANDEZ.

Lemon juice contains alpha hydroxy acids that help the skin shed its upper layer of dead cells so new ones can replace them. Seashells are a rich source of calcium and other minerals.

"My mother puts lemon juice into a seashell, then she leaves the seashell on the sill outside of the window. (You could also set the seashell in a warm place indoors.) In the morning she collects the paste from the seashell. She takes this paste and puts it around her face. This prevents wrinkles. Now my mother is seventy-seven years old. She doesn't have wrinkles."

Facial Steams

A facial sauna is an excellent way to dissolve oils, draw out impurities and toxins, moisturize, and stimulate circulation. To make one, simply bring a big pot of water to the boil, and after you take it off the fire, lean over the pot with your head draped in a bath towel. Do keep your face at a comfortable distance from the hot water—steam can burn! A handful of herbs boosts the cleansing or stimulating power. Chamomile, for example, is used for skin and hair care in places as far-flung as Eastern Europe and

Central and South America. The flowers are antiseptic and healing; they soften the skin. Mint stimulates circulation; rose and chamomile soften; calendula, juniper, comfrey, myrrh, violet, and pansy heal; orange blossom moisturizes and stimulates cell renewal; witch hazel, green and black teas, oak bark, and bearberry leaves are astringent. Some women use Swiss Kriss laxative herbs for a facial steam, claiming that the blend is an effective cleanser. **Warning:** Don't steam your face if you have broken facial capillaries—the hot steam can aggravate the problem.

A hot pack, made with a washcloth dampened with hot water, also dissolves oil and helps clean your pores. This, too, is not a cleansing method for those with broken capillaries (couperose skin).

Cleansing Lotions

Although soap was discovered by the ancient Gauls and used in Greece and Rome, until the twentieth century, "waters," most of them distilled from plants, were used for washing the face. Pineapple water would be very effective; not only does it contain an alpha hydroxy acid, the bromelain in pineapple is a digestive enzyme with great skin-softening properties. Many seventeenth- and eighteenth-century face lotions contained alpha hydroxy acids. Women also washed their faces with the juice of melons, cucumbers, beets, string beans, and strawberries; milk, buttermilk, wine, brandy, and beer foam. The water in which barley was cooked was used to tighten and soften the skin.

FROM *THE TOILET OF FLORA*, PIERRE-JOSEPH BUC'HOZ, 1799

"It is asserted that the distilled water of green pineapples takes away wrinkles and gives the complexion an air of youth."

An International Array of Cleansing Lotions

In Ecuador, women wash their face with chamomile tea and leave it on for twenty minutes before rinsing.

Haitian women boil milk until it thickens, then use the resulting "cream" as a facial cleanser.

In Burma, cucumber juice is applied, left on for fifteen minutes, then rinsed off.

A Colombian variation to this simple recipe calls for a piece of cucumber and 2 or 3 drops of lemon juice. After a minute or two, when the cucumber is saturated with lemon, it is used as a facial cleanser followed by a rinse with plain water.

A traditional American recipe to remove freckles, blackheads, and other blemishes calls for 1 teaspoon of horseradish grated into 1 cup of sour milk. Let the mixture stand at room temperature for six hours, then wash your face with it.

Deborah Rutledge, in *Natural Beauty Secrets*, writes that Erno La-zlo, a famous Hungarian dermatologist, recommended washing the face once a day with milk, and once with carrot or tomato juice.

VIRGIN'S MILK

FROM *THE ART OF PERFUMERY* BY GEORGE WILLIAM SEPTIMUS PIESSE

This popular facial cleanser had many variations. Here are a few:

1   quart rosewater
½ ounce tincture of (balsam) Tolu

ADD the water very slowly to the tincture so a milky opalescent fluid is produced, which will maintain its consistency for many years. In France this is made with tincture of benzoin.

VARIATION: Extract of elder flowers is made the same way. Add one quart elder flower water to one ounce tincture of benzoin. (Elder flowers have a reputation for whitening skin, diminishing wrinkles, and dissolving oils.)

EVENING WASH

FROM "BEAUTY RECIPES OF YESTERYEAR" BY LEONARD STOLLER

A toilette vinegar used by French court beauties.

6   ounces honey
1   quart white wine vinegar

3 drams (teaspoons) pure gelatin

½ ounce nutmeg

1 dram shredded sandalwood

DON'T leave this on the skin longer than a few minutes—it could be irritating.

SOAPWORT-AVOCADO CLEANSING LOTION

Soapwort, otherwise known as bouncing bet, a traditional cleanser in countries where it grew, is being rediscovered by people who prefer to use natural products on their skin. The entire plant contains saponins, chemicals that create suds when you swish the plant in water. Soapwort roots have the greatest concentration of saponins. This cleaner will not give you a rich lather like soap does, but it will get your skin very clean.

½ cup fresh or ¼ cup dried soapwort leaves and flowers

1 cup distilled water

½ cup mashed raw avocado

1 raw egg yolk

SIMMER the soapwort gently in the water for five minutes, strain, and cool. Using a blender or an egg beater, whip the strained liquid with the other two ingredients until the mixture is light and smooth.

VARIATION: Substitute ½ cup milk for the soapwort.

FACIAL MASKS

THROUGHOUT HISTORY IN THE UNIVERSAL PURSUIT OF BEAUTY, women in a variety of cultures have applied concoctions made with fruits, vegetables, grains, and clays to their skin in order to cleanse, tone, and condition it. Fruits and vegetables are rich in free radical scavengers that help us preserve a youthful complexion. Alpha hydroxy acids in fruits and milk help loosen dead skin cells and diminish the appearance of fine lines. Beta-carotenes in broccoli, leafy greens and deep-yellow fruits and vegetables keep our skin and mucous membranes moist and supple.

GALEN'S COLD CREAM

Galen, the renowned Attic physician, supposedly invented this cleansing cream recorded by Helen M. Fox in Gardening with Herbs for Flavor and Fragrance. *The recipe below is a somewhat updated version.*

1 cup each of almond oil and rosewater
1 tablespoon beeswax
1 teaspoon borax
a few drops rose oil

HEAT the almond oil, beeswax, and borax in the top of a glass or enamel double boiler until the wax is melted. Cool slightly, but don't allow the mixture to harden. Pour the rosewater into the jar of a ten-speed electric blender. Turn to highest speed. Add the wax mixture gradually and blend until creamy, then blend in the rose oil. Store in the refrigerator or other cool dry place.

Clay helps draw out impurities, boosting the cleaning powers of the mask. White clay, or kaolin, is milder and more suitable for dry and sensitive skin. Green or brown clay and bentonite (Fuller's earth) absorb more oil and dirt, which is helpful in cleansing oil-clogged pores. Powdered oatmeal is a soothing yet effective cleanser, excellent for sunburned or irritated skin. Honey, which soothes and moisturizes, is a popular ingredient in Central and South America

ADVICE FROM SIDNEY BRISCESE, AESTHETICIAN AT "THE BEACH," A HEALTH AND BEAUTY SPA IN NEW YORK CITY:

You don't need to spend a fortune to have healthy-looking skin. Educate yourself about skin care and don't be swept away by fads. Every week do something for yourself. If you have acne or some other skin problem, consult a doctor first.

You can have a lot of fun with face packs. Avocado is very good for dry skin; strawberries are good for oily skin. Cream that is just slightly sour is very soothing. Make a paste of the ingredients, then place them in the refrigerator for a minute or two to set. Lay a sheet of cheesecloth over your face with holes cut for the eyes, nose and mouth. Spread the paste over that. To remove the mask, peel away the cheesecloth.

and along the Caribbean. Gelatin helps seal in moisture and draw out impurities.

Once you understand how each ingredient interacts with your skin, you can have fun designing your own mask. To begin, clean your face thoroughly with soap, steam, or complexion grains. Apply the mask and let it work for fifteen to twenty minutes; then rinse with tepid water and pat your face dry with a towel. Finish off with a skin freshener or toner.

Sensitive individuals may have an allergic reaction to ingredients in a facial mask because they are unrefined and stay on the face for a time. It's a good idea to test fruits and vegetables by applying a small portion to your inner forearm or behind your ear. Cover with a bandage and leave it on for twenty-four hours. If you see pimples, bumps, redness, or other signs of allergy or irritation, don't use that ingredient.

Vegetables and fruits can be pureed or sliced, depending on consistency. Either way, since the human face is not a flat surface, the ingredients tend to slide or leak into your ears and hair. A towel wrapped around your head or—even better—a shower cap keeps this from happening. In beauty salons, a large piece of gauze or cheesecloth, with

TIPS ON FACIAL MASKS FROM AROMATHERAPIST TRYGVE HARRIS

If you are new to making beauty treatments, masks are a good cosmetic to start with. I like to use clay as a base—green clay for oily skin, white for sensitive skin. Both clays cleanse, but white is gentle. What you add to the base is even more important. To make a paste, I use hydrosol, which contains the water-soluble parts of the plant left after the plant is distilled. This liquid is very soothing; you can spray it on a sunburn. You can add chamomile flower, raspberry, or strawberry leaf tea to a mask. Honey and glycerin help retain moisture. Add a drop or two of essential oil. One drop of tea tree oil and two drops of lemon oil in a green clay or lavender mask is anti-inflammatory and works on blemishes.

My favorite mask is mashed fresh nectarine with a drop or two of patchouli essential oil. Patchouli is excellent for sensitive skin. Apple combined with oatmeal or barley is good for oily skin. White rice is an exfoliant; it makes the skin glow. Oatmeal provokes the fewest allergic reactions.

You don't need preservatives if you make only enough for one mask, but you could use grapefruit seed extract, vitamins C or E, or antioxidant extracts from sage.

FACE MASK INGREDIENTS

ACNE, PIMPLES, SPOTS: aloe vera, barley meal, a mixture of cajeput and olive oils, pureed or grated raw carrot, infusion of chervil or chickweed leaves or flowers and leaves of centaury (3 tablespoons dried herb to 1 cup boiling water); chicory flowers; leaves of costmary and adder's tongue boiled in olive oil; sliced horseradish boiled in milk; Horsetail tincture; garlic; geranium root; marshmallow root; neem oil; lavender flowers or essential oil; red rose petals or essential oil; thyme; tea tree oil; speedwell; pansy; watercress; turmeric; near-ripe banana mixed with yogurt

DRY SKIN: apricot, avocado, banana, carrots, fresh cherries, oatmeal, peach, raw potato, watermelon, sweet or sour cream, hydrogenated vegetable shortening, olive, wheat germ, avocado, peanut and other vegetable oils, glycerin, artichoke, papaya, cranberry, apple, honey, red clover, patchouli leaves or essential oil, egg yolk, mayonnaise, cream, coconut oil, castor oil, shea butter

MATURE SKIN: algae, avocado, banana, bee pollen, buttermilk, brewer's yeast, calcium carbonate, carrots, caviar, comfrey root or leaves, egg yolk, frankincense essential oil, gingko leaves, jojoba oil, rose petals, honey, buttermilk, mayonnaise, seaweed, shea butter, yogurt

SENSITIVE SKIN: tomato, apple, cucumber, fennel, celery seed, chamomile, lemon balm, lettuce, witch hazel, pine needles, cornstarch, honey, fresh or powdered milk, barley, cucumber, rain water, orange-flower water, rosewater, olive oil, castor oil

OILY SKIN: apple, barley, bentonite, brewer's yeast, cucumber, lemon, oatmeal, raw potato, strawberry, tomato, watercress, watermelon, lettuce, lemon juice, cider vinegar, wine, egg white, cabbage, melon, yogurt, buttermilk, pineapple, elder blossom, peppermint leaves, blackberry or raspberry leaves, thyme, rosemary, sage, witch hazel, yarrow

ALL SKIN TYPES: raw potato, shredded raw carrot, yogurt, buttermilk, egg white, barley, mashed cooked turnips, and carrots

holes cut for the eyes, nose and mouth, is laid over the face. See the tips from Sidney Briscese on page 52 for details.

In their more concentrated form, fruit acids are used for facial peels. The effect is similar to a severe sunburn. According to an article in *Drug and Cosmetic Industry* magazine, the long-term effect of skin peels is unknown, but it has been speculated that long-term use might thin the protective uppermost layer of skin (*stratum corneum*), increasing "sensitivity or causing subtle changes in barrier protection against steroids or other cosmetic ingredients." For this reason, it is a good idea to limit the use of acid fruit packs to once a week if your skin is sensitive, mature, or dry. Don't use a fruit pack at all if your skin is sunburned, wind-burned, scratched, or otherwise irritated. Banana or avocado are safe to use if your skin is very sensitive.

SIMPLE CLEANSING MASK FOR OILY SKIN

1 cup boiling distilled water
3 tablespoons dried mint, witch hazel, or yarrow
¼ cup green or brown clay

POUR the boiling water over the herbs. (You can use one of the herbs from the ingredients box on page 54, or combine them.) Steep for thirty minutes. Moisten the clay with enough infusion to make a paste. (Save the remainder of the infusion to use as a skin toner.) Spread the paste over your face and throat and allow the mask to set for ten minutes or so. Rinse with lukewarm water.

SIMPLE PEEL-OFF GELATIN MASK FOR ALL SKIN TYPES

Peel off masks are great for cleaning your skin. When you peel away the gelatin, impurities come with it.

3 tablespoons milk or fruit juice
1 tablespoon (1 package) gelatin

WARM the liquid and mix it with the gelatin until a paste forms. Apply the mask to your face and throat and leave it on for ten to fifteen minutes, or until it sets. Peel off and rinse with tepid water.

WARM PARAFFIN MOISTURIZING MASK FOR DRY OR MATURE SKIN

When you have an important meeting, party, or other occasion when you need to look your best, this is the mask to use. The effect is extraordinary. Not only does the mask lift out dirt and impurities, it plumps up wrinkles, stimulates circulation, and gives you a rosy glow.

$^{1}/_{3}$ block paraffin (about $^{1}/_{2}$ cup)

1   teaspoon of one of the following: oat flour, white clay
    (dry or sensitive skin) or green clay (normal to oily skin)

1   teaspoon dried lavender petals

1   teaspoon powdered frankincense

1   teaspoon dried elder blossoms

3   drops essential oil of lavender

3   drops essential oil of rose

MELT the paraffin and herbs in the top of a double boiler. Remove from fire, stir in essential oils, and cool until still warm but comfortable to touch. Spread the warm wax on your throat, hands, and face, avoiding the hair and eyebrows. Leave on for fifteen minutes, then peel off.

VARIATION: Melt pure beeswax beads instead of paraffin. Stir in a half teaspoon of almond oil.

EGG WHITE MASK

For centuries eggs have been a traditional face mask ingredient. The early Roman Christians used them. Because it absorbs oil, egg white is particularly good for oily skin and acne.

WHIP an egg white until light and frothy. If your skin is dry, add a teaspoonful of honey as a moisturizer. Spread the fluffy mixture on your face, throat, breasts, arms, and thighs. Leave on for twenty minutes and rinse with tepid water. As it dries, the egg white tightens the skin and draws moisture.

AVOCADO ANTIAGING MASK

Avocado, rich in monosaturated oils and vitamins A, C, and E, is the best ingredient to use in a mask. It tones and rejuvenates dry and aging skin. To make this mask, simply mash half of a ripe avocado, spread it over your face and throat, leave on for fifteen or twenty minutes, and rinse with tepid water. If your skin is oily, add 1 teaspoon of lemon juice.

VARIATIONS: For dry skin, add 1 beaten egg yolk to the avocado. If your skin is oily, add a beaten egg white and 1 teaspoon of lemon juice.

AVOCADO-PINEAPPLE MASK

Recommended for oily skin, pineapple contains a meat-tenderizing enzyme, brome-lain, which softens your skin. This tropical fruit is also rich in alpha hydroxy acids, which help bleach age spots.

WHIP equal parts raw avocado and raw pineapple in an electric blender. Spread over your face and throat. Leave on for fifteen minutes.

BANANA-MINT MOISTURIZER

Banana is almost as good as avocado for moisturizing and softening skin. The mint stimulates circulation and oil production and is good for all types of skin, especially dry, sensitive, or mature skin.

1 ripe banana, mashed
1 teaspoon olive oil
1 drop essential oil of peppermint

MIX ingredients and spread on face, neck and chest. Leave on for fifteen to twenty minutes before rinsing with tepid water.

EGG AND LEMON MOISTURIZER

This dry skin mask comes from Jennifer Quasha, writing in Energy Times *magazine.*

2 egg yolks
1 teaspoon olive oil
1 teaspoon lemon juice

AFTER you wash your face, leave this mixture on for ten minutes. Because lemon juice makes skin vulnerable to sun damage, all traces should be removed by thorough washing and rinsing.

STRAWBERRY REJUVENATER

For smooth, fresh-looking skin, try this homespun version of an alpha hydroxy treatment.

MASH 1 cup fresh strawberries, spread them on your face and throat, leave on for ten minutes, then rinse.

FOR A PORCELAIN COMPLEXION—KIWI CLEANSING MASK

Originally known as Chinese gooseberry, the emerald, seedy fruit was renamed by New Zealanders for their favorite bird. Not only does kiwi contain alpha hydroxy acids and antioxidant vitamin C, it contains the enzyme actidin. Like papain, actidin is a meat tenderizer. Used in a face mask, it helps dissolve dead skin cells and softens skin. The clay removes impurities, refines, smooths and tightens skin. For mature skin use white or rose clay, for oily skin brown or green.

- ½ kiwi fruit, peeled and mashed
- ¼ teaspoon olive oil
- 2 teaspoons white clay

MIX thoroughly, spread over face, leave on for thirty minutes.

PAPAYA REJUVENATING SKIN MASK

Papain, the protein-digesting enzyme in green papaya (the ripe fruit doesn't have it), helps loosen dead skin cells—a process that is aided by alpha hydroxies in the tropical fruit. The beta-carotene in papaya, which is absorbed through the skin, helps keep it supple.

- ¼ cup mashed green papaya
- ¼ teaspoon olive oil (omit if your skin is oily)

MIX thoroughly, spread onto face, and leave on for fifteen minutes before rinsing.

A shore thing

Get an ocean view (no matter where you live) with these decorating ideas inspired by the natural beauty of the beach

CAPE COD CANAL

Marine mosaic
HOW TO, *above:* Fill a bowl with sand. Create an inlaid design by pressing shells onto the surface; top with a starfish.

Conch out
HOW TO, *right:* Cut presoaked floral foam to fit inside a conch shell anchored in a dish of sand; sink blooms into the foam.

Shopping Details, page 198

For more great decorating tips, visit goodhousekeeping.com

Photo finish

HOW TO: Paint an interior shutter and glue an array of shells along its edges. Hang the shutter and place favorite pictures in the slats.

AN INTERNATIONAL ARRAY OF RECIPES

paste is applied and left on for fifteen minutes.

Haitian women grate raw carrots and leave the mask on their face for thirty minutes. Afterward the skin is "shiny and beautiful."

Turmeric has been used in India for centuries to treat a variety of disorders, including those affecting the skin. Yemenite women use this powdered root to lighten and soften their skin. They mix the turmeric with water, apply the paste to their face, and leave it on for as long as three days.

In the Dominican Republic, a mixture of cucumber and honey is applied at bedtime and rinsed off in the morning.

Women in Ecuador achieve a soft, smooth complexion by mixing honey with lemon juice. They spread the mixture on their face, leave it for thirty minutes, then rinse it off with warm water. Night is the best time to try this treatment because lemon juice makes the skin sensitive to sunlight.

Burmese women apply lime juice and leave it on for fifteen minutes before rinsing. Both lemon and lime juice are rich in alpha hydroxy acids. Be careful, though: Any citrus juice can lead to severe sunburn if you go outdoors with it on your face.

Burmese women apply a mask of crushed eggshells (a source of calcium) to obtain smooth, clear skin. The mask is left on for fifteen minutes.

Interestingly, eggshells were a favorite of Elizabethan women as well. A recipe for "cosmetic water" used by the queen herself called for powdered eggshells, egg whites, alum, borax, powdered sugar candy, "the water that runs under the wheel of a mill" and poppy seeds. Each time a new ingredient was added, the mixture was beaten for two hours. Used thrice weekly, the water was said to whiten, smooth, and soften the skin.

For an updated version, you could omit the alum and borax, whip the white of 1 egg, mix it with powdered eggshell, $1/4$ teaspoon granulated sugar, and 1 teaspoon poppy seeds, then whirr the mixture in an electric blender set at high speed.

BEFORE-DINNER FACE MASKS

*Not everyone has the time or inclination to repose under a layer of
edibles. A more casual way to feed your face is to simply rub a slice of
fresh fruit or vegetable over your face, neck, arms, the back of your
hands, or any other exposed area of skin. Some quick skin toners you
might try are these: a dab of cooked oatmeal or applesauce, citrus, or
cucumber peel; a slice of cucumber, apple, melon, raw potato, peach,
tomato or other fruit; or a splash of wine. The inside of an avocado peel
is rich in moisturizers, so don't throw the peels away if you are making
salad. Save the seed as well. You can roll it over your face as a quick
moisturizer or chop and grind it in a blender—it makes a great exfoliant.*

Elizabethans of both genders would also bathe their perspiring
faces in wine after they had taken a hot bath so they would be "faire and
ruddy."

A traditional English remedy to smooth a sun-roughened complexion: 3 ounces ground barley, 1 ounce honey, 1 egg white. Leave the
mask on overnight, then rinse with tepid water.

SKIN PROBLEMS AND DISORDERS

Acne, Blackheads, and Blemishes

All three of these skin conditions are linked with overactive oil glands.
Genetic factors can predispose you to acne; hormonal fluctuations can
cause outbreaks before menstruation and during menopause. Bacterial infections are usually at the root of an acne outbreak; stress can be
a contributing factor.

Dr. Benjamin Kligler, director of Beth Israel's Health and Healing Center in Manhattan, observes that recent studies have not borne
out the traditional view that eating too much refined sugar and chocolate cause—or at least contribute to—acne. However, in Kligler's opin-
ion, acne may be related to elevated levels of insulin, which can result
from a sugar overload, among other things. The insulin theory could
explain why chocolate has long been regarded as a culprit, Dr. Kligler

5 minute SOLUTION

SKIN FRESHENER

A skin freshener completes your facial by toning your skin, stimulating circulation and improving your skin tone.

1 tablespoon dried herbs or flowers
1 cup boiling distilled water

STEEP for five minutes, cool slightly, and apply with a cotton ball. Recipe can be doubled or tripled as needed.

FOR dry skin, use rose petals with the astringent white heels snipped off, orange blossoms, or elder blossoms. For oily skin, apply aloe vera gel, or make an infusion with 1 cup boiling water and 1 tablespoon of one of these herbs: rose petals, comfrey leaves, bay leaves, witch hazel, yarrow, sage, stinging nettles, strawberry leaves, raspberry leaves, or horsetail plant.

says. In a chocolate candy it is the sugar that causes the problem, not the chocolate. He adds that naturopathic physicians recommend chromium supplements to help balance the effect of simple sugars that can elevate insulin levels. For overall skin health, especially for people with acne, Kligler recommends a daily intake of 400 international units of vitamin E. To balance hormone production, he advises 30 to 50 milligrams of zinc.

Blackheads, whiteheads, and pimples, all acne symptoms, result from a blocked hair follicle. Blackheads occur when the oil that plugs up the follicle is darkened by exposure to air; whiteheads develop when skin grows over the plugged follicle. A break in the follicle wall may cause oil and dead cells to spill into underlying skin layers. The resulting inflammation causes pimples, and, if the break occurs deep below the epidermis, a cyst may form.

Oily skin is most vulnerable to these skin problems. It helps to keep it scrupulously clean by dissolving accumulated oils with steam or hot packs, washing with plain soap and water or complexion grains, and applying a facial mask regularly to clear away dead skin cells and absorb oils. Dark skin, however, scars easily and is subject to irregular pigmentation, so if your skin is dark, stick with a pure

YOUR FACE   61

TO REMOVE SPOTS AND *beautify face: put seven whole eggs in most*
pure and strong vinegar until shells are soft as their inner skins, mix in four
ounces mustard seed, before made in powder or stamped, then stamp [pound]
or grind them together, and therewith let the face be anointed. This hath been
proved.

Coriander seed powdered and mixed with honey and plastered upon a car-
buncle or other grievous biles [boils] destroys the same quite.

The oil of tartar doth take clean away all spots, freckles, and filthy wheals of
the face, chin, or forehead with its cleansing strength. This is proved.

From *A Thousand Notable Things,* by Thomas Lupton

bar soap and don't steam your face or apply hot packs or abrasive materials.

Dr. Kligler recommends tea tree oil to his patients. Undiluted tea tree oil can be applied directly to a boil or pimple three times a day. However, the undiluted oil can be very drying. For run-of-the-mill acne, Kligler recommends 10 to 25 percent dilutions of tea tree oil.

Natural Acne and Pimple Remedies from Various Times and Climes

Elder blossoms in a steam bath or hot pack are said to help loosen impacted oil.

Try yarrow in a face mask. This astringent herb is said to remove blackheads. Be sure to rinse off all traces of this plant before going outdoors because it can make your skin sensitive to sunlight.

Herbalist and naturopathic physician John Lust recommends tomato face packs for treating blackheads. Slice a ripe tomato in half, remove the seeds and squeeze out the juice, then lay slices over your face for fifteen minutes. For details on how to make a facial mask, see pages 51 to 55.

In Africa where it is harvested, shea butter is applied to lighten brown spots and get rid of blemishes.

You may have heard of this Scottish pimple preventative; it is synonymous with spring tonic, once an annual ritual in rural America as well as other countries where people consume a great deal of heavy, greasy food over the winter: Mix two tablespoons of sulfur with one cup molasses. Eating a daily tablespoon supposedly prevents spots and pimples.

A face mask made of bruised cabbage leaves, a sulfur-rich vegetable, is an old folk remedy for skin infection and inflammation. You could also slice a raw garlic clove or two and rub your face with it twice a day, or apply tea tree oil after you wash your face. (For details, see Dr. Kligler's remarks on page 62.)

Hugh Platt, a contemporary of Queen Elizabeth I, was Britain's first professional freelance author, as well as a gardener and inventor. The revolving barbeque spit and the alphabet block are among his most enduring inventions. Inspired by the stillroom books kept by generations of English gentlewomen, Platt specialized in the genre now known as "how to," instructing his female readers in the arts of housekeeping, cooking, and gardening. The following advice appears in his bestseller *Delights for the Ladies*, first printed in England in 1602.

TO DELAY HEAT AND CLEAR THE FACE: Three pints conduit water [distilled would do], boil in it two ounces French barley. Change the water, boil again, and repeat until the barley no longer colors the water. Boil the last three pints to a quart, then mix in one cup white wine. When cold, squeeze in two or three lemons and use for morphew [age spots], heat of the face and to cleer the skinne. [Note: Barley is a traditional skin softener and whitener. The lemon juice helps bleach age spots and suntan and clear the skin of blemishes. This exfoliant is best used at night. Be sure to wash off all traces of lemon juice before you go outdoors.]

TO HELP A FACE THAT IS RED OR PIMPLED: Dissolve common salt in lemon juice and with a linen cloth pat the patient's face that is full of heate or pimples. It cures in a few dressings.

TO TAKE AWAY SPOTS OR FRECKLES FROM FACE OR HANDS: Apply birch sap tapped in March or April. This sap will dissolve pearl.

John Parkinson, one of the greatest Elizabethan herbalists, recommends:

The juice of cowslips or primrose flowers will cleanse spots or marks on the face. Lupins will scour and cleanse the skin from spots, morphew, blue marks and other discolorations.

Most herbalists believe that blemishes indicate health neglect. For centuries they have recommended alteratives to relieve chronic conditions and favorably alter health by improving digestion, absorption, and elimination. An infusion of one or more of the following herbs, which are classified as alteratives, may help correct skin conditions: burdock, chickweed, dogwood, ginseng, goldenseal, yellow dock, sarsaparilla, wild Oregon grape, spikenard, red clover, dandelion, echinacea, indigo, neem, plaintain, sandalwood. To one cup boiling water add one teaspoon dried herbs. Steep for ten minutes.

Ayurvedic remedies include a poultice of marshmallow root or hibiscus, a daily capsule of turmeric, or external applications of neem oil. Neem, a product of the neem tree, which is native to India, is antiseptic. New York City family physician Benjamin Kligler recommends tea tree oil soap and other tea tree oil products.

Deborah Rutledge, in her fascinating book published in the late 1960s, *Natural Beauty Secrets*, offers these home remedies: Peel and chop two or three onions, cook them in lard until transparent, cool, place between layers of cheesecloth and apply to pimples. She also recommends applications of spirits of camphor or brown or yellow laundry soap. Leave the paste on until the pimples come to a head. Below is her recipe for pimple cream.

PIMPLE CREAM

1 part lanolin
1 part glycerin
1 part castor oil

MELT over low heat to blend, cool, and apply to pimple.

Bags Under the Eyes

When skin under the eyes loses elasticity, the flesh appears to sag and form pouches. The cause is often genetic, though an allergic reaction can make blood vessels swell and leak. Sleep with your head elevated, drink lots of fluids, and apply cold compresses.

Cucumber, which is cooling and astringent, is an old folk remedy for a variety of skin problems, especially around the eyes. Tea bags contain tannin, another astringent that helps shrink tissue. Sage, yarrow, witch hazel, and bearberry leaves, all astringents, would also work.

The California Avocado Commission recommends this Aztec strategy for correcting under-eye puffiness: Peel and pit an avocado, slice it into quarter-inch crescents, place the slices under each eye, and rest for about twenty minutes. Avocado boosts the skin's collagen content, thus helping to restore elasticity.

Chapped Lips

THE FINEST LIP SALVE IN THE WORLD
FROM *THE ART OF COOKERY MADE PLAIN*, BY A LADY, 1760

- 2 ounces Virgin's wax (beeswax)
- 2 ounces hog's lard
- ½ ounce spermaceti (paraffin would do)
- 1 ounce almond oil
- 2 ounces balsam of Peru (optional)
- 2 drams [¼ ounce] alkanet root cut small
- 6 new raisins shred small
- A little fine sugar

SIMMER a while and strain into little pots.

LIPSTICK

FROM *HOW TO BE PRETTY THOUGH PLAIN*, BY MRS. HUMPHREY

½ ounce alkanet

3 ounces almond oil

1½ ounces white wax (beeswax)

½ ounce spermaceti [paraffin can be substituted]

12 drops attar of roses (or their essential oil)

PUT the alkanet and oil in an earthen vessel in a warm place to melt. In another container melt the waxes. Mix the melted ingredients, add the attar of roses, and stir until thick and cool.

FOR CHAPPED LIPS

FROM *THE ART OF PERFUMERY*, BY GEORGE WILLIAM SEPTIMUS PIESSE

Glycerin softens your lips and helps prevent cracking. This mixture can also be used to make your hair glossy.

16 ounces orange flower water

1 ounce glycerin

⅛ ounce borax

Your lips are vulnerable to drying and cracking because they have no oil glands to lubricate them. Licking them aggravates the problem, especially when you are outdoors. Chapped lips may be an allergic reaction to a chemical or natural ingredient in your dentifrice. Switching to another product may clear up the problem.

Most of us deal with chapped lips by applying lipstick or a lip balm. The latter is easy to make and makes a great wintertime gift. Beauty experts recommend that you apply these products only when your lips are dry or chapped. Overuse of lip balms can make your skin dependent on them.

MEDICATED LIP BALM FOR CHAPPED LIPS AND COLD SORES

The olive oil in the recipe below helps lubricate and protect your lips from the sun.

- ½ cup olive oil
- 1 tablespoon dried calendula petals
- 1 tablespoon dried peppermint
- 2 tablespoons chopped beeswax
- 8 drops tea tree oil

IN THE top of a double boiler, heat oil and herbs over simmering water for thirty minutes, or place the mixture in a glass jar and steep on a sunny windowsill for two to three weeks, shaking daily. Strain, add the beeswax, and heat in a double boiler until wax is melted. Remove from fire, stir in tea tree oil, and immediately pour into the bottom of 3-ounce plastic cups, paper cups lined with parchment paper, or small jars.

VARIATION: Linda Pouliot, an Abenaki herbalist, makes a soothing salve for chapped lips and cold sores with this recipe: 2 tablespoons each of clary sage, violet leaves and blossoms, and mint; 1 fresh aloe vera leaf; 4 tablespoons local beeswax; ½ cup almond oil. She steeps the first four ingredients in a glass jar for six weeks, strains the oil into a bowl, adds another ½ cup oil and the melted beeswax, then pours into small containers.

ALKANET LIP BALM

Alkanet, a blue flower with a red root, was a popular Elizabethan lip balm ingredient used in Ancient Egypt, it is one of the few roots that will tint oil. In the Perfume and Paint chapter, pages 145 to 173, you will find recipes for alkanet lip gloss that will color your lips. This one does not, although it is a cheerful cherry red. It does make your lips soft and moist as soon as you smooth it on. The consistency and properties of paraffin are similar to those of spermaceti used in traditional recipes.

- 1 tablespoon shaved alkanet root
- ½ cup safflower oil

1 tablespoon chopped beeswax

1 tablespoon chopped paraffin

2 drops essential oil of rose

STEEP the first two ingredients in a warm place for two days. Strain, add paraffin and beeswax and heat until the waxes melt. Pour immediately into 3-ounce plastic cups or paper ones lined with parchment paper. Do not move the container until the wax hardens. Place in the refrigerator overnight to set.

Eczema

Eczema can be temporary or chronic. The skin is red and itchy, sometimes crusted or even blistered. Most often, an outbreak is brought on by contact with an allergen in the environment or the diet. Dishwashing soap and other household detergents can cause contact dermatitis, a form of eczema, on the hands. Dairy products, citrus fruits, nuts, fish, food additives, and fermented foods are common allergens. You may be able to avoid eczema by identifying your allergens and eliminating them from your living space or diet. Some strategies for coping with eczema include a diet rich in antioxidant vitamins A, beta-carotenes, and vitamins C and E. In addition to their vitamin content, broccoli, summer squash, shallots, and onions contain the flavenoid quercetin, believed to be helpful in relieving eczema. B vitamins, lecithin, evening primrose oil, and the essential fatty acids found in oily fish also help to relieve or prevent eczema. Dr. Benjamin Kligler, director of Beth Israel Hospital's Center for Health and Healing, recommends a 4- to 5-ounce serving of salmon, mackerel, or other fatty fish every day, or 1 tablespoon flaxseed oil.

Herbalists recommend infusions of burdock root, yellow dock leaves, or marshmallow root, and poultices made from these plants. (See the next page for details.) Native American herbalists often recommend yarrow as a cleansing and astringent herb. The late Jethro Kloss, a noted herbalist, recommended an infusion of burdock, yellow dock, marshmallow, and yarrow (1 teaspoon of the herb mixture to 1 cup boiling water). Four or five times a day, the patient sips ¼ cup of the tea, then uses the other ½ cup as a skin wash.

The herb comfrey is very effective at healing all sorts of skin problems. Both the leaves and, to a greater extent, the root contain allantoin, a natural chemical that stimulates skin renewal. This herb may be toxic to the liver if taken internally, but you could use it as an occasional poultice if the skin is unbroken. Pour boiling water over about ½ cup of dried comfrey leaves. Let the mixture sit for five or ten minutes, or until the leaves soften. Wrap the leaves in a layer of cheesecloth and apply to the eczema lesions for ten minutes three times a day.

Tannic acid, which is very astringent, is another herbal remedy; it helps dry up blisters. Steep 3 tablespoons of black tea in a cup of boiling water for thirty minutes. Apply a damp cloth saturated with the tea to the eczema lesions for fifteen minutes three or four times a day. Oak bark is also astringent. Boil a couple of tablespoons of broken oak twigs in a pint of water for fifteen minutes. Mallow root and flowers are both astringent and soothing. Follow the recipe for oak bark.

Aloe vera gel, a universal folk remedy for skin problems, is astringent, soothing, and healing. Test on a small area of skin to make sure you are not allergic to it. Apply as needed.

Apply shea butter; it heals and softens.

The Psoriasis Cream recipe on the following page is also helpful in treating eczema.

Try drinking this vegetable cocktail two or three times a day: ¼ cup each beet, celery and tomato juice.

Psoriasis

Psoriasis is usually a chronic skin condition where skin cells mature much more rapidly than normal skin cells, resulting in scaly red patches covered by dead skin cells.

The coping strategies listed in the Eczema section can also relieve psoriasis symptoms. In addition, try warm castor oil packs to help soften the skin so you can remove the cellar debris. Recent clinical studies have revealed that turmeric, used in India for centuries to treat skin conditions, is effective at relieving psoriasis. Take a capsule of turmeric orally every day and apply the Psoriasis Cream (below). For a more complete discussion of both eczema and psoriasis, see *Everywoman's Guide to Natural Home Remedies*.

ADVICE ON PSORIASIS FROM NEW YORK CITY DR. BENJAMIN KLIGLER

I have found that you can cure psoriasis by balancing omega 3 and omega 6 oils. Just about everybody needs to increase their intake of omega 3 fatty acids. You can do this by eating a 4- to 5-ounce serving of salmon, mackerel, or other oily fish once a day, or by taking a tablespoon of flaxseed oil every day. You could also take fish oil, but many of those you see on the market are oxidized (i.e., rancid). You could avoid this by buying fish oil with vitamin E (an antioxidant) added, or you could buy extracts of DHA (Docosahexaenoic acid) and EPA (eicosapeniaenoic acid) fatty acids.

Flaxseed oil, which also contains omega 3 fatty acids, is a better choice: it is easier to digest and it resists oxidation.

You also need to take in omega 6 oils found in vegetables. Corn, peanut, soy, and many others are proinflammatory, and can aggravate psoriasis. Use olive oil instead.

PSORIASIS CREAM

If you store this in the refrigerator, be sure it's clearly labeled, or it may end up in a sandwich! This cream is not toxic—all of the ingredients are edible—but it's sure to be a culinary disappointment. If you haven't made an emulsion before, see pages 8 to 10.

Turmeric lends its yellow-orange hue to mustard and curry. For best results, combine frequent applications of this cream with oral doses of curcumin, the active ingredient in turmeric, or eat lots of curry. Curcumin is sold in health food stores.

Warning: *Both goldenseal and turmeric have been used to dye clothing. You might want to wear old pajamas and sleep on old bedsheets while trying this remedy—it does stain yellow everything it touches!*

- 1/2 cup boiling distilled water
- 1/2 tablespoon powdered turmeric root
- 1/2 tablespoon powdered goldenseal root
- 1 tablespoon powdered comfrey leaves
- 1/4 teaspoon powdered myrrh
- 1/8 teaspoon powdered gum benzoin
- 2/3 cup olive oil
- 2 tablespoons chopped beeswax
- 1/3 cup aloe gel

POUR boiling water over the herbs and steep for thirty minutes. Meanwhile, add myrrh, benzoin, and wax to the oil and heat in top of double boiler until wax is melted. Remove from the fire and set aside.

STRAIN the infusion, measure out ⅓ cup, and pour into an electric blender jar along with the aloe. When wax has cooled and thickened, but not hardened, set your blender at the highest speed and add the oil mixture. When the blender sputters and labors, carefully scrape down the sides of the jar with a rubber spatula until all ingredients hold together. Whip thirty to sixty seconds more until the mixture is smooth and creamy. Pour into jars, but do not cap until cream is completely cool. Makes three 2-ounce jars.

ORANGE-GOLDENSEAL-MARIGOLD CREAM

The goldenseal in this cream may stain your skin or clothing to some extent, but much less than the above recipe. Goldenseal has been used by Native Americans for centuries to heal a range of infections and skin conditions.

⅓ cup orange water or orange blossom infusion (to make the infusion, steep 2 tablespoons dried orange blossoms in ½ cup boiling distilled water for 30 minutes)

1 tablespoon dried calendula petals

2 tablespoons chopped beeswax or beeswax beads

1½ teaspoons powdered goldenseal root

⅔ cup olive oil

A pinch of powdered gum benzoin

A pinch of boric acid

⅓ cup aloe vera gel

IF YOU are using bottled orange water, gently heat the calendula and oil in the top of a double boiler for thirty minutes, then strain. Otherwise, steep the calendula along with the orange blossoms for thirty minutes and strain. Add wax, benzoin, boric acid and goldenseal to the oil and heat gently in a double boiler until the wax melts. Remove from fire and cool until the wax mixture is thickened and opaque, but not hard. Measure out ⅓ cup flower infusion and pour into electric blender jar. Add aloe, then the oil mixture, following directions in the previous recipe.

Scars

The extent to which a burn, injury, skin infection, or disease will leave
a scar is determined largely by your genes. In general, dark skin scars
more easily than light; the darker the skin, the more easily it scars. Cocoa butter, shea butter, vitamin E, or wheat germ oil, which is rich in
vitamin E, may help some. A prompt application of aloe vera gel may
arrest scarring if you burn yourself.

DOMINICAN SCAR REMEDY

This folk remedy comes from the Dominican Republic.

- 1 part honey
- 1 part grated soap (castile or other mild, pure soap)

MAKE a paste with these ingredients. Apply the mask to your face and
leave it on for twenty to thirty minutes, then rinse thoroughly with a lot
of water. Use this treatment once or twice a week.

SUN PROTECTION

TO PREVENT SKIN CANCER AND PREMATURE AGING, DERMATOLOGISTS
recommend a layer of sunscreen (SPF 15 or higher) at all times, even
in winter. Since many chemicals are absorbed through the skin, it's a
good idea to have what you put on your skin as pure as possible. These
sunscreens can double as moisturizers. All of the ingredients condition your skin. Sesame oil absorbs 30 percent of UVA rays; coconut oil
20 percent.

Avoid the sun between the hours of 10 A.M. and 4 P.M. if you can;
otherwise, wear a broad-brimmed hat and protective clothing when
you do go out in the sun.

INDUSTRIAL STRENGTH SUNSCREEN

Although not as powerful a sunblock as some commercial ones, this homemade preparation does offer sun protection without harmful or irritating chemicals. And it works! Apply thirty minutes before going out in the sun, and renew frequently, especially if you sweat or swim. The essential oils are added to gentrify the aroma of sesame oil and caraway. They are optional. For more information on making emulsions, see pages 8 to 10.

3 tablespoons caraway seeds	$1/2$ teaspoon vitamin E oil
1 cup distilled water	3 drops essential oil of patchouli
2 tablespoons green tea	3 drops essential oil of ylang-ylang
$2/3$ cup sesame oil	2 tablespoons powdered oat flour
2 tablespoons chopped beeswax	$1/3$ cup aloe vera gel
$1/8$ teaspoon powdered gum benzoin	

BOIL caraway seeds in water for ten minutes. Remove from fire and add tea, cover and steep for thirty minutes. Meanwhile, place oil, wax and benzoin in the top of a double boiler. Heat gently until wax melts. Remove from fire, add vitamin E and essential oils. Mix two tablespoons or so of the oil with oat flour to make a smooth paste, then stir into the rest of the oil. Meanwhile, measure out $1/3$ cup infusion, discarding any remainder. Pour into electric blender jar along with the aloe. When oil mixture is lukewarm and thickened, but not hard, pour into the vortex of blender set at high speed.

WHEN blender sputters and sounds labored, stir ingredients with a rubber spatula. Be careful not to touch the blades. Continue to blend until mixture is thick and creamy, then pour quickly into sterile, wide-mouthed glass jars. Makes three 4-ounce jars.

VARIATIONS:

COCONUT-SESAME SUNSCREEN This is not as oily as the previous sunscreen, has little aroma, and is better absorbed by the skin. Because sesame oil absorbs 10 percent more UVA radiation, you will sacrifice a little sun protection, so renew frequently.

Substitute $1/3$ cup coconut oil for half the sesame oil. Omit the caraway. Instead make the infusion with 4 tablespoons of green tea rather than only two.

Aloe vera brings immediate relief from burns, sunburn, and other skin irritations and helps prevent peeling. It has been used in tropical and desert regions for centuries. Apply bottled aloe or the gel from a live plant, or spray on aloe vera juice.

To cool and soothe sunburn, splash on cold milk or vinegar, dab on yogurt, or apply slices of cucumber, tomato, or raw potato.

George William Askinson, author of Perfumes and Cosmetics, Their Preparation and Manufacture *writes: ". . . no other remedy will clear a sunburnt skin in so short a time as glycerin. Make a wash by mixing glycerin with an equal part of orange water. Do not use concentrated glycerin as a wash—it draws moisture from the skin."*

OLIVE OIL SUNSCREEN: Substitute ⅓ cup of olive oil for the sesame oil. Omit caraway and replace with 2 extra tablespoons of green tea.

OILY-SKIN SUNSCREEN: Replace sesame oil with ⅓ cup grapeseed or hazelnut oil and ⅓ cup coconut oil. Instead of patchouli oil, use 3 drops essential oil of sage.

SIMPLE SUNSCREEN

This mixture is more aromatic than the previous variations, but effective.

3 tablespoons green tea infusion (Steep 2 tablespoons green tea in ½ cup boiling distilled water for thirty minutes.) Proceed as in above recipe.

1 rounded tablespoon chopped beeswax

⅓ cup sesame oil

⅛ teaspoon powdered benzoin

3 teaspoons aloe vera gel

Take Tea and See

Black tea as well as green tea is a potent antioxidant. Researchers have discovered that tea used as a skin wash protects against sunburn.

Sunburn Remedies from Around the World

Black tea is an Irish remedy. Pour a cup of boiling water over 2 or 3 teaspoons of loose tea or tea bags. Steep for thirty minutes and apply with absorbent cotton. Tannic acid, which is used in some pharmaceutical preparations, forms a protective film over the burn so it can heal.

Soak in a lukewarm bath with a cup or two of baking soda or oatmeal added.

A honey face mask smooths skin that is roughened by exposure to sun and weather: Mix 3 ounces ground barley, 1 ounce honey, and 1 egg white. Leave on for twenty minutes, then rinse off with tepid water.

WARTS

WARTS ARE CAUSED BY A VIRUS, AND THEY SELDOM TRAVEL ALONE; IF YOU HAVE one, you undoubtedly have several. These hard, pale, skin protrusions are contagious. You can catch them from contact with the skin of a person who has them or from using their towels or clothing. Pharmaceutical preparations usually contain salicylic acid, the main ingredient in aspirin.

TRADITIONAL RECIPES TO COMBAT WARTS

PEEL A RADISH AND SPRINKLE *it with salt. Place the radish on a saucer. Apply the juice that runs from it three or four times a day for five or six days, or until the wart is gone.*

Elizabethan recipe recorded in *The Housewife's Rich Cabinet*

WOODBINE LEAVES STAMPED [*crushed* OR POUNDED] *and laid upon warts, using them six times, will quickly destroy them. The juice of elderberries destroys warts. [In clinical studies, elderberry has been found to be antiviral]*

From *A Thousand Notable Things on Various Subjects,* by Thomas Lupton

Folk remedies for fighting warts are legion. They work best applied to new warts. Abenaki herbalist Linda Pouliot breaks off a piece of milkweed stalk and applies the milky liquid that oozes from the cut plant directly to the wart. She does this three times a day until the wart is gone. "Milkweed destroys the root of the wart," she says. "You have to do that if you don't want the warts to come back. The latex from dandelion stems or fig stems are used similarly in folk medicine. Dr. Kligler observes that the latex forms an airtight film over the wart and kills it by depriving it of air.

◆ Other folk remedies include aloe vera, garlic, raw potato, green walnuts, or thuja applied several times a day until the wart is gone.

◆ The late Austrian herbalist Maria Treben recommended the fresh juice of celandine or calendula, arnica tincture, or Swedish bitters applied directly to the wart several times a day.

Family physician Benjamin Kligler, noting that warts are caused by a virus, says that we can activate our immune system to get rid of warts. In his practice, he has seen visual imagery work with patients.

"I do this with kids," he says. "Twice a day, for five minutes, they are to imagine the warts drying up and falling off their body. My father, a pediatrician, laid typing paper over the wart, had the child make a drawing of it, then burned the drawing in an ashtray. Possibly these methods work by stimulating the T cells to kill the wart virus. It doesn't work with planter's wart, though. You have to use an acid over-the-counter preparation for that."

CHAPTER 3

YOUR HAIR
GLORIOUS AND TELLTALE PLUMAGE

Our crowning glory, the object of much poetry, politics, and passion, is relatively unimpressive compared with the plumage of most birds or the pelts of other mammals. Hair does keep our body heat from escaping out of the top of our heads and protects our scalp from sunburn and other injuries, but the primary purpose of this thread-thin extrusion is decoration.

Hair is composed mostly of keratin, a protein that comprises most of our skin as well as the nails of our toes and fingers. Healthy hair is slightly acidic, with a pH ranging from 4.0 to 5.0. Each individual shaft grows out of a follicle, or pore, and is anchored by a root. Sebaceous glands lubricate the hair, blood vessels nourish it, a network of nerves runs messages to and from the follicles. ("Stand up; don't slouch," is the message hair gets in times of terror and catastrophe.)

The hair itself, slight though it appears to be, is actually composed of two or three layers. The thin, colorless cuticle protects the underlying structure from environmental damage. The cortex, or middle layer, is composed of a bundle of fibrous cells that gives hair its strength and elasticity. The shape and thickness of the cortex determine whether a hair is straight or curly, thick or thin; pigment in the cortex determines what color it will be. The medulla is the inner part of a hair. In people who have thin, limp hair, the medulla may be partially missing or not present at all.

At birth, each of us is allotted a certain number of hairs—one to a follicle. Redheads get around 90,000 hair follicles, brunettes about 100,000, blondes 140,000. Because we have only so many of these receptacles, we don't get any more hairs than that, although we can, and sometimes do, have less.

At any given time, 85 percent of our hair is growing, a process that can last from two to six or seven years, or the lifetime of an individual hair. Each hair that is in a growth phase extends about a third of a millimeter daily. The rest of our hair is either in a transitional phase, where individual hairs are moving toward the skin surface, or in a "resting" phase, where old hairs loosen and fall out and are replaced by new ones growing from the same follicle. We lose from fifty to seventy of these "resting" hairs daily.

The number of our hairs, and their color and shape, are determined by our genes, ethnic background, and—in some instances—our gender. Women's hair grows faster than men's. Because their bodies produce less testosterone, which, in excess, is associated with pattern baldness, women are far less likely to lose all of their hair.

Hair, like skin, betrays our state of health. Because minerals accumulate in the hair as it grows, it is possible to detect, through hair analysis, possible mineral imbalances in the body or the presence of mercury, lead, or other heavy metals.

Poor health habits are likely to be reflected in dull, dry, prematurely gray or thinning hair. Therefore, to maintain your crowning glory, eat well, exercise regularly, and learn to cope with stress.

To maintain your hair in top condition, you need to treat it gently. Harsh chemicals, salt, chlorine, sunlight, and intense heat from blow-dryers or curling irons can damage your hair cuticle and cause the hair to break. Grooming your hair when it is wet, pulling at your hair by teasing, back combing, fastening your hair with a tight hair tie or a rubber band, or winding it too tightly on curlers can damage or loosen it. When you swim in the ocean or a swimming pool, wear a bathing cap to protect your hair from salt and chlorine. Sunlight can dry, fade, or damage your hair, so protect it with a scarf or hat when you go outdoors. After shampooing, use a wide-toothed comb to style your hair. If you blow-dry, use the cool setting.

Because healthy hair is slightly acidic, alkaline products will dry it out, as they do your skin. Alcohol is also drying. For shine and manageability, wash your hair with soapwort or yucca root tea instead of commercial shampoo, dilute commercial shampoo with an herbal infusion, or use an acidic rinse. For more information, see pages 98 to 101.

Washing your hair too often actually makes it more oily because the sebaceous glands are stimulated to pump out even more oil to compensate. Don't shampoo more often than once a day with a mild shampoo; every other day is better. Between times, use a dry shampoo.

Some chemicals in home permanents and hair coloring are toxic. Hair dyes that are derived from coal tar are suspected carcinogens. If you can't pronounce the chemicals listed on a label—sometimes even when you can—they probably aren't good for you. If you must use these products, follow the instructions to the letter.

A daily scalp massage stimulates circulation, normalizes oil production, and encourages hair growth. Spend a minute or two massaging your scalp with your fingertips. Using firm but gentle pressure, work in tiny circles all over your scalp.

Below are discussions of common hair problems and what you can do about them.

DANDRUFF

ALTHOUGH SOME DANDRUFF IS THE RESULT OF DRY SKIN, MORE OFTEN it is a fungus infection caused by an organism similar to yeast. Like most infections, this one is contagious, so don't share combs, hats, towels, or anything else that comes into contact with scalp and hair.

Psoriasis, a chronic but not contagious skin disease, can cause an itching and scaly scalp that is sometimes mistaken for dandruff. If dandruff remedies don't work for you, check with your health care professional.

Simple neglect can also result in an itching, flaky scalp. Wash your hair at least once a week, and rinse it thoroughly. Shampoo residue on your hair and scalp can be very drying. A vinegar or lemon rinse helps get the soap out and restores a healthy acidity to your scalp and hair. If your hair is dry, add 1 tablespoon of cider vinegar to a quart of warm water; if you have oily hair, add the same amount of lemon juice. Pour the solution through your hair, then rinse with tepid water.

Dandruff Preventatives and Treatments from Around the World

In Ecuador, two aspirins are dissolved in two glasses of water. The solution is poured over the hair, then rinsed off with cool water. Aspirin contains salicylic acid, which is used in some commercial dandruff shampoos.

In the Dominican Republic, Ecuador, and Haiti, a mixture of olive oil and avocado is applied to give hair shine and prevent dandruff. A ripe or overripe avocado is mixed with a little olive oil to make a paste. This is spread on the hair and left on for an hour or two.

Africans burn papaya leaves and rub the ashes into the scalp.

Aloe vera gel is antifungal. Jamaicans rub it into the scalp once a day until the dandruff is gone.

◆ In places as far-flung as Senegal and Haiti, women anoint their scalp with palm oil as a lubricant and dandruff preventative. Haitians apply the palm oil the day before a shampoo so it can work overnight.

◆ In Burma women apply coconut oil to prevent or eliminate dandruff and make their hair strong, glossy, and healthy. This oil locks in moisture, thus hydrating the hair.

◆ For instant medicated oil, add ¼ teaspoon essential oil of basil, sage, geranium, juniper, rosemary, or tea tree to 2 ounces carrier oil. Massage your scalp with the mixture at least once a day, preferably at bedtime. The oil can also be used for a preshampoo conditioner.

HERBS AND/OR THEIR ESSENTIAL OILS THAT COMBAT DANDRUFF

aloe vera gel, birch bark oil, burdock root, cedar wood, catnip, chamomile blossoms, clary sage leaves, fennel seeds, juniper berries, stinging nettle leaves, patchouli leaves, rosemary leaves, sage leaves, tea tree oil, thyme leaves, willow bark, wintergreen leaves and berries

Make a strong infusion using 3 tablespoons of one or more of these herbs to 1 cup boiling water. Steep for thirty minutes, then strain and add to a shampoo base (see the Shampoo section on pages 98 to 100) or use as a rinse.

You could also use one or more of these herbs to make a medicated oil. Place 3 tablespoons of one or more of these herbs in a glass jar. Add 1 cup of olive or jojoba oil. Seal the jar and leave it in a sunny place for two weeks, shaking daily. If you want medicated oil in a hurry, place 3 tablespoons herbs and 1 cup olive or jojoba oil in the top of a double boiler. Heat gently over simmering water for thirty minutes, then strain and bottle.

ANTIDANDRUFF SHAMPOO

At least as far back as medieval times, the leaves, flowers, and root of soapwort have been used for bathing, shampooing, and laundering clothes. The plant, also known as "bouncing bet" is easily grown and pretty. The petals resemble pink phlox, but they are somewhat square and rather ragged.

A shampoo containing only soapwort and water is one of the best you can use. It doesn't lather much, but it does get your hair clean and it deposits a waxy coating that softens, enhances color, and reflects light. If you insist on lather, add liquid castile soap (2 tablespoons to 1 cup of water). Although less effective than pure soapwort, this is an excellent shampoo:

½	cup dried or 1 cup fresh soapwort leaves and flowers
1	cup water
2	tablespoons dried rosemary leaves
1	tablespoon dried thyme leaves
1	tablespoon dried patchouli leaves
2⅓	tablespoons liquid castile soap (optional)
2	tablespoons fresh aloe vera gel
10	drops tea tree oil

GENTLY simmer soapwort in water for ten minutes. Strain and pour over rosemary, thyme, and patchouli. Steep thirty minutes. Strain, add castile soap, aloe, and tea tree oil. Whir in a blender for about thirty seconds, or until ingredients are completely mixed.

VARIATIONS:

FOR BLOND HAIR, substitute 1 tablespoon chamomile for half the rosemary.

FOR WHITE HAIR, omit thyme, and substitute 1 tablespoon of cornflower petals. Instead of 2 tablespoons of rosemary, use 1 tablespoon of rosemary and 1 tablespoon of chamomile.

DRY HAIR

The causes of dry hair can be hereditary, hormonal, or environmental. Thin people are more likely to have dry skin and hair. After menopause a woman's hair is likely to be dry. Dry winter air, forced air heating, summer sunshine, salt, and chlorine can also rob your hair of moisture.

The strategies for preventing or treating dry hair are similar to those for dry skin: Keep hydrated by drinking eight glasses of water every day. Keep lubricated by including at least a tablespoon of mono-saturated oil in your diet and frequent servings of salmon, mackerel, or other oily fish. When you don't eat fish, take in a tablespoon of flaxseed oil or supplement with fish oil capsules.

It also helps to moisturize your indoor environment with a hu-midifier, vaporizer, houseplants, or open containers of water. When you go outdoors, protect your hair from sunlight with a scarf or hat, and from salt and chlorine with a bathing cap.

Brushing your hair distributes sebum along the hair shaft and helps cleanse it of dust and soil. It's a good thing to do several times a week, especially before shampooing it. The traditional hundred strokes a day is really not necessary, contemporary hair experts say; overbrushing can result in split ends and dryness.

Shampooing your hair too frequently strips it of its natural oils. Dry, mature, colored, or permed hair should not be washed more than twice a week with a gentle shampoo. Avoid alkaline shampoos—they are very drying.

Universal Folk Remedies for Dry Hair

In the Dominican Republic, a mixture of coconut oil and egg yolk is ap-plied as a conditioner an hour before a shampoo.

Women in Puerto Rico slice a ripe avocado in half, mash it, and work the paste into their hair. They cover their hair with plastic and let the mixture sit for a half hour before washing it out.

Mayonnaise is another tried and true conditioner for dry hair. Work the mayonnaise into your hair and scalp, cover with a shower cap, and let the mixture work for a half hour or more.

For centuries various cultures all over the world have used one or more of the following herbs to correct dry hair: comfrey root or leaves, plantain leaves, patchouli leaves, southernwood leaves, orange blos-soms and orange peel, calendula, rosemary, lavender, sandalwood, and burdock root.

Shampoo your hair with a raw egg to strengthen, condition, and moistur-
ize. Whip the egg until it foams and either add it to a commercial sham-
poo, or mix it with ¹/₄ cup of warm water. One egg will do if your hair is
long. Contrary to what you might expect, washing your hair with egg
doesn't make it sticky. The egg doesn't lather, of course, but it does leave
your hair clean and tangle-free. If possible, dry your hair in the sun after
shampooing. Refrigerate the unused portion of your egg mixture. Shake or
whip when ready to use again.

→ To add moisturizing action to commercial shampoo, add about 1 teaspoonful of wheat germ oil or mashed, fresh avocado to each portion of
shampoo every time you wash your hair.

→ Science writer Deborah Chase, in her *New Medically-Based No-Nonsense*
Beauty Book, writes that coconut, wheat germ, jojoba and avocado oils,
balsam of Peru or lanolin, when applied to the hair, lock in moisture and
protect hair from water evaporation.

Hot-Oil Treatment

Hot oil is another traditional and universal treatment to give the hair gloss
and strength. Castor oil is the best strengthener; next best are lanolin, olive oil, and
corn oil. The amount you use depends on the length, thickness, and texture of your
hair.

¹/₄ to 1 cup vegetable oil
3 tablespoons of one or more of the herbs listed above
under "Universal Folk Remedies for Dry Hair" (optional)

STEEP the herbs and oil in a sealed jar for two weeks, shaking daily, or
gently warm the oil in the top of a double boiler for thirty minutes and
strain. Massage the oil gently into your hair and scalp, then cover your
head with a hot, wet towel for at least fifteen minutes, soaking the towel
in hot water every time it cools. To get the oil out of your hair, rinse with
tepid water. To restore your hair's natural acidity, follow your shampoo
with a vinegar rinse (1 tablespoon cider vinegar to 1 quart warm water).

BRIGHTENING YOUR HAIR

Martha Sanchez, hair stylist at Astor Place Haircutters in New York City, has these suggestions:

Beat an egg white into a cup of shampoo. Leave the mixture on your hair for fifteen minutes before you wash it.

If you have red hair, add about ¼ cup of crushed fresh raspberries to a cup of
shampoo and use the mixture for washing your hair.

If you have dark hair, use blackberries instead.

Strong, freshly brewed black coffee makes black hair shiny. Mix it half and half
with shampoo.

For blond hair, mix shampoo with an equal amount of strong chamomile tea
(2 or 3 tablespoons to 1 cup of water).

DRY HAIR SHAMPOOS

*Here are two quick and easy recipes suitable for dry hair. You will find more shampoo
recipes for dry hair on pages 99–100.*

- 1 cup boiling water
- 3 tablespoons of one or more of the dried herbs listed
    under Universal Folk Remedies on page 83.

POUR boiling water over the herbs and steep for thirty minutes. Strain
and add to a cup of commercial shampoo. You could also use the infusion as a conditioning rinse.

BASIC CASTILE SHAMPOO

- 2 tablespoons liquid castile soap
- 1 cup herbal infusion (see recipe above)

PLACE ingredients in a recycled shampoo container, shake, and use.

Dull Hair

Hair that is either too dry or too oily can become dull and lifeless. See
the section on dry or oily hair for recipes and suggestions on coping

FOR DULL HAIR

After shampooing, rub in a mixture of olive oil and egg yolk, lemon juice and beer. Leave on for five minutes and wash out.

with either of these problems. Stress, trauma, illness, and poor nutrition can erase the glow of health from your hair as well as your skin. Sun exposure, chemicals, and overprocessing can also dull your hair. Be sure to include plenty of fresh, raw vegetables, dairy products, and other foods rich in calcium, and monosaturated oil in your diet.

Sometimes the hair color you were born with is just plain uninspired. Herbs that enliven dull blond hair include red clover blossoms, chamomile blossoms, cornflowers, green tea, rosemary leaves, southernwood. Black tea and clove buds perk up darker hair; red onion, madder root or orange pekoe tea enliven red hair. Plantain, shepherd's purse, marshmallow leaves, mullein leaves and malva work for all shades. For more suggestions, see page 85.

Gray Hair

The color of our hair depends on how much melanin, a black pigment, is sent from our hair root where it is manufactured to the cortex of the hair shaft. The older we grow, the less melanin we produce. Our hair shade becomes lighter until it appears to be gray. This illusion is created by the presence of white hairs among pigmented ones. They are more noticeable in dark-haired people than in blonds. Trauma or a vitamin deficiency can cause hair to gray prematurely, but usually this event is genetically programmed. As to when your hair will gray, find out when your mother's did.

Getting enough copper, vitamin D and the B complex vitamins can delay graying. Liver, kidneys, shellfish, nuts, mushrooms, and broccoli are rich in copper. Vitamin D, which is added to fortified milk, is also manufactured by our bodies when we are exposed to summer sunlight. B vitamins are present in whole grains, nuts, meat, fish, and dairy products. Some people have actually recovered their original hue by taking large doses of B vitamins (check with your doctor regarding recommended dosages), but the more likely scenario for most of us is a gradual absence of color.

A gleaming cap of healthy gray hair can be stunning. If this doesn't suit you, you could try gradually darkening your hair with a sage rinse.

HAIR-DARKENING RINSE

- 1 quart boiling water
- 2 tablespoons dried stinging nettle leaves
- 2 tablespoons dried rosemary leaves
- 2 tablespoons dried sage leaves

POUR boiling water over the herbs and steep for thirty minutes

IF YOU use this rinse regularly, it is said to gradually darken your hair.

VARIATIONS: Use ⅓ cup dried sage leaves instead of the herbal mixture. If your hair is blond or very light brown, steep 3 tablespoons each calendula and chamomile in 1 quart boiling water for thirty minutes.

For information about dyeing your hair, see pages 102 to 106.

Hair Loss

Although thinning hair is more commonly a male affliction, a woman can have a genetic predisposition to hair loss and even baldness. The most dramatic and sudden hair loss a woman experiences is after radiation or chemotherapy. Both weaken the hair roots. The remedy is waiting a few months for the hair to grow back.

Hormonal changes during pregnancy and menopause are the most common causes of hair loss for women. Starting or stopping birth control pills may also result in more shedding than usual. Other hair loss triggers include physical or emotional trauma, rapid weight loss, psoriasis, and allergy. Harsh chemicals in shampoos, dyes, permanent waving, or hair straightening lotions can also weaken the roots so the hair falls out. Pulling your hair back in a tight ponytail or winding it tightly on curlers can loosen your hair.

Anemia, an underactive thyroid, or insufficient protein intake can also be accompanied by hair loss. To avoid these problems, it helps to include plenty of iodine, sulfur, and iron in your diet. Protein is to

HERBS THAT STIMULATE HAIR GROWTH

Many herbs and essential oils that are recommended as hair restorers work by stimulating the hair follicles. Some, like bittersweet and other members of the nightshade family, are toxic; others, like peppermint and juniper, make your scalp tingle. Herbs traditionally used as hair restorers include arnica blossoms, basil leaves, bittersweet berries, black elder blossoms, boxwood leaves, burdock root, calendula blossoms, juniper berries, lavender spikes, peppermint leaves and blossoms, mullein leaves and blossoms, parsley leaves, rosemary leaves, soapwort leaves and root, sage leaves, southernwood leaves, stinging nettle leaves, white birch bark, white onions, white willow bark, and wormwood leaves. In addition, Kathi Keville and Mindy Green, in their excellent book, *Aromatherapy,* recommend the essential oils of basil, cedar, peppermint, rosemary, or tea tree.

be found in meat, poultry, fish, dairy products, and combinations of grains and legumes. Iron is present in red meat, leafy greens and legumes. Seafood and seaweed, sea salt, and iodized salt are excellent sources of iodine. Broccoli, cabbage, and cauliflower are rich in sulfur. Whole grains rich in riboflavin, and seafood, a source of zinc, are also important dietary weapons against hair loss.

Alternative treatments for thinning hair that have worked for some people include a daily dose of 100 milligrams of vitamin B_6 and drinking three cups of green tea daily.

HOMEMADE HAIR RESTORER

3/4 cup vodka

1 tablespoon dried lavender

1 tablespoon dried rosemary

1 tablespoon dried southernwood

1 tablespoon burdock root

1 tablespoon dried stinging nettle

1 tablespoon dried basil

1 tablespoon dried peppermint

POUR the vodka over the herbs and let them steep for two weeks in a warm place, shaking daily. Strain and bottle. Gently massage into your scalp morning and evening.

FATHER KNEIPP'S HAIR RESTORER

Father Kneipp was an Austrian herbalist who is considered the father of hydrotherapy.

200 grams of nettle veins
1 liter water
½ liter cider vinegar

BOIL the mixture for thirty minutes and rub into the scalp nightly.

STIMULATING HAIR RESTORER

4 ounces ground cayenne pepper
1 pint of grain alcohol (vodka)

MIX, seal, and steep for ten days, shaking several times a day. Strain and rub a small amount into your scalp morning and evening.

JOHN LUST'S HAIR RESTORER

The late, great naturopath and herbalist drew on traditional hair loss remedies for this formula.

1 part fresh nettle leaves
1 part raw onion
100 parts 70 percent alcohol

STEEP for several days, strain, and use for a daily scalp massage.

Dr. Zhao Zhangguang's 101 Hair Regeneration Liniment

In the mid-1970s, one of rural China's barefoot doctors invented this hair restorer which in 1987 won him the top prize in the 36th Brussels Eureka World Fair. He was chosen from an international array of inventors for his herbal potion that he claims has a 90 percent success rate at producing hair on the most stubbornly bald heads. The liniment, Dr. Zhao says, contains ginseng, the root of membraneous milk vetch, Chinese angelica, a type of *Aconitum*, dried ginger, walnut meat, safflower, the root of red-rooted salvia, a Psoralea, and alcohol.

Historical Recipes

HOW TO KEEP THE HAIR CLEAN AND PRESERVE IT
BY HANNAH WOOLLEY, *THE COMPLEAT SERVANT-MAID*; QUOTED IN *THE HOUSEWIFE'S RICH CABINET*

TAKE 2 handfuls of rosemary and boil it softly [gently] in a quart of spring water til it comes [reduces] to a pint. Let it be covered all the while. Then strain it out and keep it. Every morning when you comb your head, dip a sponge in the water and rub up your hair, and it will keep it clean and preserve it. It is very good for the brain and will dry up the rheum.

From Yemen and from Haiti come stories of people who use a special soil for washing their hair. Supposedly it makes the hair strong and beautiful. If a mud pack can nourish the skin with minerals as well as soften and remove impurities, perhaps it can do the same for hair.

Raw onions are a universal folk remedy for thinning hair. In Haiti, a finely chopped raw onion is applied to the scalp. A traditional British recipe calls for three onions steeped in 1 quart of rum for twenty-four hours. Rub into the scalp every other day.

The three folk remedies below are from Leonard Stoller's article "Beauty Recipes of Yesteryear."

TO STIMULATE HAIR

BOIL 2 handfuls chamomile in 2 quarts water for fifteen minutes or until the mixture is coffee-colored. Pour it into 2 more quarts cold water and place in a gallon jar. Massage into scalp after a shampoo.

If none of these home remedies work for you, there are a few tricks that will make your hair appear fuller than it is:

Greasy hairdressings flatten your hair, so don't use them for styling. Try a styling mousse or plain water instead. Clean hair appears to have more volume, so shampoo twice weekly if your hair is dry, every other day if it is oily. The Soapwort Shampoo recipe on page 100 stimulates hair growth. Between shampoos, if your hair flattens down, use a dry shampoo (page 101) to absorb the oil.

If you dye your hair, go for the lighter shades, never black—your scalp will show through. If your hair is straight, consider curling it, cutting it, or styling it so it appears to have more volume.

OILY HAIR

OILY HAIR, LIKE OILY SKIN, IS CAUSED BY OVERACTIVE SEBACEOUS glands. It is most likely to occur in our teens and twenties. A diet low in fats, especially saturated fats, and high in fresh produce, proteins, and whole grains gives you the nutrients recommended for healthy hair: B vitamins and antioxidants A, C, and E.

If your hair is oily, it is important to keep it clean; otherwise, it can look dull and limp. However, overwashing isn't good for it either because the sebaceous glands are stimulated to pump out even more oil to compensate. A daily soaping with a mild shampoo is enough for even the oiliest hair; every other day is better. Jojoba oil is thought to help normalize oil production because the waxy substance resembles sebum. If the hair follicles produce too little sebum, jojoba moisturizes; if you have too much sebum, jojoba keeps it from building up on your scalp. Between washings, use a dry shampoo to absorb oil.

HERBS BENEFICIAL TO OILY HAIR

Lemon juice, sage leaves, burdock or comfrey root; strawberry, raspberry, blackberry, stinging nettle, rosemary, or patchouli leaves; linden, lime, elder, red clover, or chamomile blossoms; kelp and other seaweeds; lavender spikes; birch bark oil; cornflowers; green, black, or pekoe tea; witch hazel; lemongrass, aloe vera gel

Remember: Tepid water does a better job of washing away oils than hot or cold. Add lemon juice or cider vinegar to your rinse water—a tablespoon or two to a quart, or make a rinse with one or more of the herbs listed on page 93. You will find instructions in the following section.

HAIR MASKS, RINSES, AND CONDITIONERS

CONDITIONERS HELP LOCK IN MOISTURE, PREVENT SPLIT ENDS, AND shrink or coat the hair shaft to give it strength and gloss. Certain vitamin-rich hair masks, such as those made with avocado (see page 94), nourish and strengthen hair. Silica, milk, eggs, and other proteins repair damage caused by overprocessing or exposure to sun, chemicals, or other environmental hazards. Most conditioners soften the hair. Others coat the shaft, making it appear thicker, or cause it to swell, giving it more body. Some conditioners are applied before a shampoo in the form of a hair mask or pack; others after a shampoo as a rinse.

HERBAL INFUSIONS

Infusions are effortless to make, and they help to condition your hair.

1 pint boiling water
¼ to ⅓ cup dried herbs (consult the box on page 93 for which one[s] to use)

POUR the water over the herbs, cover, and steep for thirty minutes. You can acidify the mixture by adding vinegar or lemon juice (see next page). When possible, leave the solution on your hair for a few minutes before you rinse it out.

ACID RINSE

2 tablespoons cider vinegar or lemon juice

1 pint warm water

TO BOOST the conditioning effect, add 6 or 8 drops of essential oil. For suggestions on which oils to use for your hair, see the chart below.

BEER RINSE

Flat beer, which is somewhat acidic, is a simple, classic hair rinse that leaves your hair soft, shiny, and easy to manage. Makes a good setting lotion. You can use it on all types of hair, but it is especially good for brunettes.

One 12-ounce can or bottle of beer

OPEN the beer and let it stand for several hours. Apply after shampooing as a final rinse. The brewery aroma should dissipate once your hair dries.

HERBAL RINSES FOR VARIOUS HAIR TYPES

RINSES FOR OILY HAIR: Lemon juice; vinegar; sage; comfrey or burdock root; stinging nettle, rosemary, patchouli, strawberry, raspberry, or blackberry leaves; linden, lime, elder, red clover, or chamomile blossoms; kelp and other seaweeds; lavender, birch bark oil; cornflowers; green, black, or pekoe tea; witch hazel; lemongrass; aloe vera gel; Kathi Keville and Mindy Green, authors of *Aromatherapy,* **the** book on the art, recommend these essential oils for oily hair: lemongrass, patchouli, clary sage, cypress, and cedar wood.

MOISTURIZERS FOR DRY HAIR: Burdock root, comfrey root and leaves, kelp and other seaweed, lavender, rosemary, sandalwood, southernwood, and ylang-ylang.

Aromatherapy's recommendations for essential oils that benefit dry hair: chamomile, clary sage, geranium, lavender, myrrh, rose, rosemary, rosewood, sandalwood, and spikenard.

HERBS TO BRIGHTEN DULL HAIR: Red clover, chamomile, or malva blossoms; cornflowers; rosemary, marshmallow, or mullein leaves; green, black, or pekoe tea; clove buds; red onion; madder root; plantain; shepherd's purse. Essential oils recommended by *Aromatherapy:* chamomile, juniper, lemon, lemongrass.

HAIR MASKS AND FLORAL PACKS

A HAIR MASK IS AN OIL, CREAM, OR PASTE THAT COATS ALL OF YOUR hair just like a facial mask coats your skin. Masks are especially beneficial to dry hair; you will find several variations of the hair mask in the Dry Hair section. Floral packs are similar.

HERBAL HAIR MASK

3 tablespoons dried herbs (see chart on page 93 for suggestions)
1 cup olive, jojoba, or other vegetable oil

STEEP for 30 minutes, keeping the mixture warm in the top of a double boiler. Spread the mixture over all your hair, including the ends. For neatness sake you may want to cover your hair with a shower cap or plastic bag, but this is optional.

FRUIT OR VEGETABLE MASK

MASH a banana, melon, berries, an avocado, or a cooked vegetable such as potato, squash, or carrots. Proceed as above.

COLOMBIAN HAIR MASK

Thanks to Colombia native Miriam Sanchez for this recipe, which she uses once a week. Unless your hair is very long and thick, this should be enough for one application. Discard the remainder or use it as a facial mask.

½ avocado
1 tablespoon aloe vera
1 tablespoon olive oil
1 egg yolk
A dash of honey
A little piece of banana

PLACE all ingredients in the blender and mix. When blended, put mixture in hair one hour before you wash it. Later you will have beautiful and shiny hair.

TO MAKE A HAIR PACK

1 part water
1 part dried herbs or flowers (see chart for suggestions)

GENTLY simmer for ten minutes, cool to room temperature, drain off excess water, and work the herbs or flowers into your hair, making sure that all of it, including the ends, is covered. Put a shower cap or a plastic bag over your hair and give the herbs an hour to work their magic. In India hibiscus flowers are made into a paste and applied to the hair to stimulate growth and give it a healthy glow.

FOR HANDSOME HAIR

4 egg whites
½ cup rum
½ cup rosewater

BEAT egg whites to a froth and rub the mixture thoroughly close to the roots of the hair. Let the mixture dry, then wash the head and hair with rum and rosewater.

CITRUS HAIR PACK

This hair conditioner leaves your hair soft and silky with reddish highlights. The citrus fruit restores natural acidity to hair that is dulled and dried by alkaline shampoos. This recipe makes enough to cover medium-length hair. Use more or less depending upon the length of your hair.

Juice of 1 fresh orange
Juice of 1 fresh grapefruit

REMEDIES FOR THE HAIR WHEN IT SPLITS

WHEN YOU GO TO BED, *take oil and water, a like quantity, put them into a bottle, and incorporate them well together. Anoint the hair well with it going to bed. Next morning wash it with . . . marsh mallows, fleabane, willow bark boiled in spring water.*

From *Artificiall Embellishment* by Thomas Jeamson, 1665;
quoted in *The Housewife's Rich Cabinet*

POUR the citrus mix into a squeeze-top bottle. Shampoo your hair and blot with a towel until it is damp. Saturate your hair with the solution and leave it on for an hour or so or until your hair dries. Rinse with warm water.

VARIATION: If your hair is blond and you don't fancy reddish highlights, use only grapefruit juice.

SPLIT ENDS AND DAMAGED HAIR

HAIR DYE AND PERMANENT WAVES ERODE THE STRUCTURE OF YOUR HAIR, making it more porous. This type of hair is easier to perm and color, but it is also fragile and vulnerable to split ends and other damage. Shampooing too often with harsh shampoos, blow-drying, styling your hair with hot rollers or a curling iron, and overbrushing can also damage your hair. Most of the treatments for dry hair also help to repair damaged hair. See pages 82 to 85. See also the section on hair packs, rinses, and conditioners, above.

Protein, the stuff our hair is made of, is particularly good for damaged hair. Protein shampoos, it is claimed, will repair split ends and other damage and strengthen the hair shaft. However, most commercial shampoos don't contain enough protein to do much good. You can better condition your hair by adding a raw egg or cow's or goat's milk to a store-bought shampoo. You could also use these high-protein conditioners by themselves or incorporate them into a home-made conditioner. For more information, see the Shampoo section beginning on page 97, or the Conditioners section on pages 92 and 93.

SHAMPOO RECIPES

... A key shampoo ingredient which can, even at neutral pH, denature protein of the eye is sodium lauryl sulfate (SLS). ...

ROBERT GOLDEMBERG, WRITING IN THE JANUARY 1995
ISSUE OF *DRUG AND COSMETIC INDUSTRY*

If you read the label on a bottle of shampoo, even a so-called "herbal" one, you will note a very long list of ingredients. Some, like sodium lauryl sulfate, are petroleum-based detergents that are harsh on the skin and very irritating to the eyes. To counteract the irritation, other chemicals are added. Then there are the stabilizers, emulsifiers, preservatives, and coloring agents. The amount of "botanical" ingredients, if there are any, is quite small. Moreover, the botanical ingredients don't stay on your hair long enough to have much effect.

Shampoos are among the easiest cosmetics to make at home, requiring no special equipment and few ingredients. For a base, you can either use a natural shampoo you buy in a health food store or castile soap. To give your hair a longer exposure to the beneficial ingredients, apply the shampoo as soon as you step into the shower or sit down in the bath. Do not rinse your hair until you have finished bathing. Apply about a tablespoon of shampoo. If you are using a store-bought shampoo, dilute it with an equal part of warm water before using. Work the shampoo into your hair and scalp with your fingertips. Rinse thoroughly with warm water, and finish with a simple acid rinse made with a tablespoon of vinegar or lemon in a quart of warm water, or try one of the homemade rinse recipes below. Some hair experts recommend two soapings. If you have overactive sebaceous glands or an oily residue from a hair mask or a hot-oil treatment, this is a good idea. However, shampooing does strip oil from your hair. If your hair is dry, color treated, permed, or shampooed daily, one soaping should be enough.

After shampooing, blot your hair lightly with a towel and let it dry naturally rather than using a blow-dryer. Because the chemical bonds that hold it together separate when hair is wet, it is vulnerable to damage at this time. To avoid stretching or breaking, wait until your hair is dry to style it. Pulling at your hair can loosen it or cause it to fall out, so don't tease or back comb it, pull it back tightly with a rubber band, or wind it too tightly on curlers.

SHAMPOO MIXES

CASTILE SHAMPOO

You can make your own quick shampoo base by adding two tablespoons castile soap to one cup warm water or an herbal infusion. Instead of an herbal infusion, you could add 10 drops or so of essential oil to the castile shampoo base. See Conditioners chart on page 93 for suggestions on which oils to add.

Liquid castile soap is sold in health food stores. You can buy the bar soap in supermarkets. Originally, castile soap was made from olive oil—hence the name. Now, both bar and liquid castile soaps are a blend of olive and coconut or jojoba oils for improved lathering action. Although castile soap does produce a rich lather and usually gives hair shine and softness, combined with hard water or certain herbs such as horsetail, it can leave your hair stiff and dull. You may want to experiment with small batches to see which herbs work for you.

YOU can also customize a store-bought shampoo by adding an infusion of single herbs or a mixture of them. Pour 1 cup boiling distilled water over 4 tablespoons dried herbs or twice that amount of fresh herbs. Steep in a teapot or other closed container for thirty minutes. Strain and mix with 1 cup shampoo. For suggestions on which herbs would be beneficial to your hair, see Dry, Oily, Thinning, Gray Hair, or Conditioners sections.

QUICK SILICA SHAMPOO

The primitive plant horsetail is rich in silica, which shampoo manufacturers add to their product to give hair strength and shine. Sandalwood and jasmine soften and moisturize.

2   teaspoons dried horsetail
2   teaspoons powdered sandalwood
2   teaspoons dried jasmine flowers
½ cup boiling distilled water
½ cup mild shampoo base (don't use castile soap)

PLACE herbs in a teapot or other ceramic vessel, add water, cover, and steep for fifteen minutes. Strain and mix with shampoo. Produces about a cup of fragrant, golden shampoo that makes a rich lather.

CONDITIONING SHAMPOO FOR OILY HAIR

1   tablespoon dried elder blossoms
1   tablespoon dried patchouli leaves
1   tablespoon dried witch hazel leaves
1   tablespoon green (for blonds), orange pekoe (for redheads), or black tea (for brunettes)
1¼ cups distilled water
1   cup shampoo base

PLACE herbs in a teapot or similar container. Bring water to the boil and pour over herbs. Cover and steep for thirty minutes. Strain and mix with shampoo base.

CONDITIONING SHAMPOO FOR DRY OR NORMAL HAIR

1¼ cups distilled water
1   tablespoon powdered burdock root
1   tablespoon comfrey
1   tablespoon red clover blossoms
1   fresh egg
1   cup shampoo base

POUR boiling water over the herbs. Steep in a closed container for thirty minutes. Strain. When the infusion is cool, beat egg and add it to infusion, then beat in shampoo, mixing thoroughly.

Color-Enhancing Shampoos

To bring out your natural color or touch up artificial color, add 1 cup of one of these solutions to 1 cup shampoo. For more recipes see page 86 in the Dull Hair section.

Blonds: Steep 1 tablespoon chamomile, calendula, powdered rhubarb root, or green tea in 1 cup boiling water for thirty minutes

Brunettes: Add 1 cup strong black coffee or 1 cup water in which you have steeped 1 tablespoon powdered black walnut shells, allspice, or clove for thirty minutes

Redheads: Add 1 cup red wine and/or orange juice, or 1 cup water in which 1 tablespoon red hibiscus or 2 tablespoons red clover have been steeped thirty minutes

SOAPWORT HAIR RESTORER

This invigorating shampoo stimulates circulation and gives hair golden highlights. All of the herbs in the recipe, including soapwort, are recommended for stimulating hair growth. If you are lucky enough to have soapwort growing in your garden or a nearby field, you can use the fresh plant. For best results, let the fresh plant wilt for a couple of days before you use it. The greatest concentration of saponins are in the root, which is harvested in October. You can add finely chopped root to the blend. (See antidandruff recipe on page 82 for more information about soapwort.) This shampoo is better without the castile soap, but add it if you insist on lather.

2   cups fresh or 1 cup dried soapwort leaves and blossoms

2   cups distilled water

4   tablespoons fresh or 2 tablespoons dried rosemary
    leaves

2   tablespoons fresh or 1 tablespoon dried peppermint
    leaves

2   tablespoons fresh or 1 tablespoon dried stinging nettle
    leaves

1   tablespoon powdered sandalwood

4   tablespoons liquid castile soap (optional)

SIMMER the soapwort in water gently for five minutes if fresh, or ten minutes if dried. Meanwhile, place the herbs in a teapot or other ceramic or glass container. Strain soapwort and pour the hot liquid on the herbs. Cover and steep for thirty minutes, strain again, and add the soap. Beat until thoroughly mixed.

VARIATION: For light-colored hair, substitute 2 tablespoons dried chamomile and 2 tablespoons dried calendula for nettle and rosemary.

PROTEIN CONDITIONING SHAMPOO

Shampoo manufacturers add milk or chemical substitutes to condition hair that has been damaged by heat, chemicals, or sun. Milk contains lactic acid that helps restore the hair's natural acidity and leaves hair soft and manageable.

¼ cup sour or sweet milk (the former has more lactic acid)

¼ cup mild shampoo base

4 drops grapefruit skin oil

BEAT ingredients thoroughly and bottle.

YUCCA ROOT SHAMPOO

In the Southwest, Native Americans used the root of this bristling desert plant to make shampoo. So fond were they of yucca root that they incorporated it into their wedding ceremonies where the bride and groom washed each other's hair. On occasion, the entire tribe would get together and have a shampoo party. Like soapwort, yucca contains saponins that make suds when the plant is swished in water. Hair washed with yucca is clean, soft, and free of tangles. Although this shampoo does a better job without the castile soap, add it if you insist on lather.

¼ cup dried yucca root

1 cup distilled water

2 tablespoons castile soap (optional)

SIMMER the yucca in water for about fifteen minutes, or until the broth is reddish and slightly thickened. Let the mixture sit for a half hour after you take it from the fire, then strain and bottle or mix with castile soap and use.

DRY SHAMPOO

½ to 1 cup barley flour (You can make your own barley flour by powdering flaked barley in a blender, coffee grinder, or spice mill.)

1 tablespoon dried lavender or rose petals or 1 tablespoon
   dried orrisroot mixed with two drops of your favorite essential oil

PLACE the barley flour in a metal or glass container with a tight-fitting lid. Make a sachet of the flowers or the orrisroot and oil mixture by placing them in cheesecloth, then add the package to the container. Let the mixture marry in a closed container for a couple of weeks or until evenly scented, shaking every day or two. Work the flour thoroughly into your hair and scalp as you do when washing your hair. Next, brush the barley out of your hair using the traditional long, sweeping, 100 strokes of the brush. The barley removes excess dust and sebum, giving your hair shine and body.

HAIR COLORING

PEOPLE HAVE BEEN DYEING THEIR HAIR FOR CENTURIES. CAPTAIN JAMES Cook, the famous eighteenth-century explorer, noted in his journals that Pacific Islanders, both male and female, dyed their thick, straight black hair orange, brown, or purple. Long before, in ancient Greece, women used mullein flowers to dye their hair blond. In ancient Rome, some people used vinegar lees or quince juice mixed with privet leaves to achieve flaxen tresses. Others used a mixture of oil, ashes, and earthworms to keep their hair from turning white. A few more adventurous types dyed their hair blue. Meanwhile, in Asia, Africa, and the Middle East, women used the powdered leaves of the henna plant as a hair and body dye. The practice spread to Europe, and it became the rage there as well. Queen Elizabeth I used it. Henna continues to be the most widely used botanical dye in use today—for good reason. It is widely available, relatively inexpensive to buy, nontoxic to use, and it works.

If you have seen fabrics dyed with berries, nuts, or flowers, you have an idea of what a vegetable dye can do for your hair. The color is more subtle. It doesn't last quite as long as chemical dye, but fades gradually, so your hair roots remain the same color as the rest of your hair. Even more important, pure vegetable dyes are not hazardous to your health. Some chemical hair dyes have caused cancer in rats and are suspected of causing some cancers in humans.

HAIR POWDER TO COLOR HAIR

IN THE TIME OF EMPRESS *Eugenie who wore it first in 1860, crushed gold leaf was used to lend golden sparkle to the hair. Coarse bronze powder was also used, or powdered glass. The powders were applied with a hare's foot fitted with handles.*

From *The Art of Perfumery,* by George William Septimus Piesse

In just about all parts of the world, people have used an array of roots, nuts, berries, and flowers to bring out highlights or dye their hair a rainbow of hues. Some that are easy to gather or buy in this country include chamomile, calendula, tea, coffee, mullein, saffron, yellow broom, rhubarb root, Saint John's wort, honey, cloves, lemon juice, goldenseal, turmeric, mullein flowers, black walnut hulls, madder root, alkanet root, red onion slices, red hibiscus flowers, elderberries, indigo, sage leaves, saffron, red wine, and malt or cider vinegar. If you live in a rural area, you may have discovered others through experimentation.

Hair coloring easily can be done at home. The supplies are those you are sure to have on hand: an old towel to protect your clothing, salad oil or petroleum jelly to grease the area below your hairline so you won't stain your skin, a hairbrush for applying henna, or a squeeze-top bottle for applying other kinds of dye. You'll also need a clock or timer, measuring cups and spoons, and two mirrors so you can see both the front and the back of your head. Depending on which dye you are using, the process takes about an hour to an hour and a half.

Your hair should be in good condition when you color it. If the texture is porous, damaged, overly dry, or if you have dandruff, condition your hair for a week or two to get it back in shape. Wait also for at least a week after a permanent to color your hair. No dye—natural or chemical—should be applied if your scalp is irritated or the skin is broken.

Eliminate split ends by trimming, or have your hair cut and shaped before coloring—there's no point in coloring hair you don't intend to keep.

Before you get to work, remove all jewelry, apply oil or cream around your hairline, and drape an old sheet or bath towel around your shoulders. Hair coloring can be a bit messy, so it's a good idea to do it in the bathroom where cleanup is easy.

To avoid a patchy look, be sure to cover all of your hair with dye. A second mirror helps. Pay attention to timing, especially when using henna, or you may end up with a hair color you didn't expect.

Even if you are using vegetable dye, your hair after coloring should be handled gently. Wash no more than three times a week, less often if your hair is dry. Protect your hair from sun, salt, and chemicals by wearing a scarf or hat when you are outdoors, and a bathing cap when swimming.

Most people who want natural color choose henna. It conditions as well as colors hair, and the color lasts from six to eight weeks. Be careful where you buy it, though. A trusted herbal purveyor is your best source of pure, unadulterated henna. Some brands, according to *Milady's Standard Textbook of Cosmetology*, contain metallic salts such as copper, lead, and silver, which react with keratin to turn the hair brown. These salts, Milady tells us, "have been known to cause headaches, scalp irritation, contact dermatitis, facial swelling, hair breakage and loss, lead poisoning . . ." Ingested, Milady goes on to say, metallic salts can be fatal.

Henna comes in a variety of colors, ranging from neutral to shades of blond, brown, and black. Your safest choice is to buy a neutral henna, then make a custom blend, depending on what color you want. Henna does not lighten hair, although it does bring out golden highlights. If your hair is white or gray, choose a blond shade. The Rainbow Research Corporation recommends adding 2 tablespoons of cider vinegar to the henna mixture to help fix the color on gray hair.

HENNA MIX

2   parts vegetable color (see suggestions below)
3   parts neutral henna
5   parts liquid

REDUCE the vegetable color to powder in a blender, coffee grinder, or spice mill. Combine this powder thoroughly with the henna, then add water gradually until your mixture is the consistency of porridge. For special effects, you can substitute another liquid for water. According to herbalist Roy Genders, hot red wine gives hair a satiny sheen. The Rainbow henna people recommend using black coffee if you want to subdue reds, deepen browns, or cover gray; they recommend Red Zinger Tea to enrich reds and lemon juice to lighten blond tones.

BLOND HAIR DYE

Although shampooing before applying henna is often recommended, it actually works better if your hair is not squeaky clean, so omit the pretreatment shampoo unless your hair is oily.

1   tablespoon green tea

About 1 cup boiling water

⅓ cup neutral henna

2   tablespoons calendula

1   tablespoon chamomile

1   tablespoon rhubarb root

1   tablespoon turmeric

STEEP tea in water for ten minutes, strain, and add slowly to the henna and herb mixture, stirring until smooth and the consistency of porridge. Apply to small sections of hair with a fairly stiff hairbrush. Make sure you cover all the layers and strands. Check in a mirror to make sure, or, better, have a friend help you. Cover your head with a plastic

VEGETABLE COLORING

BLONDS For golden tones add chamomile, calendula, turmeric, and/or rhubarb root, and moisten with green tea. For honey tones add a little ground clove, allspice, or powdered black walnut hulls.

BRUNETTES Add clove and/or walnut hulls and moisten with freshly brewed black coffee or black tea. For raven hair add indigo.

REDHEADS AND AUBURNS Add madder root, alkanet root, hibiscus, red clover, red onion, and moisten with orange juice, red wine, coffee, or Red Zinger tea.

GRAY HAIR To darken add sage, stinging nettle, and/or rosemary, and moisten with water and 2 tablespoons of cider vinegar. To remove the yellow from white hair, add cornflowers. For golden gray hair see Blonds section.

TO BRIGHTEN ANY SHADE OF HAIR, add blue malva, red clover, southernwood, mullein, or marshmallow leaves.

bag or shower cap and leave the mixture on for fifty to sixty minutes.
Shampoo and rinse thoroughly, lathering twice. To let the color get a
grip, don't use rinse or conditioner for at least a week.

VARIATIONS: Instead of the four herbs in the above recipe, use 5 tablespoons
of the herb of your choice, alone or in combination. Select from the ones
listed on the preceding page.

Historical Recipes

TO DYE HAIR YELLOW

FROM *DELIGHTS FOR LADIES* BY HUGH PLATT, 1602

> 4 ounces turmeric, rhubarb [root], or barberry bark or dog-
>   berrie
> A pottle [2 quarts] of water

BOIL [for 15 minutes] and strain.

TO DARKEN HAIR

> 4 ounces black tea
> 1 cup vinegar

SIMMER in an iron pot for fifteen to thirty minutes.

FOR RICH BROWN COLOR

BY COSMETIC CHEMIST DOROTHY CRISP, WRITING IN *THE HERBALIST* MAG-
AZINE

> 50 grams walnut skins
> 250 to 300 milliliters water

SOAK [the mixture] twenty-four hours, then boil for one hour until
thickish brown liquid results. Apply and leave on the hair for thirty to
sixty minutes.

CHAPTER 4

YOUR BODY

FROM CLAVICLE TO TOE
"THE BODY IS YOUR HOME."

So said Ettia Tal, of Ettia Holistic Day Spa in New York City. "All beauty comes from the inside," she reminds us. "Food creates your health, it creates your death. This didn't happen yesterday, but twenty years ago." She gives an example: "Age spots are caused by too much sugar in the blood.

Your liver is the last stop on the train station, the cemetery of dead cells. When we accumulate toxins—and sugar is toxic—the excess comes as dark spots."

She adds: "Coffee dries out your skin and other organs; many decaf beverages are chemicalized. Barley tea is very calming, soothing, and good for the digestion. Bancha tea is also good for the digestion. If you have good digestion, you will have good skin."

Ettia's remedy: "Surround yourself with green plants and walk in nature at least a half hour every day. Eat mostly grains and vegetables, some olive or sesame oil, and chew your food well, until it becomes liquid in your mouth. In cooking, it's your energy that's important."

Ettia's philosophy reflects some of the basic tenants of contemporary holistic and complementary medicine, which in turn have been inspired by the centuries of Asian, European, and indigenous medicines that preceded them. The payoff for sensible health habits is that you not only feel good, you look good.

The American Cancer Society recommends five to nine servings of fruits and vegetables daily. Not only are these foods rich in bioflavenoids and other phytochemicals that help prevent cancer, cardiovascular disorders, and other chronic illnesses, they are our main sources of vitamins. Vitamin A, in particular, is important for healthy skin. Retin A, which some regard as a miracle drug for acne, age spots, and related problems, is derived from vitamin A. The raw material for this vitamin is beta-carotene, distributed most abundantly in leafy greens and deep-yellow and orange fruits and vegetables. Broccoli, apricots, papaya, and other melons, as well as squashes, are rich sources. Beta-carotene and vitamins C and E are antioxidants. By scavenging free radicals, antioxidants help prevent premature aging.

The effects of exercise are reflected in your over-all appearance: bright eyes, rosy cheeks, smooth skin, and a well-toned, resilient body. You need at least thirty minutes of aerobic exercise daily. Not only does it increase circulation, tone your muscles, and keep you slim, it keeps your skin thick and supple so it resists wrinkling. Rapid walking is splendid aerobic exercise, requiring no training or equipment. A park or forest is an excellent place to do it because trees and plants give off oxygen. Like other forms of exercise, walking also releases endorphins, the "feel-good" hormones.

Hatha yoga—the form of yoga most familiar to Westerners—consists of poses or postures that stretch the joints and muscles and may help regulate the endocrine system. Both yoga and regular meditation are excellent for relieving stress. In addition to daily exercise and stretching, it is important to keep your musculoskeletal system in alignment by regular visits to a chiropractor or osteopath, or through classes in the Alexander or Feldenkrais methods. Spinal alignment helps maintain your nervous and immune systems and improves the flow of energy through your body. The results are increased health and vitality, a fluid gait, and release from stress and tension. How often you do this depends on a number of factors, including the amount of stress you put on your neck and spine. It goes without saying that the earlier in life you start these practices, the longer you will maintain a youthful appearance.

Sleep is another essential. Again, how much you need depends on the individual, but recent studies show that most people don't get enough. Researchers have discovered a correlation between sleeping patterns and longevity: She who sleeps most lasts longest. Sleep is when cellular renewal takes place. If you don't believe this, just look at your face in the mirror after a night or two of little or no sleep.

Finally, a diet of sugar, caffeine, and chemicals affect your appearance as well as your state of health. As you read in Chapter Two, salt, sun, and tobacco are the enemies of beauty; they dry out your skin. Smoking and imprudent sun bathing contribute to premature aging.

CELLULITE

DIMPLED SKIN ALONG THE THIGHS, HIPS, AND BUTTOCKS OCCURS when the connective tissue between upper and lower skin layers breaks down, allowing fat cells to clump together. Cellulite is often associated with obesity, rapid weight loss, and aging, but formation is largely the result of individual biochemistry. Daily aerobic exercise and a low-fat diet rich in fresh fruits and vegetables are preventatives. Massage is also helpful because it stimulates circulation and helps to break down accumulated fat. A massage oil containing rosemary is very good for this purpose. You will find the recipe in Chapter Six, page 191.

Whole herbs are preferable to essential oils because they contain phyto-chemicals not extracted by distilling. Essential oils, however, are more convenient to use, and their concentrated scents do have aromatherapy benefits.

ANTICELLULITE MASSAGE OIL

FILL a clear glass jar with one or more of the following dried herbs: juniper berries, horsetail, strawberry leaves, ginger root, cypress, peppermint, yerba mate, geranium leaves. Cover the herbs with cold-pressed, organic almond, grapeseed, or other oil. To avoid moldering, be sure the top layer of herbs is covered. Let the mixture steep in the sun for two weeks, then strain it. If you are using fresh ginger, add only a tablespoon of the chopped root to each cup of oil; ginger is strong and can irritate your skin.

INSTANT ANTI-CELLULITE OIL

10 drops essential oil of grapefruit peel, thyme, fennel, lavender, geranium, juniper, cypress, or fennel

1 ounce of almond or other carrier oil

USE one or more of these essential oils in a massage oil, or add eight drops to your bath.

KIWI CELLULITE MELT

External applications of kiwi fruit is a Puerto Rican folk remedy.

1 ripe kiwi
1 sheet of plastic wrap

MASH the kiwi, spread it over the cellulite area, cover with a sheet of plastic, and leave on for thirty minutes. Repeat as often as necessary.

Seaweed is rich in iodine, essential for proper functioning of the thyroid gland, which in turn regulates metabolism. Our metabolism determines how efficiently we burn calories and how much fat is deposited. Add a cup of seaweed to your bath water; try using granulated kelp as a seasoning. Don't go overboard, though—seaweed does contain sodium.

Drinking several daily cups of fennel tea is a traditional treatment, centuries old, to accelerate weight loss by stimulating the body to burn fat. Fresh grapefruit has a reputation for doing the same.

THE BATH

IN MANY PARTS OF THE WORLD, THE BATH IS A SACRED RITUAL, A prelude to a major undertaking such as marriage, or a purification following a significant biological event such as menstruation or childbirth. Sometimes the bath *is* the significant event, as in a baptism or christening, although today these ritual ablutions are most often observed with a symbolic sprinkle rather than a full immersion.

Cleopatra is said to have bathed in ass's milk. In Elizabethan England, elder ladies bathed in wine, the younger ones in milk. During the French Revolution, one of the age's great beauties "bathed in strawberries and raspberries, then was gently rubbed with sponges saturated with milk and perfumes."

Such bathing luxuries were not without purpose. The lactic acid in milk and the glycolic acid in wine are both alpha hydroxies. In more concentrated form, these acids are used in skin peels to rejuvenate and clarify the skin. Cosmetics manufacturers use milk protein to hydrate the skin and help it to retain water; the skin softening properties of whey have been known to dairymaids for centuries. (Whey is the colorless liquid that remains after curds form in sour milk.)

To most busy and harried contemporary Americans, however, the bath is a room, not a daily or even weekly event. Our flesh and sometimes creaking joints are as deprived of a hot soak as those of any desert anchorite. There is something, hisses the Puritan conscience, self-indulgent and maybe even sinful about such a sensual pastime.

A regular regime of baths is not only good for what ails you, it can actually prevent disease from developing. Hydrotherapy is often recommended for arthritis. Heat from the bathwater soothes muscle aches and softens the joints so they become more supple. A hot bath with Epsom salts added is often recommended by massage therapists as a way to cleanse the lymphatic system. Sitting in a tub of hot water stimulates perspiration so the body can release toxins. (A quick shower after the bath helps rinse those toxins from your skin so they won't be reabsorbed.)

A boon to insomniacs, a warm bath, paradoxically, cools you down by heating you up. Your body compensates for the artificial rise in temperature by turning down the thermostat. In consequence, your temperature drops—a condition that heralds sleep.

If you live with others, soaking in a warm tub offers you a time to be alone. In most households the bath may be the only room where privacy is respected. It's a great place to relax or even meditate. By deliberately emptying your mind, you leave space for creativity. Solutions to work-related or personal problems are more likely to occur when you are relaxed.

Even the most demanding schedule should allow for a weekly bath. Make your bathroom inviting by bringing in some pretty stones or seashells, homemade soaps, and glass bottles filled with fresh herbs floating in oil. Light a candle. Light several. Put on some uplifting music. Pour in a few drops of your favorite essential oil or bath oil, a handful or two of bath salts, or some herbs. Close the door. A bath can be therapy for your physical, sensual, and spiritual selves.

While you are bathing, have a glass of cold water handy to replace the fluids lost by perspiration. If you are alone, limit your bath to twenty minutes. Otherwise, you can soak for up to an hour. To avoid lightheadedness, rise from the bathwater slowly. Sleep, or at least rest after you bathe. When that is not possible, follow your bath with a quick, cool shower. Hot baths are not recommended for diabetics, people with high blood pressure, or pregnant women.

Getting Clean

Sidney Briscese, aesthetician at The Beach spa in New York City, offers this advice:

Your skin's best lubricant is its own natural oils. Forget soap if your skin is dry. For oily skin I like Neutrogena because the pH is about 5.5, the same pH as our skin. Don't scrub. If your skin feels squeaky clean, you've gone too far and removed the entire lipid layer.

The water for your bath or shower should be warm, not hot. Dissolve a few drops essential oil in a carrier oil such as jojoba or grapeseed and add it to your bath. Eight drops is enough because essential oil is very active; too much can irritate your skin. Mix in a few drops of milk as an emulsifier so the oils won't bead up on the surface of the water.

When you get out of the bath or shower, pat your skin with a towel until it is almost dry, then apply a moisturizer. Warm, damp skin absorbs a moisturizer more completely. In winter, even if your skin is oily, apply a little bit of moisturizer.

If you prefer to shower, you can use aromatherapy there, too. I like to hang a fresh branch of eucalyptus in my shower. In big cities you can buy eucalyptus just about any place where they sell flowers. I wash it first to get rid of any pesticides.

Most people shower or bathe too often. For example, you don't need to shower both before and after you work out in the gym. It is enough to shower once a day, and keep it short—no longer than two minutes. The water should be tepid, not hot. At least once a week give your skin a rest by skipping your shower. This allows the natural oils to replenish themselves.

Cosmetic Vinegar

Like milk and wine, vinegar contains alpha hydroxy acids. Also, the pH helps restore the natural acidity of healthy skin. Below are three modern adaptations based on George William Septimus Piesse's recipes for cosmetic vinegar.

BATH VINEGAR

1   cup cider or wine vinegar
1   tablespoon gum benzoin

1 tablespoon balsam of Peru (optional)

4 tablespoons orange blossoms

1 tablespoon freshly grated nutmeg

¼ cup rosewater

¼ cup vodka or brandy

PLACE the first five ingredients in a glass jar with a tight lid. Steep in a warm place for two weeks. Strain through a coffee filter to remove all solid matter. Add the rosewater and brandy, shake, store in dark glass or a dark cupboard. Add ¼ to ½ cup to the bath.

HENRY'S VINEGAR

Who was Henry? Piesse doesn't say.

1 tablespoon powdered gum benzoin

1 tablespoon each dried leaves of rosemary, sage, and mint

1 tablespoon dried lavender flowers

¼ cup white wine

1 cup white vinegar

¼ cup orange water

STEEP the benzoin and herbs in the wine for twenty-four hours. Add the vinegar and steep for one week longer. Strain through a coffee filter, add orange water, and bottle. Use ¼ to ½ cup in a full bath.

AROMATIC VINEGAR

1 tablespoon powdered benzoin

1 tablespoon each camphor, powdered nutmeg, and clove

¼ cup brandy

1¼ cups wine vinegar

FOLLOW directions for Henry's Vinegar above.

WINE SPLASH

The recipe below is an excellent way to use up leftover red wine that is too old to be drinkable.

1 cup red wine
1 cup water

POUR the two fluids into a squirt-top bottle, shake, and squirt all over your body after you bathe. Leave on for five minutes, rinse with tepid water, and pat your skin dry.

MILK BATH

1 quart cold water
4 cups dehydrated, full-fat milk

ADD water to the dry milk gradually and stir until dissolved. Add to a tub of warm water. When bathing, be sparing with soap, and lather only the necessary. Upon emerging from the tub, do not rinse off the milk. Pat your skin dry and moisturize. This is best done at bedtime.

FLORENTINE BATH LOTION

10 drops essential oil
1/2 cup fresh whole milk

STIR your favorite oil or oils into the milk and add to the bath.

Exfoliants

Perhaps for as long as humans have roamed the earth, women have sought to whiten, soften, and moisturize their skin with various concoctions. Such preparations contain acids and/or abrasives that stimulate renewal by removing dead skin cells on the epidermis.

Leonard Stoller writes that belles of the Spanish court whitened their neck and arms with well-sifted bran that had been infused for four hours in white wine vinegar. Egg yolks and ambergris were added, then the mixture was distilled and allowed to age for a couple of weeks. Used as a scrub, the bran mixture added a fine polish and luster to the skin.

SPANISH EXFOLIANT

Here is an updated version of the above recipe.

- 1 cup well-sifted bran
- 1 cup white wine vinegar, or enough to make a loose paste
- 5 drops of your favorite essential oil
- 1 raw egg yolk

MIX the bran with vinegar and let it sit for four hours. Mix the oil and egg yolk and add it to the bran. Spread the paste over your neck, arms, chest, and back. Leave it on for fifteen minutes, then rinse with tepid water.

USED regularly, exfoliants minimize the appearance of fine lines and help keep your skin looking soft and youthful. However, they should not be overused, because they can irritate your skin. Once every week or two should be sufficient, especially if your skin is sensitive.

Body Scrubs

A blender or spice mill turns just about any grain or nut into a satisfying scrub. The object is mild abrasion—too coarse a texture can injure your skin. Powdered rice is an Asian favorite; in this country, pulverized almonds or apricot seeds are often used in commercial preparations.

AVOCADO SCRUB

Another exfoliant that is excellent for sensitive or dry skin is avocado pit.

The seed of 1 ripe avocado

REMOVE the seed from the avocado, peel it, and let it dry for a few days. Chop it into pieces about the size of your little fingernail. Grind the

Some of the best skin scrubs come ready-made:

◆ Cornmeal and sour milk (if your skin is dry) or cornmeal and yogurt (if it is oily) are miraculously effective, leaving the skin satin smooth.

◆ If your skin is very sensitive, use oatmeal as an exfoliant. Moisten the powdered meal with cream that has just begun to sour.

◆ Other abrasives you can moisten with milk, buttermilk, water, fruit juice, or wine include bran, brewer's yeast, Cream of Wheat, or granulated seaweed. You could also rub on a few handfuls of un-moistened table salt or sugar.

pieces in an electric blender for a few seconds, or until the seed is the texture of coarse coffee grounds.

PRESHOWER SCRUB

This recipe makes enough for one application. It is best done in the shower because it is a bit messy.

½ cup pulverized grain, nuts, or seeds—one type or several

½ cup milk, cream, sour cream, sour milk, buttermilk, wine, or fruit juice. (The amount will vary according to the ingredients. You want enough liquid to make a loose paste.)

SCOOP up a handful of the paste and rub it, using a circular motion, over your face and neck. Do the same with the rest of your body, working up from the feet and avoiding the more sensitive areas. Use firm but gentle pressure, but don't scrub—the nuts or grains do the scrubbing for you. Rinse thoroughly with tepid water. Pat your skin with a towel until almost dry, then smooth on a generous amount of moisturizer.

Dry Brushing

This technique gets rid of dead skin cells. It is neater than the treatment above, but you don't get the benefits from the ingredients in the preshower scrub.

Using a soft-bristled body brush and a circular motion, gently but firmly brush your skin, working upward from the feet. This stimulates blood and lymph circulation.

A Word About Loofahs

Although loofah sponges look like something that must have been plucked from the sea, they are actually plants. Some people use the rough surface of the plant as an exfoliant. Not recommended. The critters can harbor bacteria and viruses and give you a skin rash. One way to avoid this problem is to keep your loofah clean. Sterilize it with boiling water at least once a week. Putting it in the dishwasher works. Otherwise, use the loofah to scrub only the tough areas of skin on your heels and elbows.

SALT GLOW

Standard treatment in many spas, a salt glow increases circulation, sloughs off dead skin cells, and renews and polishes the skin. Sidney Briscese uses this recipe at The Beach spa in Manhattan. Those who come to his spa claim that the salt scrub is great for their skin. People with sensitive skin should not use this treatment, he says.

2 tablespoons sea salt or Dead Sea salt (The latter has a
   higher mineral content.)

2 tablespoons refined jojoba oil, or enough to make a paste

TAKE a handful of salt and gently rub it on the skin using a circular motion. Working from the feet up, rub the paste over the skin until it is rosy. To whiten your elbows, heels, and knees, slice a lemon in half, dip the cut lemon in the salt paste, and rub it over these areas.

Do not use lemon juice on any other areas of your skin. This treatment is best done at night because lemon makes your skin sensitive to sunlight.

COSMETIC BATH

Bran is a traditional exfoliant. This recipe is from The Toilet of Flora *by Pierre-Joseph Buc'hoz. Add about a cup to your bath and refrigerate or freeze the remainder. You should have enough for several baths or many friends. Of course, you can also halve or quarter the recipe.*

2 pounds barley or bean meal
8 pounds bran
A few handfuls borage leaves

BOIL ingredients in spring water (about 2 parts water to 1 part grains). Cook very slowly in a double boiler over low heat for about forty-five minutes, or until thickened, stirring frequently. Use to clean and soften skin.

The Salubrious Benefits of Mud

Mud cleansing does seem to be an oxymoron until you consider that the wet dirt that constitutes mud is actually ground up rocks. This abrasive material scours and polishes the skin. Moreover, a warm mud bath encourages sweating, which in turn relieves you of toxins. In addition, some of the minerals from what once were rocks, and possibly the faded phytochemicals that once were vegetables, are absorbed, to some extent, through your skin.

Should you try this at home? Unless you are convinced of the purity of your local mud supply—i.e., this dirt is uncontaminated by feces and toxins—it is best not to mine for it in your backyard or the environs. Many beauty emporiums will be happy to sell you mud, but enough to wallow in is rather costly, especially if you go for the more exotic varieties such as Dead Sea mud or goop from a prehistoric moor. Even if you don't mind paying big bucks for this stuff, consider, gentle reader, what the ancient moor must look like after the mud has been extracted.

An excellent substitute is clay. Add some water and you've got mud. Compared to mud from the exotic locales, clay is cheap. Try bentonite. Also known as Fuller's earth because people who work with fabric have used it to remove natural oils from wool, bentonite consists of ancient algae deposits left on the ocean floor millions of years ago. It is largely composed of silica, and is commonly used in mud packs and facials.

Mix the bentonite with fresh herbs or an herbal infusion. Add some olive oil if your skin is dry. If you wish to simulate the effects of a steamy wallow, apply a layer of the warm, resulting mud. (This is best done in the bathtub because it's messy. If you don't care what the neighbors think, in summer you could do this outdoors.) Over the mud lay plastic wrap (here's a chance to recycle all those wrinkled grocery bags you've felt guilty about throwing out), then pile on a blanket or two. Twenty minutes is long enough, as the heat can be debilitating.

Body wraps are similar to face masks: they exfoliate, moisturize, and deliver valuable nutrients to your skin. Peel and finely dice a large cucumber and moisten with buttermilk. Lie in the bathtub and spread the mixture over your body. It helps to have a partner do the spreading. Cover the body mask with a sheet of plastic, then a blanket, and steam for twenty minutes. For more information about body wraps, see page 193 in the Gifts chapter.

Herbs are another universal therapeutic or cosmetic bath additive.

FOR THE BATH

FROM *ARTIFICIALL EMBELLISHMENTS* BY THOMAS JEAMSON, 1665; QUOTED IN *THE HOUSEWIFE'S RICH CABINET*

THIS bath is very good. Take 2 handfuls of sage leaves, the like quantity of lavender flowers and roses, a little salt. Boil them in spring water and therewith bathe your body, remembering that you are never to bathe after meals for it will occasion many infirmities. Bathe, therefore, 2 or 3 hours before dinner. It will clear the skin, revive the spirits, and strengthen the body.

Elizabethan Hugh Platt, ever the pragmatist, has a five-minute solution for making a washing water:

3 or 4 drops essential oil of clove, mace, cinnamon, or
   nutmeg
1 pint fair [pure, clear] water

MIX and use.

COCONUT BATH

IN AREAS all over the world where it grows, coconut is used to moisturize the skin and hair. It helps the skin hold water. Thanks to Rosa Howard, who is from the Panama Republic, for this recipe.

MY GRANDMOTHER used to spread grated fresh coconut all over her body as a moisturizer. After a while she rinsed it off with coconut milk that had been diluted with water.

TO SCENT BATHWATER

FROM *THE TOILET OF FLORA,* BY PIERRE-JOSEPH BUC'HOZ

PUT flowers in a large jar, layer by layer, mixed with salt until the jar is quite full. Cork it tight and let it stand in a cellar or other cool place for forty days. Empty the whole into a sieve or straining cloth stretched over the mouth of an earthen or stone pan to receive the essence that drains from the flowers upon squeezing them gently. Fill a glass bottle two-thirds full of essence, cork it tight, and expose to the heat of the sun in fine weather for twenty-five or thirty days. A single drop can scent a quart of water.

Bath Salts

Bath salts help you relax, soften your skin, and soothe aches and pains. A long soak in a warm bath laced with Epsom salts can nip a cold in the bud and stimulate the release of toxins through perspiration. Do not bathe in salt more than once a week, however; it will dry out your skin.

SLEEPYTIME BATH SALTS

A warm bath at bedtime raises your temperature. To compensate, your body lowers its thermostat. The cooling-down process prepares your body for sleep. The Epsom salts are a time-tested home remedy for aches and pains. They are also an excellent source of tension-relieving magnesium. Sea salt, especially Dead Sea salt, has a high mineral content. Baking soda soothes skin itch and irritation. The herbs in this mix calm you down and prepare you for sleep. If you don't have on hand some of the flowers in this recipe, simply increase the proportions of the others to make ½ cup. You can also use 10 drops of the essential oil of each of the flowers.

2 cups Epsom salts

¼ cup sea salt, Dead Sea Salt, or table salt

¼ cup white clay or bentonite

¼ cup baking soda

2 tablespoons orrisroot

2 tablespoons dried lavender spikes

2 tablespoons dried chamomile flowers

2 tablespoons dried hops flowers

2 tablespoons dried orange blossoms

MIX in a ceramic bowl with a wooden spoon, or put all the ingredients into a metal container with a tight lid—a coffee can works fine—and shake vigorously. Let the bath salts stand overnight before using. Add ¼ to ½ cup to the bath.

VARIATIONS:

STIMULATING BATH SALTS: Use the above recipe. Substitute 3 tablespoons of peppermint, 3 tablespoons of eucalyptus, and 2 tablespoons of juniper, or 15 drops each of the essential oils.

APHRODISIAC BATH SALTS: Use the Sleepytime Bath Salts recipe. For the four flowers substitute 1 tablespoon each of dried patchouli leaves, jasmine blossoms, sandalwood chips, and vanilla bean, or add these essential oils: a few drops of jasmine, 15 drops of patchouli, 15 drops of sandalwood, and 5 drops ylang-ylang.

SEA BREEZE THERAPEUTIC BATH SALTS

Good for aching muscles and warding off colds and flu if used at the first sign of a sniffle.

- 2 cups Epsom salts
- ¼ cup baking soda
- ¼ cup kaolin
- 2 tablespoons powdered orrisroot
- ½ cup ground kelp, bladder wrack, or other seaweed

MIX thoroughly and store in a glass container with a tight-fitting lid.

SPIKENARD BATH SALTS FOR LUNGS AND SKIN

Native Americans sipped tea made from the root of the woodland plant spikenard to clear up skin conditions and lung problems.

- 1 cup Epsom salts
- ½ cup sea salt
- 2 tablespoons bicarbonate of soda
- 3 tablespoons bentonite
- 1 tablespoon powdered orrisroot
- 1 tablespoon spikenard

MIX ingredients in a large bowl with a wooden spoon. Enclose ¼ to ½ cup bath salts in an old cotton sock or a net or muslin bag, then immerse in your bathwater.

LINDA'S BATH SALTS

Borax is often added to homemade bath salts to prevent it from caking. It can, however, irritate the skin. If the recipe below works for you, you might want to experiment with other essential oils, adding them in the same proportions as the ones in this recipe. It comes from Linda Buck, a massage therapist who lives in Maine. The lavender relaxes; white thyme soothes aching muscles.

2½ cups Epsom salts

2½ cups borax

¼ cup French white clay

½ teaspoon essential oil of white thyme

½ teaspoon essential oil of lavender

USING a wooden spoon, mix all the ingredients in a large glass or ceramic bowl. Work the oils through the mixture with your fingers until it is distributed throughout. Ladle into moisture-proof containers such as glass jars with screw-top lids or airtight tins. Shake well before adding ¼ to ½ cup to your bath.

FIVE-MINUTE BATH SALTS

You don't really need unusual ingredients to improve your bath. You probably have the makings of a batch of bath salts on your kitchen spice shelf. This one helps ward off cold and flu and eases stiff and sore muscles.

1 cup kosher salt, sea salt, or plain old iodized salt

1 tablespoon baking soda

1 tablespoon dried marjoram

1 tablespoon dried basil

1 tablespoon dried thyme

½ tablespoon dried rosemary

MIX ingredients by shaking or stirring. Use ¼ to ½ cup for the bath.

VARIATIONS: You can use any of these herbs alone or in combination to make up a quarter cup. If you prefer to use essential oil, add 10 drops of marjoram, 5 drops of basil, 6 drops of thyme, and 4 drops of rosemary.

Soaps

The history of soap making goes back to the early Gauls, who made it from tallow and ashes. Even today, the basics remain pretty much the same: You need an animal fat or vegetable oil, and a catalyst that saponifies the fat, or makes it lather. Traditionally, this has been lye—hence, the Gallic recipe for animal fat and ashes, the source of lye.

Making soaps from scratch is a lot of fun, but quite a production, and too complex a subject for the scope of this book. You can find excellent advice on how to go about it by reading Susan Cavitch's *The Natural Soap Book*, and consulting Miller's Homemade Soap Page at http://www.silverlink.net/~timer/soapinfo.html. See the appendix for more information.

Remilled, or rebatched soap, however, is a quick, easy, and time-honored way to create luxury soaps. The process is similar to the one used by fine soap manufacturers. It consists of grating a basic, unscented soap, melting it with water, milk, an herbal infusion or similar liquid, and adding essential oils, herbs or spices, and/or glycerin or vegetable oil before pouring it into a mold.

Castile soap is a perfect candidate for reworking because it is relatively pure, melts fairly quickly, and makes a rich lather. For a mold you can use just about anything, even a cardboard box or a recycled yogurt carton as long as it is clean. To prevent sticking, line your container with freezer paper, baking parchment, or mylar, or dust it with cornstarch.

Miller's Homemade Soap Page has some dandy ideas for remilling soap. Here are a few:

The texture of remilled soap depends on how finely you grate it—an electric shredder is helpful.

One correspondent claims great success from microwaving soap. She puts 1 to 1½ pounds grated soap in a 2-quart heat-proof measuring cup, nukes it for two minutes, stirs, lets it cook for another two minutes, then adds liquid, but only if necessary.

Another soaper remelts her soap in the oven. She breaks the soap into chunks, places them in a large pot (preferably glass or enamel), covers the pot, and sets the oven thermostat at its lowest temperature. Two hours later, when the soap has melted, she stirs it, leaves it in the oven for another two hours, then pours it into loaf pans.

A third correspondent remelts her soap in the top of a double boiler. She gets smooth, hard soap by adding powdered milk. Her never-fail recipe calls for ¾ to 1 pound of grated soap, enough water to equal half the weight of the soap, and about ¼ cup powdered milk. To keep the soap from browning, she adds the milk near the end and doesn't let the temperature of the soap get too hot.

A fourth correspondent wrote that her perfect solution for rebatching is to put the grated soap, along with a little liquid, into a boiling bag intended for melting candle wax. Once the soap is melted, she adds color and fragrance, mixes it in by squeezing the bag, and fills her molds by cutting a hole in the bottom of the bag and squeezing the soap into it. She lets her soap set in the freezer overnight.

Kathy Miller, the web master, stresses that it is important not to let your soap get too dry, or it will be too thick to remill properly. You should also be careful to mix the soap gently—vigorous stirring incorporates air into the soap and makes it spongy.

A pinch or so of powdered turmeric gives soap with a natural creamy color. (More than a pinch can stain because turmeric is a strong natural dye.)

To increase the lather, some soapers add a little sugar or castor oil to the batch.

SAGE SOAP FOR OILY SKIN

One 4-ounce bar castile soap
⅔ cup distilled water
14 drops essential oil of grapefruit skin
16 drops essential oil of sage

GRATE the soap and place it in the top of a glass or enamel double boiler. Add water and simmer gently until the soap is melted, stirring occasionally. Remove from the fire and cool slightly. Mix the oils together, stir them into the soap, and pour the soap into molds dusted with cornstarch. Recycled 8-ounce yogurt cartons make good molds. Leave the soap undisturbed until it hardens, then place in the refrigerator overnight to set.

VARIATION: **Dry-Skin Soap.** Substitute orange water for the distilled water; instead of sage and grapefruit, add these essential oils: 5 drops of ylang-ylang, 10 drops of rose, and 15 drops of patchouli.

SEAWEED SOAP

This soap does wonders for all types of skin. The peppermint stimulates circulation. Seaweed, an abrasive, loosens dead skin cells so underlying new cells can emerge, moisturizes the skin, and nourishes it with a wealth of minerals.

3/4 cup grated castile soap

1/4 cup herbal infusion:

   1 tablespoon elder blossoms

   1 tablespoon shredded marshmallow root

   1/2 cup boiling distilled water

1 teaspoon castor oil

1 teaspoon glycerin

2 teaspoons dried, ground kelp, bladder wrack or other seaweed

12 drops peppermint oil

STEEP the herbs in the boiling water for thirty minutes. Strain the infusion and measure out 1/4 cup. Pour it into the top of a double boiler, preferably a glass one. Add grated soap and melt very slowly over simmering water. When the soap is dissolved, remove from the fire and stir in the seaweed, oil and glycerin. Let the mixture cool slightly, then stir in the peppermint oil. Pour into a mold dusted with cornstarch, let the soap harden undisturbed, and leave it in the refrigerator overnight to set.

A DELICATE WASHING BALL

FROM *DELIGHTS FOR THE LADIES* BY HUGH PLATT

This classic recipe is slightly more labor intensive than the others. However, perfuming a soap when it is cool produces a more intense fragrance. Using this method, you can make scented soap from other flowers when they are in season. Calamus and orrisroot are fixatives.

3 ounces orrisroot

1/2 ounce cypress

2 ounces calamus aromaticus

1 ounce rose petals

2 ounces lavender flowers

BEAT in a mortar, press through a sieve. Grate some castile soap, dissolve it with some rosewater, then incorporate all your powders therewith by laboring them well in a mortar. (To make this recipe, melt a couple of 4 ounce bars of grated castile soap in about 1½ cups rosewater. Put the paste in a large bowl, add the scented ingredients, and mix with a wooden spoon or a stick blender. Shape into egg-sized balls and let them dry on a sheet of paper for a couple of days.)

VALENTINE LIQUID SOAP

Orange, rose, patchouli, and sandalwood heal and moisturize sensitive, dry, and mature skin. The aromas of each of these herbs are considered aphrodisiac.

¾ cup herbal infusion:

    3 tablespoons sandalwood chips

    1 cup distilled water

2 ounces grated castile soap (about ¾ cup)

2 tablespoons orange water

12 drops essential oil of patchouli

7 drops essential oil of rose

BRING the sandalwood and water to a simmer, simmer one minute, then turn off the heat and steep for thirty minutes. Strain and measure out ¾ cup fluid. Place soap and infusion in the top of a glass or enamel double boiler. Simmer very gently until the soap melts, stirring occasionally. Remove from fire, cool slightly, add the orange water. When the soap is lukewarm, mix the oils and add them, too. Pour into a pump-top bottle.

ANTIBACTERIAL LIQUID SOAP

Unlike the much-touted antibacterial soaps you see in drugstores and supermarkets, this soap has a fresh, clean aroma and no harsh chemicals. Use it as a hand soap or in the bath or shower as a deodorant soap.

2   ounces (³/₄ cup) grated castile soap

³/₄   cup distilled water

2   tablespoons aloe vera gel

5   drops essential oil of tea tree

15   drops essential oil of lavender

2   drops essential oil of peppermint

MELT the soap in the distilled water in the top of a double boiler over low heat, stirring now and then. Remove from the fire, cool slightly and add the aloe. When the soap has cooled to lukewarm, mix the oils and stir them into the mixture. Pour into a pump-top bottle.

Deodorants

Perspiration is usually odorless unless garlic, fenugreek, or some other aromatic food has been eaten. Although deodorants do occur in nature—baking soda, lemon, clay, and the herb lovage are examples— what you most need is an antiseptic to kill the bacteria that cause offensive odor. So-called antiperspirants contain astringents that irritate the skin around the pores, causing it to swell so less perspiration is released. In case neither of these ingredients is effective, fragrance is there to mask the scent.

Advertising has taught us to fear the aroma of our humanity. We are admonished to scrub it away with deodorant soap so we will be "nice to be near." Once our personal aroma is eradicated, an attractive person whom we might "like to know better" might be enticed to "come a little closer." In contrast, the Elizabethans used to present their significant others with "love apples" they had tucked under an armpit until imbued with their personal aroma. In other cultures, people slipped their hands into each other's armpits when they greeted and bid others farewell.

Inoffensiveness is not without its risks. Chemicals in deodorants can sting, burn, and irritate your skin. Science writer Ruth Winter reports that people have died from intentionally inhaling deodorant sprays. (We'll assume this was done to induce euphoria, not deodorized breath.) In 1971, Winter writes, seven cases of lung tumor were attributed to deodorant sprays. More recently, it has been specu-

It's a hot and busy day and you're out of deodorant. You probably have something just as good in your kitchen.

◆ The **aloe vera plant** you may have sitting on your windowsill is antibacterial as well as antifungal. Split a leaf with a knife or fingernail and rub some of the gel under your arm. Tuck a leaf into your purse or pocket to refresh later.

◆ Like aloe, the skin and juice of a **fresh lemon** deodorizes by killing bacteria. It also imparts a fresh, appealing scent. Rub the peel—not the juice—under your arm. Don't use if you have just shaved—it stings! **Fresh orange peel** is another good quickie deodorant. **Baking soda,** which appears in many a toothpaste and deodorant advertised as "natural," neutralizes your sweat, which is slightly acidic, and absorbs odor. Rub some of the dry powder into your armpits. If your feet perspire, sprinkle some into your shoes.

◆ **Powdered clay,** also used in face masks and complexion grains, absorbs both moisture and odors. Rub some under your arms. First be sure the skin is dry.

◆ For a quick mix, put equal parts baking soda and clay in a large container. To a cup or so of this mixture, add a handful of powdered lavender or rose petals, or a few drops fragrant essential oil such as rose, patchouli, or lavender. The oil should be worked into the mixture with your fingers until it is completely dispersed through the dry ingredients. Close the container and shake vigorously.

◆ A splash of cold witch hazel (keep some in the refrigerator), very refreshing on a sultry summer day, is both astringent and deodorant.

lated that chemicals in underarm deodorants may be harmful to breast and lymph tissue. Recent research suggests a link between antiperspirants and breast cancer.

These are reason enough to make your own deodorants. In addition to being nontoxic, homemade products are more aesthetically pleasing because they are scented with plants, not chemicals. Another advantage is that most of the preparations described here are alcohol-free and can be used without irritation immediately after shaving.

INSTANT SPRAY DEODORANT

If you have some vodka and essential oils on hand, you can whip up an instant spray deodorant in no time:

- 3 tablespoons vodka
- 3 tablespoons distilled water
- 2 drops essential oil of rose
- 2 drops essential oil of lavender
- 2 drops essential oil of ylang-ylang
- 1 drop essential oil of grapefruit

POUR ingredients into a spray-top container. Store in a cool, dark place or a dark glass bottle. Shake well before using.

VARIATIONS: Instead of the essential oils listed above, try one of these combinations:

Two drops each essential oils of tea tree, peppermint, and sage

Two drops each essential oils of patchouli, lavender, and bergamot

Two drops each essential oils of rose, lavender, and geranium

Three drops each essential oils of grapefruit and tea tree with $\frac{1}{2}$ teaspoon baking soda

SPRAY DEODORANT

Although not as effective as the solid or cream deodorants below, spray deodorants are light, easy to apply, and cooling in summer. They also last a long time because the alcohol acts as a preservative.

- $\frac{1}{3}$ cup vodka
- 1 tablespoon dried yarrow leaves and flowers

1   tablespoon chopped orrisroot

1   tablespoon dried bergamot leaves

⅓ cup distilled water

PLACE the alcohol and herbs in a clean, transparent, screw-top jar. Let the mixture steep on a sunny windowsill for a week, shaking daily. Strain through a coffee filter and add water. Shake well before using and apply with a spray-top bottle or cotton balls.

UNISEX SOLID DEODORANT

Fragrant and woodsy, this effective deodorant is satisfying to both genders, and appealing even to people who don't ordinarily wear deodorant. Unlike store-bought solid deodorants, this one can be applied immediately after shaving without causing irritation. Grapeseed and hazelnut oils are astringent. All of the herbs in this recipe are deodorant. In addition, the sage is astringent, thyme is a potent antibacterial, and patchouli is fragrant and sooth-ing. Because there is no water in the recipe, the deodorant lasts for months. Prepa-ration is quick if you have infused the herbs and the oil a couple of weeks beforehand.

1   tablespoon dried sage leaves

1   tablespoon dried patchouli leaves

1   tablespoon dried thyme leaves

½ cup grapeseed, hazelnut, or safflower oil

3   tablespoons chopped or grated beeswax

⅛ teaspoon powdered gum benzoin

1   tablespoon powdered clay—preferably green

3 drops essential oil of tea tree

PLACE the herbs and oil in a clear glass jar with a screw-top lid. Leave the mixture to steep on a sunny windowsill or radiator for two weeks, shaking daily. A quicker infusion method is to gently warm the herbs and oil over simmering water in the top of a double boiler for thirty minutes. When the infusion is ready, strain out the herbs, pour the oil into the double boiler, add wax and benzoin, and heat gently un-til the wax melts, stirring occasionally. Remove from the fire. Working rapidly, add about a tablespoon of the hot oil to the clay and mix thoroughly until a paste is formed. Stir the paste into the wax mixture, add the tea tree oil, and pour immediately into two 3-ounce plastic cups or sturdy paper cups lined with baking parchment. Leave the mixture undisturbed until the wax is set. Refrigerate overnight to harden. To use, peel away the top of the cup until about a quarter inch of its contents are exposed, then apply as you would any solid deodorant.

QUICK UNISEX DEODORANT

This recipe almost qualifies as a five-minute solution. The scent is similar to the deodorant above, but less intense. This deodorant also lasts for months.

- ½ cup grapeseed, hazelnut, or safflower oil
- 3 tablespoons finely chopped beeswax or beeswax beads
- ⅛ teaspoon benzoin
- 3 drops each essential oils of tea tree, sage, patchouli, and bergamot

MELT oil, wax, and benzoin in double boiler. Meanwhile, mix the essential oils together. When the wax is melted, stir in the oils. Pour immediately into 3-ounce plastic cups or sturdy paper cups lined with parchment paper. Leave undisturbed until the wax sets, then place in the refrigerator overnight to harden. To use, trim the cup to just below the wax. Keep trimming as you use the wax.

LEMON-FRESH SOLID DEODORANT

The title says it all: this one is light, refreshing, and appealing to both genders.

- ½ cup grapeseed, hazelnut, or safflower oil
- 1½ tablespoons dried grated lemon peel
- 1 tablespoon dried lovage leaves
- 1 tablespoon powdered orrisroot
- 3 tablespoons chopped beeswax

⅛ teaspoon powdered gum benzoin

⅛ teaspoon powdered myrrh

INFUSE the lemon peel, lovage and orrisroot in oil for thirty minutes in top of a double boiler over simmering water, or in a glass jar on a sunny windowsill for two weeks, shaking daily. Strain off the herbs, add wax, benzoin, and myrrh. Heat gently until wax is melted. Remove from the fire and immediately pour into 3-ounce plastic cups or sturdy paper cups lined with parchment paper. Place in refrigerator to set overnight.

VARIATION: Substitute orange peel for lemon peel. Omit orrisroot. Add ½ tablespoon baking soda and ½ tablespoon white clay.

HERBAL CREAM DEODORANT

This is the queen of deodorants. It stays fresh for months and keeps you fresh all day. A little goes a long way.

⅓ cup herbal infusion:

⅛ ½ cup boiling distilled water

1 tablespoon dried patchouli leaves

1 tablespoon dried yarrow leaves and flowers

⅔ cup safflower or hazelnut oil

2 tablespoons chopped beeswax

¼ teaspoon powdered gum benzoin

A small pinch of boric acid

1 teaspoon powdered white clay

1 teaspoon baking soda

⅓ cup aloe vera gel

POUR boiling water over the herbs and steep for thirty minutes. Place the oil, wax, benzoin, and boric acid in the top of a glass or enamel double boiler. Heat over simmering water until the wax melts. Remove from heat. Mix a tablespoon or two of the thickened oil with the clay and soda and stir until you have a smooth paste. Stir the paste into the wax mixture. Cool until thick and opaque, but not hardened. Meanwhile, strain the herb infusion, measure out ⅓ cup, and pour into the jar of a high-speed electric blender. Add the aloe. Turn to the highest speed. Gradually pour the wax mixture into the vortex. Because of the clay, the mixture may be slow to emulsify. You will need to stop the blender a time or two and mix the clay in with a rubber spatula. After a bit of coaxing, the mixture will emulsify into a cream. Pour immediately into a glass jar with a tight lid. Do not cap the mixture until it cools.

THE MANICURE

AS ANY SHERLOCK HOLMES DEVOTEE KNOWS, MUCH CAN BE LEARNED about a person by observing the hands. Loose, wrinkled skin betrays the real age of a youthful-seeming face; tough, calloused palms reveal physical work or exercise; ragged cuticles and dirty or broken nails proclaim self—neglect. The solution to any of these problems is inexpensive, and it won't take up very much of your time—maybe thirty minutes a week devoted to giving yourself a manicure.

Supplies are simple: absorbent cotton, an orangewood stick, a glass bowl big enough to accommodate your hands, a couple of hand towels, some olive oil or milk, and accompanying herbs.

A preliminary soak will soften your skin, your cuticles, and the nails so you can work with them more easily. Here are some choices:

If time is limited, soften your nails by rubbing them with peroxide.

If there is no rush, prepare your nails the night before a manicure by applying a nail ointment at bedtime.

BEDTIME NAIL OINTMENT

4 ounces petroleum jelly
½ ounce grated castile soap
a few drops essential oil bergamot or other essential oil (optional)

MELT the first two ingredients over a low fire. Remove from fire, add oil. When the mixture cools, spread over hands, cover with rubber gloves, and leave on overnight.

KIWI FRUIT, green papaya, and pineapple all contain digestive enzymes that can soften your cuticles. Immerse your hands in mashed fruit or fresh pineapple juice for ten minutes.

PROTEIN NAIL TREATMENT

The protein in milk softens skin; the calcium strengthens nails. Fresh herbs make a more sensual soak, but dried will do.

one cup of warm milk
1 tablespoon dried or 2 tablespoons fresh rosemary
1 tablespoon dried or 2 tablespoons fresh rose petals

POUR ingredients into a bowl large enough to accommodate all your fingers. Immerse your fingertips for 10–30 minutes. For a soothing hand treatment, double ingredients.

HORSETAIL NAIL STRENGTHENER

Olive oil softens and moisturizes your skin and cuticles. A weekly immersion prevents hangnails. The herb horsetail contains silica, a mineral that strengthens nails.

¼ cup olive oil
1 tablespoon dried or 2 tablespoons fresh horsetail

STEEP the mixture for at least three hours in a warm place such as a radiator, a sunny windowsill, or over hot water in the top of a double boiler. Strain out the herbs and soak your hands for ten minutes in this oil.

WHEN you finish soaking your nails, massage the oil into your wrists and fingers, using a circular motion. If you used milk instead of oil to soak your hands, massage them with your oil of choice. Olive or jojoba oils are best, but any vegetable oil will serve.

REMOVE the excess oil from your hands with a warm, damp towel, then use the towel to gently push back your cuticles. Stubborn tissue can be eased back from the nail with an orangewood stick wrapped in cotton.

VARIATION: If your nails are brittle, substitute glycerin for all or part of the olive oil.

Buffing your nails stimulates circulation. You can do this with a soft cloth or a nail buffer. To make your nails shiny, dust on some kaolin or rub some beeswax into the nails before buffing. If you like, you can tint the beeswax pink by melting it with a little alkanet root. This will not produce anything like a red nail polish, but it will give your nails a healthy pink glow.

NAIL-STRENGTHENING POLISH

Martha Sanchez, a hair stylist with Astor Place Haircutters in Manhattan, gives this recipe for strong fingernails:

1   clove fresh garlic
1   bottle nail polish

CRUSH the garlic clove and add it to nail polish before you paint your nails. If you don't mind the garlic odor, you could apply the garlic directly to your nails.

THE PEDICURE

YOUR FEET, TOO, WILL BENEFIT FROM A LITTLE TLC. THINK OF ALL they do for you. You can treat them using the instructions for the manicure. In addition, you will want to smooth away any roughness with a pumice stone. If you don't have one, scrub away accumulated dead skin cells with a paste made from ground almonds or sunflower seeds or cornmeal moistened with milk or olive oil, or use a loofah.

Damp skin attracts fungus infections. To prevent athlete's foot, dry the skin thoroughly, especially between the toes, then apply cornstarch, baking soda, or dusting powder. Make sure your socks are dry, and keep your feet dry by going barefoot as much as you can.

If you do have athlete's foot, apply aloe vera gel, which is antifungal. Allow the gel to dry before dusting your feet with powder and putting on your socks. Tea tree oil is also antifungal. Thoroughly mix a few drops into your cornstarch or dusting powder before applying.

HAND AND BODY LOTIONS
AND POTIONS

CAMPHOR ICE FOR ROUGH SKIN

FROM *THE ART OF PERFUMERY*, BY GEORGE WILLIAM SEPTIMUS PIESSE

- 2 ounces paraffin
- 8 ounces petroleum jelly
- 2 ounces camphor

MELT paraffin, add Vaseline, then camphor, pour into jars while melted, then color and perfume to suit.

The two traditional recipes below were recorded by Leonard Stoller.

FOR HAND CREAM

- ½ pound soft soap
- 1 gill [½ cup] salad oil
- 1 ounce mutton tallow [lanolin]

BOIL until thoroughly mixed. While still warm, add 1 gill [¼ cup] wine spirits [brandy] and 1 gram musk or a few drops essential oil.

FOR BEAUTIFUL HANDS

- 6 ounces rosewater
- 4 ounces honey
- 2 ounces beeswax
- 1 ounce myrrh

PLACE the last three ingredients in the top of a double boiler and melt them over simmering water. Before electric blenders were invented, the rosewater would have been beaten into the honey mixture a few drops at a time. Nowadays, all you have to do is pour the rosewater into

MOISTURIZERS

Jojoba oil *is often used in skin and hair preparations because the texture resembles human sebum. The oil is well absorbed by dry skin. For best results, apply the oil immediately after you wash or bathe, while your skin is still warm and slightly damp. Rub in as much as you can, let it sit a minute, then remove excess oil with a tissue or soft cloth.*

◆ Even oily skin benefits from the application of a little moisturizer. Showers and baths strip your skin of oil. Oily skin replenishes the lost sebum by producing more oil. A light application of oil helps to balance oil production. **Hazelnut** or **grapeseed** are best for oily skin because they are slightly astringent.

◆ Almond oil is slight and smooth—good for all types of skin.

◆ In tropical countries where coca trees grow, **coco butter** is used to moisturize the skin and eliminate scars and stretch marks.

◆ **Coconut oil** is another ready-made moisturizer. For best results, apply very sparingly; too much coconut oil actually dries out your skin.

◆ Vegetable shortening is relatively pure, and it softens and moisturizes.

a blender and add the wax mixture gradually until emulsified. Apply at night. Put on rubber gloves two sizes too big and punctured as freely as the top of a pepper box.

LAVENDER HAND AND BODY LOTION

½ cup lavender infusion:

  2 tablespoons dried lavender blossoms

  ½ cup plus 2 tablespoons boiling distilled water

¼ cup almond oil

¼ cup safflower oil

¼ teaspoon powdered gum benzoin

1 teaspoon chopped beeswax, firmly packed

10 drops essential oil of lavender

HAND TREATMENTS FROM AROUND THE WORLD

"The white of an egg well beaten, and mixed with the Powder of Mastick, helps chapt hands, if they be anointed therein."

From *A Thousand Notable Things on Various Subjects,* by Thomas Lupton

"To remove stains from the hands, wash the stain with sorrel juice."

From *Delights for the Ladies,* by Hugh Platt

In Mexico, granulated sugar moistened with a few drops of lemon juice is rubbed into the hands at bedtime. Afterward, the hands become very soft.

STEEP lavender in water for thirty minutes, then strain and measure out ¹/₂ cup infusion. Set aside. Meanwhile, place oils, benzoin, and wax in the top of a double boiler. Heat gently over simmering water until the wax is melted. Remove from the fire. Pour the lavender infusion into the jar of a high-speed electric blender. When the wax mixture is thick and opaque, but not hardened, beat in the essential oil. Set the blender at its highest speed and add the wax mixture. When the motor slows, scrape down the sides of the jar with a rubber spatula, being careful to avoid the blades. Continue blending until the mixture is creamy. Pour immediately into 2-ounce glass bottles. Wait until the lotion is cold before you cap the bottles. Lasts longer if you store in the refrigerator.

GARDENERS' HEALING HAND CREAM

Suitable for both genders, this rich golden cream soothes, softens and heals chapped, irritated, dry, or weathered skin. Smooth it on your hands after gardening or other outdoor work, or use it to cream your body after a bath or shower for all-over softness.

³/₄ cup olive oil
2 tablespoons dried calendula petals
1 tablespoon dried comfrey leaves
1 tablespoon dried patchouli leaves
1 tablespoon red clover blossoms
¹/₈ teaspoon powdered myrrh

⅛ teaspoon powdered gum benzoin	4 tablespoons aloe vera gel
1½ tablespoons beeswax	4 tablespoons rosewater
1 tablespoon powdered oatmeal or oat flour	1 teaspoon honey

INFUSE the first five ingredients in a glass bottle placed in the sun for two weeks. A quicker infusion method is to warm these ingredients in the top of a glass or enamel double boiler for thirty minutes. Strain the oil, pour it into the double boiler, add myrrh, benzoin, and beeswax. Heat gently until the wax is melted. After you take the mixture from the fire, mix about a tablespoon of it with the oatmeal or oat flour to form a smooth paste, then stir the paste into the oil. Set aside until opaque and thick, but not hardened. Pour the rosewater and aloe into an electric blender jar, add honey, and turn the blender to top speed. When the mixture is thick and creamy, pour into wide-mouthed glass jars immediately. Cap when the cream is completely cool. Store in the refrigerator.

LEMON BALM LOTION

The ingredients in this cream are healing and soothing, especially good for sensitive skin. The lotion has a fresh lemon scent. It is quickly absorbed and is not oily.

1 cup herbal infusion:	1 cup safflower oil
1⅓ cups boiling distilled water	2 teaspoons chopped firmly packed beeswax or beeswax beads
1 tablespoon dried shredded calendula blossoms	A pinch of boric acid
1 tablespoon dried crushed lemon balm	½ teaspoon powdered gum benzoin
	2 teaspoons powdered oats
1 tablespoon dried, crushed linden blossoms and leaves	1 teaspoon honey
	4 drops grapefruit seed extract

STEEP herbs in water for thirty minutes, strain, measure out 1 cup and set aside. Heat oil, wax, benzoin, and boric acid in top of a double boiler until the wax melts. Remove from fire, stir about a tablespoon of the oat flour into wax mixture. When a smooth paste forms, stir it into the wax mixture and cool until thick and opaque. Pour the infusion into blender jar. Add honey, set blender at highest speed, add wax

SUNSCREENS FROM AROUND THE WORLD

◆ Sesame oil is very effective—it blocks 30 percent of UVA rays.

◆ Olive and coconut oils absorb about 20 percent of UVAs.

◆ Aloe vera gel is an excellent sunblock and sunburn remedy.

◆ The antioxidant effect of green tea is fairly well known by now. An application of green tea has been clinically proven to delay burning.

mixture slowly. Beat until creamy and thoroughly emulsified, add grapefruit extract, and continue to blend for another minute.

SUN SENSE

TOO MUCH OR TOO LITTLE SUN CAN BE BAD FOR YOU. YOU NEED A certain amount of sunlight on your skin to manufacture vitamin D. The best way to get it is to expose your bare skin (no sunscreen) to the sun before 10 A.M. or after 4 P.M. In winter, if you live in a northern clime, this won't do you any good because the angle of the sun is too low in the sky. To some extent our bodies do store vitamin D from summer sunning, but northerners will probably need vitamin D supplements in winter.

That's the good news about sun exposure. The bad news most people know by now: A thinning ozone layer admits solar radiation that at the very least makes your skin age prematurely, and at the most degrades your immune function and can cause skin cancers.

The much-admired, healthy-looking tan is actually the skin's response to sun damage. A little goes a long way. To be safe, toast yourself no longer than twenty minutes a day before 10 or after 4. In a little while you will acquire a light tan and a healthy glow.

You will find recipes for homemade sunscreens on pages 73–74 in chapter two.

5 minute | SOLUTION

SUNBURN REMEDIES

Despite our good intentions, sometimes we do get sunburned, especially if we have fair skin. Below are some quick home remedies that will take the sting out of the burn and prevent peeling.

◆ Split a fresh aloe vera leaf with a knife or your fingernail and smooth the gel on the burn. You can also use bottled aloe gel.

◆ Dip absorbent cotton in a strong infusion of black tea (use 3 tablespoons of loose tea or tea bags of black tea infused in 1 cup boiling water for ten minutes) and apply to the sunburn.

◆ Splash on a few handfuls of cider vinegar.

◆ A layer of fresh yogurt soothes and cools.

◆ Mash and spread a layer of raw tomatoes or papaya on the burn.

◆ An Elizabethan sunburn remedy called for a handful of salt dissolved in the juice of two lemons. This was rubbed on both the hands and face and allowed to dry.

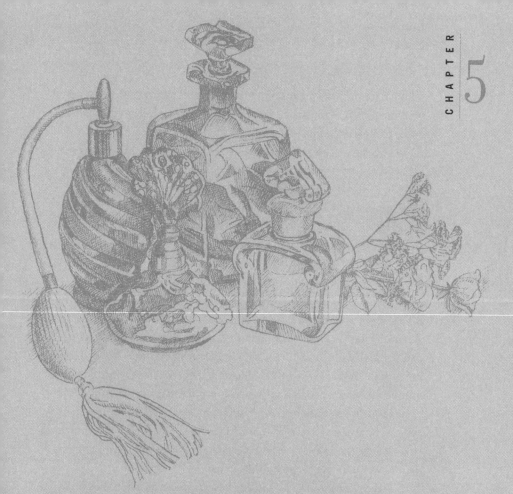

CHAPTER 5

FRIVOLITIES

PERFUME AND PAINT

FACE PAINT

Through all ages, times, and climes, both men and women have embellished their faces and bodies with pigment, dyes, tattoos, scar patterns, and a range of synthetic chemicals. Compared to the brilliant plumage of birds and the dazzling patterns on scales of tropical fishes, the human body is tinted with a limited palate. Even compared to some other mammals such as the baboon, the leopard, and certain whales, we humans make a rather poor showing in the animal beauty parade.

So we paint ourselves. We've been doing it for centuries, probably at least since we lost most of our fur. The initial purpose was camouflage. Body paint enabled a prehistoric hunter to stalk his next meal undetected by his prey. A bit later, when killing evolved from dispatching animals for food to dispatching neighbors for territory, the paint was incorporated into war regalia. After that, people decorated their faces and bodies with colors and patterns as a way to express emotion and to attract the opposite sex.

From early Germanic tribes the ancient Brits learned to use the leaves of woad (Isatis tinctoria) to dye their bodies blue for aggressive and decorative purposes. Long before that time, in ancient Egypt, women applied malachite, a copper ore, galena, a lead ore, and other ground minerals to their eyelids, and kohl to outline their eyes. The purpose was as much medicinal as decorative—to prevent eye irritations and infections brought on by the searing desert sun. They used different tones of color at various times of day according to how the light fell, varying the shade of eye shadow at different times of year. Cleopatra is said to have painted her upper eyelids blue-black, her lower lids green.

According to Max Wykes-Joyce's Cosmetics and Adornment: Ancient and Contemporary, South Sea Islanders were the first to come up with the idea of decorating their bodies permanently with tattoos. They made incisions in the skin with bone and filled in the indentations with a mixture of oily nut ash and water.

Scarification (wounding the flesh in such a way that the resulting scars will form patterns) is another ancient and contemporary attempt at personal adornment. Some indigenous peoples curled or frizzed their hair and, long before punk made such hues famous, bleached their hair or dyed it orange, blue, brown, or purple.

Catherine Corkery, former Peace Corps volunteer, gives a close-up view of the art of adornment she witnessed during the four years she spent in a village in Senegal:

"Women wear makeup for special occasions. Young women and children put charcoal around their eyes and draw with it on their cheeks and chest. Adult women use henna to produce the orange-red dye they use for a sort of tattoo. For Ramadan a woman might dye the palm of her hands with henna paste. Using surgical tape to make a stencil, she might also use the paste to paint circles, diamonds, or rectangles on the soles of her feet.

"By painting her hands, a woman announces her superior social status: she does not have to work with her hands, nor does her husband. Henna is great for fingernail polish. The entire finger is painted up to the first knuckle. The toenails are painted, too. In Morocco, the henna is applied with an ink pen, an instrument similar to a syringe.

Pular girls, a Senegalese indigenous people, tattoo their gums with blue dye. Older Pular women draw tattoos under their lips. They also do scarification on their temples. They make an incision with a razor blade and insert grains of rice to keep the wounds open so the scar will be wide."

You will find information on the later history of makeup in chapter one. Through the ages, a variety of concoctions, ranging from the bizarre (frog's blood, goat fat) to the lethal (lead, arsenic) have been dabbed on the face in the pursuit of beauty. You could say the same about some of the cosmetics that are sold today. The current trend toward "natural" cosmetics is no guarantee of purity. The only way you can be sure of what goes into your face paint is to make it yourself.

Ann Wolven Garrett, reporting on the 1994 annual meeting of the American Academy of Dermatology for *Drug and Cosmetic Industry* magazine wrote that "allergies to various [cosmetic] ingredients are common, with preservatives causing these exceeded in percentages only by fragrances." The article goes on to say that preservatives that contain forms of urea ". . . moved high on the list of allergy-triggers probably because it releases formaldehyde. . . ."

Most homemade face and body paint, because it contains little or no liquid, does not require any preservative. Some makeup, such as eye shadow, which you'd pay a high price for at a department store, can be made in less time than it takes to tell about it. Lip gloss and other homemade products are particularly kind to mature skin, which can look masklike under a layer of chemical makeup. Some, such as lavender eye shadow, have a calming and uplifting aroma. Below you will find a sampling of recipes to get you started. Your garden or local health food store or herb shop will give you lots more ideas.

EYE SHADOW

EYE SHADOW IS ONE OF THE MOST EXPENSIVE COSMETICS TO BUY AND THE easiest to make at home. Simply reduce the plant material to a powder in a spice mill or coffee grinder. Some plant parts reduce to powder easily; others do not. You may have to experiment to learn which plants work best.

Apply the powder to your eyelids with the tip of your pinkie finger or a Q-tip. Be careful not to get it in your eye! For a smoother and more adherent eye shadow, mix in a little gum tragacanth. Smooth it on your eyelids after you have applied moisturizer. Your eye shadow can last for several hours if you mix a few drops of glycerin with the powdered plant material to make a loose paste. Omit the tragacanth if you are using glycerin.

BROWN EYE SHADOW

You can buy black walnut shells already powdered. They make a splendid dark-brown eye shadow.

- 1 teaspoon powdered black walnut shells, or powdered, dark-roast coffee beans
- ½ teaspoon gum tragacanth

GRIND in a stone mortar until thoroughly mixed and pulverized. If you don't have a mortar and pestle, use a small glass and the round handle of a wooden spoon. Pour the mixture into a small, airtight container.

GREEN EYE SHADOW

Nettle leaves make a soft, fine powder that is about the consistency of face powder. The color is forest green. Adding gum tragacanth lightens it somewhat.

- 1 teaspoon powdered nettle leaves
- ¼ teaspoon gum tragacanth

PROCEED as in the above recipe.

LAVENDER EYE SHADOW

Lavender petals produce not a lavender but a gray eye shadow. It doesn't reduce to a fine powder; the effect is rather grainy, but it smells so good you probably won't care.

1   teaspoon powdered lavender
¼ teaspoon gum tragacanth

FOLLOW directions for making brown eye shadow.

If you are an organic gardener you might like to experiment with some of your flowers. Pansies, violets, and iris are all good for your skin. Dry the petals and remove the part with the color you want. Use the remainder of the petals in a skin freshener. A few flower species such as larkspur or monkshood are toxic and not for internal or external use.

Before you use any plant on your skin, do some research to ensure that the plant is not toxic or otherwise harmful to your skin. Try a little on the inside of your wrist or behind your ears to test for an allergic response before you put any of these powders on your eyes.

EYEBROW DARKENER

A LITTLE POWDERED BLACK WALNUT HULL APPLIED TO THE EYEBROWS with a small toothbrush gives you lasting and natural-looking color. As with eyeshadow, apply only a small amount and be careful not to get it in your eye.

If you don't happen to have any walnut shells, try finely ground dark-roast coffee.

KOHL

Kohl, a centuries-old eyeliner used in Africa, parts of Asia, and the Middle East, is actually a form of soot. The word is derived from the Hebrew verb for "to paint." Imports to this country, science writer Ruth Winter tells us in A Consumer's Dictionary of Cosmetic Ingredients, *may contain lead. You could make your own more safely with a bit of charcoal. If you have a woodstove or fireplace, you have a ready source of black pigment—the charred remains of a log you have burned. Reduce a piece of the charcoal to powder and use as above. You could also try George William Septimus Piesse's recipe below (India or Chinese ink is sold in art supply stores):*

1   stick Chinese or India ink (about ½ ounce)
1   cup rosewater

IN A mortar reduce the ink to a fine powder. Heat the rosewater until it is hot but not boiling. Rub the rosewater into the powder until it is uniformly liquid. Stir repeatedly for two days and apply to eyebrows and lashes with a camel hair pencil. (Note: You could make short work of the stirring process with an electric blender.)

LIP GLOSS

IN DAYS OF YORE, LADIES TEMPORARILY ACHIEVED ROSY LIPS AND cheeks with berry juice or pressure—a bite on the lips, a pinch on the cheek to bring the blood to the surface. A more lasting effect was achieved with red ocher mixed with animal fat.

If you want only to soften, not color, your lips, try the alkanet or the medicated lip balm recipe in Chapter Two, pages 65–68. Most plants—beets, for example—do not give up their color to oil. Alkanet root and annatto are exceptions. The kind of oil you use is also important. If you want the plant to stain not only the oil, but your lips, you need to use castor oil, the primary ingredient in commercial lipsticks. The wax must be colored at the same time as the oil, and all of the ingredients must be kept warm and liquid for at least five hours. The actual preparation will take you about three minutes. The infusion is what takes time, but it can be easily accomplished on a woodstove, radiator, or warming plate. You do not need to simmer the infusion. In fact, it is best not to because it might burn.

The root of alkanet, a blue flower, was used to make lip gloss in Elizabethan England. Depending on how much you use and how long it is infused, alkanet yields a red dye ranging from cherry to burgundy. The use of this, or a similar plant, can be traced to ancient Egypt, and later, to Rome. (In Attic Greece, the right to wear makeup was reserved for courtesans.)

The scent and taste of annatto is also rather pronounced, so you will probably want to lighten it by adding scented oils.

STEEPED ALKANET LIP GLOSS

This lip-softening gloss will give your skin some color, but it is subtle and you will need to renew it frequently. It requires next to no effort to make.

- 2 tablespoons shaved alkanet root
- 3 tablespoons almond oil
- 2¼ teaspoons shaved beeswax
- ¼ tablespoon shaved paraffin

STEEP the alkanet and oil for a couple of days, in a sunny place, if possible. Add wax and paraffin and heat gently until wax is melted. Pour immediately into the bottom of 3-ounce plastic cups or sturdy paper cups lined with cooking parchment. Leave the mixture undisturbed, then refrigerate overnight to set.

VARIATION: This recipe gives somewhat more color: 2 tablespoons alkanet root, 2 tablespoons castor oil, 1 tablespoon almond oil, ¾ tablespoon beeswax. Proceed as in recipe above. Let the mixture cure, uncovered, for 6 weeks.

COCONUT OIL LIP GLOSS

This recipe makes a beet red lip gloss. If left uncovered for a few days, the color darkens to a brownish red. This lip gloss is soft and easy to apply. However, at warm room temperatures it will liquefy, so be sure and keep it in a cool dark place. Alkanet has a heavy aroma when it is heated for a long time—hence the essential oils.

- 2 tablespoons castor oil
- 2 tablespoons coconut oil
- 3 tablespoons alkanet root

1 teaspoon shaved beeswax

4 drops each essential oils of patchouli, lavender, and
   ylang-ylang

PLACE all the ingredients except the essential oils in top of a double
boiler, in a 1-cup glass or enamel saucepan or stainless steel measuring cup. Heat over hot water or place the saucepan on a radiator or similar very warm place for five hours. Meanwhile, mix the essential oils
together. After you remove the wax mixture from the heat, stir the oils
in thoroughly. Pour immediately into tiny containers or the bottom of
3-ounce plastic cups or sturdy paper cups lined with cooking parchment.

VARIATION: For a softer hue and a milder taste, proceed as above, but use
only 1½ tablespoons of alkanet.

OLIVE OIL LIP GLOSS

This lip gloss has a deep red stain.

3 tablespoons castor oil

2 tablespoons olive oil

4 tablespoons alkanet root

1 tablespoon shaved beeswax

4 drops each essential oils of patchouli, lavender, and
   ylang-ylang

FOLLOW directions for making Coconut Oil Lip Gloss.

VARIATION: 2 tablespoons each of castor oil, olive oil, and alkanet; 1 tablespoon of beeswax; 4 drops each essential oils of ylang-ylang, patchouli, and
lavender. This lip gloss is darker than the variation to Coconut Oil Lip Gloss
and it is milder-tasting than Olive Oil Lip Gloss.

ALKANET ROSE LIP GLOSS

1 tablespoon almond oil

2 tablespoons olive oil

1	tablespoon castor oil
3	tablespoons alkanet root
1	tablespoon beeswax beads
10	drops essential oil of rose

KEEP first five ingredients warm for five hours. Remove from fire, add rose oil, and pour immediately into small containers.

ANNATTO-ALKANET LIP GLOSS

Gives an orange-red lip stain.

1½	tablespoons chopped dried annatto
1½	tablespoons shaved alkanet root
1	tablespoon castor oil
1	tablespoon safflower oil
2	tablespoons olive oil
4	drops each essential oils of patchouli, lavender, and ylang-ylang

KEEP first five ingredients warm for five hours. Remove from fire, add essential oils, and pour immediately into small containers.

VARIATION: For a less pronounced orange tint, use 1 teaspoon annatto, 2 tablespoons plus 2 teaspoons alkanet.

FRAGRANCE

NO COSMETICS CATEGORY IS AS ROMANTIC AND EVOCATIVE AS PERFUMERY. Jasmine, sandalwood, acacia. . . the very names of some of the ingredients are like poems, each conjuring up a landscape, a memory.

The art of perfumery began in Asia, probably as a burnt offering during religious ceremonies. Piesse writes that in Egypt porcelain jars bearing Chinese inscriptions were found in the ruins near pyramids. The jars contained cosmetics and scents dating back three or four thousand years. In Arabia, perfumes were kept in seashells to release their fragrance into the room where they neutralized unpleasant environmental odors.

odors coincide, like the keys of an instrument. Almond, heliotrope, vanilla and clematis blend together, each producing different degrees of a nearly similar impression. Similarly, citron, lemon, orange peel and verbena. . . . Odors of some flowers resemble others; some are identical in composition, i.e., cajeput and clove, cinnamon, anise, lavender."

From *The Art of Perfumery* by George William Septimus Piesse

Originally used in Egyptian embalming, most early Egyptian and Persian perfumes were in the form of powdered gum resins. One dry mixture unearthed from an Egyptian catacomb was discovered to be still fragrant after 3,000 years!

Eventually, through trade between East and West, and warfare, which inevitably fostered a great deal of cultural intermingling, perfumes made their way to Athens. There, Piesse tells us, perfumery was "brought to a higher pitch of refinement than it has ever enjoyed before or since." Athenian perfume shops became gathering places, like cafés would later become in Paris. Citizens kept their clothing in scented chests, and perfumed their rooms with scent bags and their wines with violets, roses, and other aromatic flowers. For each part of their body they used a different fragrance: mint for the arms, marjoram for the hair and eyebrows, ground ivy for the knees and neck. When they left home, they carried on their persons alabaster boxes filled with scented oils.

The Romans, who often emulated the Greeks, but with far less subtlety, took up perfumery with enthusiasm. They added perfumed oil to the bath and scented their beds, bedrooms, and amphitheaters. Before going into battle, the warriors surreptitiously dabbed on a fragrant oil for courage.

The steam distillation method of obtaining essential oils originated in Arabia around the fourth century. Five centuries later, the Persian herbalist, alchemist, and philosopher Avicenna perfected the technique.

During the Middle Ages, in the old cathedrals that had also served as burial grounds, the smoke of burning incense camouflaged the odor of moldering corpses. As the plague decimated the population of Europe, incense was burned to fumigate the sickroom and halt the spread of disease. (Piesse, writing centuries later, theorized that the smoke, which is acidic, neutralized pestilential odors, which are alkaline. He noted that ". . . fever will rarely travel from one room to another if incense is burned.") Aromatic and balsamic herbs were planted for the same purpose, and people avoided contagion by carrying bags of camphor, bundles of lavender, and bits of cloth soaked in aromatic vinegar.

Throughout the history of perfumery, boxes made of precious metal or marble were filled with perfumed pastes and worn as pendants or carried in the pocket in the belief that aromatic substances could protect the wearer from infection. Dr. George William Askinson, in *Perfumes and Cosmetics: Their Preparation and Manufacture*, notes that the practice has scientific validity, observing that workers in perfume laboratories and residents of French flower-growing districts are

FOUR THIEVES VINEGAR

LEGEND HAS IT THAT THE *inventors of this famous potion lived in Marseilles at the time of the bubonic plague. They made their living by robbing the sick and the dead. To survive this highly contagious and usually fatal disease, they inhaled an aromatic vinegar.*

One of the thieves, when apprehended, saved himself from the gallows by revealing the formula: ³/₄ oz. each fresh tops of common wormwood, Roman wormwood, rosemary, sage, mint, and rue, 1 ounce lavender flowers, 1 dram [1 teaspoon] each garlic, calamus aromaticus, cinnamon, cloves, and nutmeg; ½ ounce camphor, 1 ounce alcohol [e.g., vodka] or brandy, 4 pints strong vinegar.

Steep all but the camphor and spirits in a closely covered vessel for two weeks at summer heat; press and filter, add camphor previously dissolved in spirits.

From *The Art of Perfumery* by George William Septimus Piesse rarely troubled by respiratory infections. He adds that tests done at the Pasteur Institute in the early twentieth century "confirmed that evaporation of essential oil or vapor from their burning killed many bacteria."

The recipe below is typical of those used to fill scent boxes.

SPANISH PASTE

FROM *PERFUMES AND COSMETICS: THEIR PREPARATION AND MANUFACTURE*
BY GEORGE WILLIAM ASKINSON

The ambergris (from the sperm whale) and musk (from the musk deer) are used in perfumery as fixatives. The former was used in light floral scents, the latter in heavier floral scents. If you wish to make this recipe but object to the animal ingredients, you could omit them or use synthetics instead.

$3/4$ ounce ambergris

$1 1/2$ ounces benzoin [powdered]

$3/4$ ounce musk

$3/4$ ounce vanilla

$3/4$ ounce orrisroot

$3/4$ ounce cinnamon

$1 1/2$ ounces [essential] oil of bergamot

$3/4$ ounce [essential] oil of rose

$1 1/2$ ounces gum acacia

$1 1/2$ ounces glycerin

MIX in porcelain mortar and add water drop by drop until a doughy mass results.

During the Renaissance, perfumery flourished along with the more enduring arts. In England, inspired by Queen Elizabeth I, who had an exquisite "nose," perfumes were rich, delicate, elaborate, and costly. Each manor house was equipped with a stillroom, which functioned as the estate's apothecary shop. Here the lady of the house presided over the manufacture of fragrant waters made from distilled flowers and the preparation of home remedies. Milady recorded her recipes in a stillroom or receipt book, which was handed down in families for generations.

On the Continent, various monarchs prohibited or encouraged the use of scent. In Europe during the Inquisition, all cosmetics were viewed as diabolical; it was also true in pre–Victorian England, although the art flourished in Germany and France.

Paris was established as the center of perfumery during the fifteenth century. In the court of Louise XIII, the use of perfume was the height of fashion. In the time of Louise XV, a lady's lover wore the same perfume as she did.

During the nineteenth century, synthetics replaced some of the more rare and costly ingredients. Most contemporary perfumes are a mixture of synthetic and natural ingredients. Since the late twentieth century, there has been growing concern about the effect of synthetic fragrances and other chemicals on individuals and their environment. Synthetic fragrances are responsible for the majority of allergic responses to cosmetics, which can range from mild skin irritation to anaphylactic shock.

Natural essential oils are attracting increasing interest because of their purity and their cosmetic and medical value. The concept of treating certain physical and psychological disorders was introduced in the 1920s and came into its own during the late 1970s. Since then, aromatherapy has made its way into mainstream American medicine as well as the health spa, the boudoir, and the bath.

Learning to Work with Fragrance

A thrifty way to get started on the scented path is to start with small quantities of herbs and spices. Don't overlook the ones in your

> "The FDA is particularly concerned about synthetic musklike fragrances that have been associated with damage to the central and peripheral nervous systems."
>
> From *Aromatherapy,* by Kathi Keville and Mindy Green

kitchen. Fresh orange, lemon, or lime peels give zest to a blend and a lift to your spirits. Tarragon, in the right proportion, smells like new mown hay. Marjoram has been used since earliest times in perfumes and as a bath additive. The warm, slightly licorice scent of basil is sacred to Hindus who grow it around their temples. It seems to open the senses along with the sinuses. The heavenly aromas of vanilla, cinnamon, and clove awaken your sensuality as well as your appetite. You can use any of these ingredients to scent a room or make a toilet water or cologne.

A PERFUME FOR A CHAMBER

FROM *THE TREASURIE OF HIDDEN SECRETS* BY JOHN PARTRIDGE; RECORDED IN *THE HOUSEWIFE'S RICH CABINET*

TAKE rosemary, sweet marjoram, bay leaves (of each a handful), a penny's worth of cloves, vinegar, and rosewater (a sufficient quantity). Boil these in your perfuming pot, which smell is sweet and wholesome.

QUEEN ELIZABETH'S PERFUME

FROM AN UNDATED MANUSCRIPT, RECORDED IN *THE LITTLE BOOK OF CONCEITED SECRETS FROM SIXTEENTH TO EIGHTEENTH CENTURY STILLROOM OR RECEIPT BOOKS*

8 spoonfuls of compound water or vodka
The weight of tuppence [or a half teaspoon] of fine powder
    of sugar
Half an ounce of sweet marjoram dried in the sun
The weight of tuppence of the powder of benjamim (gum
    benzoin)

BOIL on hot embers and coals softly. The perfume is very good and sweet for the time.

ROSEMARY COLOGNE

ADAPTED FROM A RECIPE IN *THE HEALING POWER OF HERBS* BY MAY BETHEL

- 6 tablespoons dried rosemary leaves
- 1 teaspoon dried lemon peel
- 1 teaspoon dried orange peel
- 1 tablespoon dried mint leaves
- 1 tablespoon dried lemon balm leaves
- ¼ cup strong rosewater
- ¼ cup vodka

MIX and steep for eight to ten days.

LAVENDER WATER

- 1 part fresh lavender petals
- 1 part high-proof vodka
- 1 part distilled water

COVER the lavender with vodka. Steep for two weeks. Strain and add an equal part of distilled water. Pour into a bottle until the container is filled. Store in a dark place or in a dark glass bottle.

SCENTED OILS

The classic methods of extracting essential oils are these: distilling, which forces steam through flowers or leaves; enfleurage (see the recipe below); or maceration, where flower petals are steeped in warm oils for several hours, discarded, and re-placed with fresh ones a dozen times or more. A few, notably citrus oils, are extracted by pressure.

Enfleurage is an old French perfumer's technique. Glass plates were coated with lard or beef suet, then overlaid with fresh flower petals that were renewed every day or two when the old ones withered. An alternate method was to cover a cotton cloth with olive oil. On top of that went a layer of fresh flower petals. The fragrance was extracted by pouring rectified spirits, usually brandy or vodka,

*over pomade made from the scent-impregnated suet, or the olive oil squeezed
from the cotton cloth. This is a wonderful way to preserve a fleeting scent such as
lilacs, which flower for only a couple of weeks. The recipe below is a modern adap-
tation.*

For each fragrance you need:

One glass saucer

Two glass plates or saucers or a wide, shallow glass jar with
　　screw-top lid

Enough absorbent cotton to cover the saucer or jar to a
　　depth of about ½ inch

Flower petals—enough to form one layer over the cotton

Cold-pressed canola or safflower oil—enough to saturate the
　　cotton

SPREAD cotton over bottom of plate or jar. Gradually add oil until the
cotton is saturated. Over this spread a layer of fresh petals—lilacs,
roses, apple blossoms, or whatever is in season. Cover with jar lid
or inverted plate or saucer and place on a sunny windowsill. In a day
or two, when the petals wither, remove and replace them with a
fresh layer of flowers. Continue throughout the flowering season,
then gently strain the oil through a clean cloth and store in a dark bottle.

Using Essential Oils

A fragrance may be energizing, stimulating, calming, or uplifting; it
can set a mood—a characteristic that perfumers have exploited for centuries. As you become more familiar with an array of scents, you may
want to invest in an essential oil or two and experiment with making
perfume.

Trygve Harris, whose aromatherapy shop, Enfleurage, is one of
New York City's finest, has this advice for neophyte perfumers: "Start
with one oil and get to know it: find out what it does and how it interacts with other ingredients. Lavender or rosemary are good ones to begin with. Various essential oils are good for different things. They are
interesting by themselves, and they combine well with other fragrances.

"You need to learn to use essential oils safely. They are not for internal use, and you shouldn't apply them to your skin undiluted. Cinnamon bark oil should never be used on your skin—it can literally eat through the surface. Use cinnamon leaf oil instead."

Because essential oil is so concentrated, it is hard to get an idea of how it will smell in a perfume until a small amount is exposed to the air. To do this, cut a coffee filter into slivers, moisten each sliver with a drop of essential oil, and label it. After you have spent some time sniffing individual fragrances, you will begin to get an idea of how they play against each other. Try different combinations. A great perfumer can spend years creating a new fragrance, so take your time. Find out what scents are most pleasing to you: floral, fruity, or resinous. Are you most likely to choose a fragrance that is light and subtle, rich and sensuous, or earthy and woodsy? The type you like best is what should determine what you put in a blend.

Your nose is your guide to creating a perfume. Add a drop or two at a time, sniff the results, and keep adjusting the mixture until you get a scent you like. Come back to it a day or two later, and if you still like the scent, add vodka or brandy. To accurately measure each drop of oil and to keep the odors separate, use a different pipette (a long-stemmed dropper) for each oil. You can buy plastic pipettes for about 50 cents apiece.

Perfumers classify aromas as having a top, middle, or bottom note. The middle note is the most predominant. Some scents fall into two categories; rose can serve as all three notes. The top note, usually a citrus or floral scent, is predominant, the one you notice first. Base notes are, as the name implies, a foundation and fixative for other scents in the blend. Most often they will be a wood or a resin. The middle note is the bridge uniting the top and bottom notes. For more information, see the chart below.

Some combinations you might try are those recommended by Edith G. Bailes in *An Album of Fragrance:* bay leaf with rosemary, lavender, or citrus; lavender with orrisroot and vetiver; orrisroot with lavender and rose; vetiver (also called khus khus) with rose, lavender, patchouli and sandalwood.

George William Septimus Piesse used these combinations in some of his perfumes: lavender and clove; musk, rose, tonka bean, and

AROMA CLASSIFICATIONS

SCENT	CONTRASTING OR COMPATIBLE SCENTS
Basil	thyme, mint, bay leaf, rosemary
Bay leaf	lavender, rosemary, citrus
Bergamot	most other scents, floral and spicy mixtures
Chamomile	bergamot, geranium, lavender, rose
Cinnamon	clove and other spices, bergamot, lavender, frankincense, ylang-ylang
Eucalyptus	bergamot, lavender, tea tree, mint, sandalwood
Geranium	most other scents, especially herbal, citrus, and floral blends
Grapefruit	patchouli, sandalwood, and most fruit, spice, and floral blends
Jasmine	bergamot, geranium, rose, ylang-ylang, tangerine
Lemon	most other scents
Lemon verbena	citrus
Lime	citrus
Mandarin	citrus
Orange	citrus, clove, cinnamon, and herbal blends
Palmarosa	violet, lavender, patchouli
Peppermint	bergamot, geranium, tea tree, lavender, sandalwood, herb and citrus blends
Rose	chamomile, geranium, tea tree, lavender, sandalwood
Rosewood	violet, lavender, vanilla, tonka bean, jasmine, patchouli
Tangerine	bergamot, frankincense, patchouli, sandalwood, vanilla
Tea tree	bergamot, lavender, sandalwood, mint, eucalyptus

MIDDLE NOTES

Almond	vanilla, rose, musk, tonka bean, orrisroot, clove, cinnamon, allspice
Bay leaf	see **TOP NOTES**
Birch bark	juniper, rosemary, peppermint, tea tree, eucalyptus
Chamomile	see **TOP NOTES**
Cinnamon	fruity and spicy scents, almond, vanilla, lavender, rose
Clary sage	juniper, lemon, orange, lemongrass, thyme, basil

Clove	spicy and woody blends
Geranium	see **TOP NOTES**
Jasmine	see **TOP NOTES**
Juniper	rosemary, marjoram, basil, thyme, birch, mint, eucalyptus
Lavender	clove, patchouli, rose, most other scents
Lemongrass	orange, lemon, mint, juniper, vetiver, lavender
Marjoram	sage, lemon, basil, thyme, rosemary, lemongrass
Neroli	most scents
Palmarosa	see **TOP NOTES**
Peppermint	see **TOP NOTES**
Rose	see **TOP NOTES**
Rosemary	lavender, bergamot, basil, all citrus oils, herb blends
Rosewood	see **TOP NOTES**
Sandalwood (santalwood)	most scents
Tea tree	see **TOP NOTES**
Ylang-ylang	bergamot, jasmine, lavender, tangerine, woody blends

BASE NOTES

Balsam of Peru	most scents
Balsam of Tolu	most scents
Benzoin	rose, sandalwood, most other scents
Cedarwood	rosemary, patchouli, vetiver, sandalwood, bay leaf
Frankincense (olibanum)	lavender, patchouli, rose, sandalwood, tangerine
Neroli	vanilla, acacia, tonka bean, fruit, and spices
Patchouli	bergamot, geranium, lavender, frankincense, rose, sandalwood, tangerine
Rose	
Spikenard	
Spruce	juniper, eucalyptus, tea tree, mint
Vanilla	bergamot, sandalwood, tangerine, citronella, rose, citrus
Vetivert	rose, lavender, patchouli, sandalwood, jasmine

RIMMEL'S CLASSIFICATION OF ODORS

One way of creating a new scent is to use ones that are similar. The effect is more subtle than with contrasting scents. There are fewer surprises. This chart is from George William Askinson's *Perfumes and Cosmetics: Their Preparation and Manufacture*.

CLASS	TYPE	OTHERS IN CLASS
Rose	rose	geranium, sweetbriar, rhodium, rosewood
Jasmine	jasmine	lily of the valley
Orange flower	orange flower	Acacia, syringa, orange leaf
Tuberose	tuberose	lily, jonquil, narcissus, hyacinth
Violet	violet	acacia, orrisroot, mignonette
Balsamic	vanilla	balsam of Peru, balsam of Tolu, benzoin, styrax, tonka bean, heliotrope
Spice	cinnamon	acacia, nutmeg, mace, pimento, clove, pink, carnation
Camphor	camphor	rosemary, patchouli
Sandalwood	sandalwood	vetiver, cedarwood
Citrine	lemon	bergamot, orange, limette
Lavender	lavender	spike, thyme, serpolet, marjoram
Mint	peppermint	spearmint, lemon balm, rue, sage
Aniseed	aniseed	badiane, caraway, dill, coriander, fennel
Almond	bitter almond	laurel, peach kernels, mirbane
Musk	musk	civet, musk seed, musk plant
Amber	ambergris	oak moss
Fruit	pear	apple, pineapple, quince

camphor; sandalwood, acacia, orange flower, and camphor; acacia, orange water, and orrisroot; vanilla bean, tonka bean, benzoin; camphor, rosemary and patchouli; sandalwood, vetiver, and cedarwood; lemon, bergamot, and orange; patchouli, sandalwood, vetiver, verbena, and rose; rose, tonka bean, vanilla, orrisroot, and acacia.

The best way to sample the wide range of essential oils is to take a workshop in aromatherapy that includes hands-on experience. A local aromatherapy shop or even a well-stocked health food store can also help you expand your repertoire of fragrance possibilities.

When making a blend, you will probably find it easiest to start with fragrances that are similar. For suggestions, consult the chart on page 164.

Begin with the top note, round it out with the middle note, and ground it with a base note: a drop or two of base note, twice that amount of middle note, and up to five times that amount of top note. For perfume, add about four times that amount of vodka; more if you are making toilette water or cologne.

With the possible exception of plastic pipettes, use glass, not plastic, for all of your oil and fragrance containers. This is particularly true when you are making something as concentrated as a perfume. Be sure not to get essential oil on your bare skin. Exercise caution also in breathing in the scent of undiluted essential oils; they may give you a headache.

After working with essential oils for a while, your nose will get tired. Take a break, preferably in fresh air.

As you no doubt have discovered, the same cologne or perfume often smells different on different people. The only way to find out how a fragrance interacts with your particular biochemistry is to apply it.

Colognes, Perfumes, and Waters

LAVENDER WATER FOR BEAUTY AND FRAGRANCE
FROM *THE ART OF PERFUMERY* BY GEORGE WILLIAM SEPTIMUS PIESSE

- 4 ounces essential oil of English lavender
- 3 ounces spirit [preferably vodka]
- 1 pint rosewater

POUR into a glass container, shake, and apply.

FLOWERS OF ERIN

A Victorian cologne that smells like summer roses.

- 2 tablespoons rose water
- 35 drops (¼ teaspoon plus ten drops) vanilla extract

If you happen to be out of perfume and would like something nice to dab behind your ears, head for your spice shelf. A drop or two of vanilla, almond, lemon, or orange extract can impart a citrus zing or an almond or vanilla sensuality. Be sure the extract brand you use has no added sweetener. You could also mix and match vanilla with orange or almond, or orange with lemon. Food-grade orange water or rosewater can also be used straight from the bottle as a fragrant and refreshing skin toner or body splash. Add a drop or two of your flavoring extract for a dash of mystery or piquancy. Who knows, perhaps you'll start a trend.

LAVENDER-ROSE PERFUME

6 drops essential oil of rose
1 drop essential oil of lavender
⅓ teaspoon vodka

RONDELETIA

Piesse considered this perfume to be "one of the most gratifying to the smelling nerve ever made." The recipe below is adapted from The Art of Perfumery.

8 drops essential oil of lavender
2 drops essential oil of clove
2 drops essential oil of rose
4 drops essential oil of bergamot
2 drops musk oil
8 drops vanilla extract
1 teaspoon vodka

TONKA BEAN EXTRACT

6 tonka beans
2 tablespoons vodka

STEEP the beans in vodka for forty-eight hours. Remove five of the beans and use them for the sachet recipe on page 173. Steep the remaining bean in the vodka for one week, strain, and use in the recipe below or one of your own devising.

TROPICAL RAIN PERFUME

- 1 teaspoon tonka bean extract
- 1 drop essential oil of ylang-ylang
- 2 drops essential oil of bergamot

CITRUS GROVE PERFUME

- ½ teaspoon vodka
- 6 drops essential oil of grapefruit
- 2 drops essential oil of bergamot
- 1 drop essential oil of patchouli
- 1 drop essential oil of rose

Dusting Powder

Contrary to what you may have thought, dusting powder is not just for little old ladies. Your recipe can be simple—a handful of cornstarch straight from the box to soothe itches and irritations, or it can be complex—a medley of dried flowers, essential oils, and various starches and clays formulated to produce a lingering scent that can be as subtle or exotic as you wish.

This toiletry is easy to make and hard to ruin. Even if you add too much of a particular ingredient such as scent, all you have to do is lighten it up by adding more powdered grain or flour. A dusting powder is rather like soup, accommodating a range of dried and powdered materials, from the marjoram or basil flowers you may pluck to encourage the leaves to grow, to the pine spills that litter your lawn, the sweet fern that may fringe it or the bouquet of homegrown flowers that has become too withered to display.

Dusting powder ingredients, like those in a soup, are not too fussy about what company they keep. If an ingredient is unobtainable,

Here's a quick fix from your pantry shelves. Blessed with a robust fragrance reminiscent of pine, marjoram has been used in perfumery and as a bath additive since earliest times.

substitute one that you have on hand. Basically, you want this toiletry to keep you dry and fragrant. To do that requires a scent, a starch, and maybe a deodorant. To find them, you seldom have to look further than your kitchen shelves. Instead of, or in addition to, the more obvious floral fragrances from essential oils or dried flowers, how about scenting your mixture with dried, powdered citrus peel; ground cinnamon, allspice, or a pinch of clove; or maybe some vanilla bean or almond extract? Besides cornstarch or arrowroot starch, which you may not have on hand, there is oatmeal, tapioca, or barley, all of them soothing to the skin, each one easily reduced to powder in a kitchen blender or coffee grinder. As for deodorants, a tablespoon or so of baking soda will do.

ANCIENT-AIRS DUSTING POWDER

You can use this powder immediately. It has a green and herby woodland fragrance. If you choose wheat flour as your base, use pastry rather than bread flour because the lower gluten content makes it less sticky.

2 tablespoons dried marjoram leaves
½ cup cornstarch, oat flour, or wheat flour

POWDER the marjoram in a spice mill or blender. Put into a container with a tight lid. Add the starch or flour. Shake and use.

Another ingredient that appears in the finest powders is corn silk, which does make your skin feel silky. When corn is in season, instead of throwing away the tassels, spread them out on an old bed sheet or some paper bags in a warm, dry place until crumbly dry. Home-dried under the right conditions, corn silk should remain a delicate shade of gold.

Other bath powder ingredients can be found in your local health food store, food co-op, or herbal outlet, or you can search for them over the Internet. Slippery elm, used by herbalists to treat cough and sore throat, also soothes skin irritations. Orrisroot, which comes from the Florentine iris, is absorbent and aromatic. In perfumery it is used as a fixative to prolong the fragrance of other scents. Clay, especially green clay, is absorbent and deodorant; although the noncolor of white clay may better suit your purposes if you are adding floral ingredients. Fuller's earth, or bentonite, has properties similar to those of clay.

In addition to the recipes below, you will find others in the Gift chapter on pages 185–186.

LAVENDER-SPICE DUSTING POWDER

The fragrance of a freshly made powder is somewhat raw compared to the more subtle aroma that emerges a few weeks later after the scents have time to mingle, mellow, and marry. Therefore, it's a good idea to give a powder about a month to age before you use it—something to bear in mind if the powder is to be a gift. The powder below is a good example: What emerges is an interesting, rather exotic fragrance that is unlike that of any individual ingredient.

- 1 cup cornstarch
- ½ cup barley flour
- ½ cup bentonite
- ½ cup corn silk
- 2 tablespoons powdered orrisroot
- 2 tablespoons powdered allspice
- 2 teaspoons coriander
- 2 tablespoons powdered lavender
- 1 lemon peel left whole or in large pieces

COMBINE the ingredients in a glass or metal container with a tight-fitting lid. Let the mixture steep for a month, shaking daily or as often as you remember. Before using, remove the lemon.

LINDA BUCK'S AFTER-BATH POWDER

1 cup French white clay

1 cup cornstarch

1 cup powdered slippery elm bark

½ cup powdered rose petals

¼ teaspoon essential oil of rose

PLACE all of the ingredients in a large container, such as a coffee can, with a tight-fitting lid. Work the oil through the dry ingredients with your fingers until no lumps remain. Shake the container vigorously, then let it steep for a week or two before using. Store in an airtight, moisture-proof container such as a glass jar with a tight-fitting lid or a decorative tin.

DAMASK POWDER

These two powders are very aromatic, more a solid perfume than a dusting powder. The damask is a variety of rose. Both these recipes are from Hugh Platt's Delights for the Ladies. *All of the ingredients should be thoroughly dried before adding them to the mixture.*

5 ounces orrisroot

2 ounces cypress

2 ounces calamus

½ ounce cloves

1 ounce benzoin

1 ounce rose petals

1 ounce storax calamitum

½ ounce spike (lavender) flowers

IN A spice mill, coffee grinder, or blender, reduce each ingredient to a powder. Measure and mix them together in a large bowl. Store in a glass or metal container with a tight lid.

DAMASK POWDER

For centuries musk and civet have been used in perfumery to enrich and extend the scent of other aromatics. Synthetics are recommended: Not only are they less costly, they are much better for the musk deer and the civet.

½ pound orrisroot

4 ounces rose petals

1 ounce cloves

2 ounces Lignam rhodium (rosewood)

1½ ounces storax

10 grains each musk and civet

BEAT together. Store in a glass or metal container with a tight lid.

Environmental Perfumes

A simple way to try out a scent and its effect on you is with a potpourri burner. Warmed by a small tea light candle, these two-part ceramic devices consist of a receptacle for a tea candle with another receptacle for oil or water and herbs on top of that. They are inexpensive and readily available. If you have a woodstove, oil heater, or old-fashioned metal radiator, you could simmer the herb or a drop or two of the oil in an enamel or stainless-steel saucepan partly filled with water. A Crock-Pot is an excellent way to diffuse scent through a room. To every cup of water, add a teaspoon of dried herb or a drop or two of oil. You could also put a drop or two of oil on a diffuser ring. These ceramic devices fit onto a lightbulb, which, when turned on, warms the essential oil so its fragrance is released into the room.

As you become familiar with the properties of an essential oil, or otto, try different combinations of herbs and oils. For example, a teaspoon of dried rosemary and a drop of cedarwood otto keep you intellectually focused and grounded at work. Rose is said to open the heart; lavender and chamomile ease tension; ylang-ylang, patchouli, jasmine, sandalwood, vanilla, and rose are all considered aphrodisiac.

Cassolette

FROM *THE TOILET OF FLORA*, BY PIERRE-JOSEPH BUC'HOZ

The author of this recipe notes that the use of orange-flower water was very extensive. It was highly esteemed for its aromatic perfume and used with success for hysteric complaints.

Mix powders of Florentine orris, storax, benzoin, and other aromatics. Moisten with orange-flower water, and put the paste into a silver or copper box lined with tin. When you want scent, put this on a gentle fire or hot ashes.

Sachets

Back in "the old days," before clothes were scented by chemical perfumes in laundry detergents and fabric softeners, they were stored with a few sprigs of dried lavender or a sachet containing several dried flowers. Some plants, notably cedar, lavender, and eucalyptus, were stored among woolens to repel moths.

A Sweet Bag to Scent Clothes

FROM *THE WHOLE DUTY OF A WOMAN; OR A GUIDE TO THE FEMALE SEX*, WRITTEN BY A LADY; RECORDED IN *THE HOUSEWIFE'S RICH CABINET*

Take tops of hyssop, winter savory, rosemary, lavender, and the chippings of cassia ligna [a bark resembling cinnamon, which you could use as a substitute], cedar, and sassafras. Sew them up in thin bags, and lay them among your garments, and they will not only give them a curious scent, but preserve them from worms, moths, or any other insects.

HELIOTROPE SACHET

George William Septimus Piesse, who records this recipe in The Art of Perfumery, *considers it "one of the best sachets ever made."*

- 2 pounds powdered orrisroot
- 1 pound ground rose leaves
- ½ pound ground tonquin [tonka] beans
- ¼ pound vanilla beans
- ¼ ounce musk grains
- 5 drops almond otto

MIX, enclose in muslin bags, and store among your clothes.

TONKA BEAN SACHET

The rich, vanilla scent of tonka beans is ideal for sachets.

- 5 dried tonka beans, crushed (See Tonka Bean Extract recipe, pages 166–167.)
- 2 tablespoons dried orange rind, chopped small
- ½ cinnamon stick, broken into small pieces

PLACE all the ingredients into a small muslin bag with a drawstring top. Refresh or replace when the scent fades.

Once you have been surrounded by fragrance, your life won't be the same without it. A lemon studded with cloves in your closet, a handful of lavender or a few tonka beans stored among your bed linen, sachets tucked among your sweaters and lingerie—all, or at least one or two, of these habits may become indispensable to your sense of well-being. Enjoy them in good health and a joyous spirit.

CHAPTER 6

Thanks so much for
the hospitality, here's
some dusting powder
to make you feel
SPeCial! Fred

GIFTS OF NATURE

GIFTS OF BEAUTY

There is no gift that you can buy from the most elegant emporium that can equal the purity and freshness of a homemade toiletry. A lotion, face cream, shampoo, dusting powder, or bath salt that you have put together yourself is a creative and original gift, and one of the most welcome. In fact, don't be surprised if one or more happy recipients urge you to start a cottage industry just to get you to continue making the stuff.

A handcrafted cosmetic can be as quick and simple as adding a few drops of essential fragrance oil to a jigger of vodka for a custom-made birthday cologne, or as festive and labor intensive as teaming up with a friend or two to create an assorted few dozen lotions and potions to give at holidays and other special occasions.

If you intend to mail your gift, you have a few things to consider before you choose what to make. Face cream is a universal favorite among all ages and both genders. The orange aloe moisturizer on pages 36–37 holds up for a long time under adverse conditions such as those encountered during shipping. Of the body lotions, the Gardener's Healing Hand Cream (pages 140–141) and the Lavender Lotion (pages 139–140) are the most durable.

Whatever you send, be sure to pack it well, especially if the container is glass. Wrap the jar in bubble wrap or several layers of crushed paper and cradle it in more Styrofoam or crushed paper. Layers of popcorn make a good cushion, too.

The next consideration is where your package is going. If you are sending your gift to someone who lives in the tropics or an overheated apartment and who can't be bothered to refrigerate the cream or wash her hands before sticking them in the jar, choose a less perishable item.

Because they are dry and virtually indestructible, not to mention easy to ship, dusting powder, bath salts, and complexion grains fall into this category. So do herbal sleep masks, pillows, and sachets. Lip balm, solid deodorants, and soaps, because they do not contain water, hold up well under adverse conditions, as do shaving lotions, hair re-storers, floral waters, perfumes, spray deodorants, and other products containing alcohol. Dry shampoo is one of the easiest gifts to make, re-quiring only that you store a few sprigs of lavender, rosemary, or other fragrant herb with cornmeal or barley until the grain absorbs the scent. When the unexpected happens—no water, no time, or a sudden head cold—this modest gift is priceless.

Is the person who is getting the gift a do-it-yourselfer? Instead of the finished product, you could send a packaged mix. You provide the dry ingredients and instructions on how to use them; the recipient adds the liquid. Assembly is quick and easy, and you can put together a number of these gifts at the same time. Seal the dry ingredients in zipper lock bags or paper envelopes. All of the ingredients that are added at the same time go in the same envelope. Mix ingredients might include dried herbs, grated soap or beeswax, powdered gum benzoin, borax, and perhaps a tiny vial of essential oil. Package the entire mix in a decorated box or larger envelope and paste a handwritten or typed copy of the recipe on the front. If you anticipate that your recipient might have trouble finding a certain liquid ingredient such as orange water (not to be found in any store in the state of Maine), you could include that, too.

A special gift for someone who loves homemade cosmetics is a toiletry kit containing a face cream, hand and body lotion, shampoo, bath salts perhaps, and maybe a fragrance item such as a cologne, perfume, or dusting powder. If you are making a quantity for a holiday, and especially if you have a partner or two to make gifts with you, the toiletry assortment is easily accomplished.

Other gift possibilities are illustrated recipe cards or—a more elaborate gift—a "stillroom" or "receipt" book. Forerunners of the modern cookbook, the former dating back to the thirteenth century, these were family recipe collections handed down from mother to eldest daughter. Each new generation tinkered with existing recipes and expanded the repertoire. Why not start a family tradition that may turn out to be an heirloom? You can find supplies for handmade books in craft shops, art supply stores, and on the Internet. Here you will find acid-free cardboard for your book cover, beautiful paper with which to cover it, and fine, durable material for the pages. Along with your recipe cards or book, you could include an exotic herb or two such as alkanet or patchouli.

If you have the time and inclination, a very special gift to a friend or loved one is a spa day. Essentially this consists of a few structured hours of nurturing that includes a facial, massage, manicure and pedicure, hair conditioning, and a long soak in a hot, therapeutic bath. You will find details below.

Before you set about gift production, map out your plan on paper, listing the items you will make and the ingredients you need. Even in a major metropolis, tracking down certain items takes time. Therefore, write a detailed shopping list and factor in a little extra of everything to compensate for possible mishaps.

In scheduling your work, begin with the date when you expect to present or mail the gift and work backward. If you are ordering supplies over the Internet, allow at least a couple of weeks for them to arrive, up to a month at Christmas. The same is true if you are ordering through a local dealer—during the Christmas rush, deliveries are sometimes delayed.

Shaving lotion, massage oil, fragrance oils, floral waters, and similar items that need to be steeped for a period of time should be started at least two weeks before you present them. This is also true of the infused oils you will use in a lip balm, face cream, or body lotion.

A word about large batches and how they affect ingredient proportions in a recipe: Usually they don't. Baby powder and dusting powder tend to pack down when you make a lot, so it doesn't seem as if you have as much as you expected. Face creams, body lotions, and other emulsions work best in two-cup batches. If you put less than a cup or more than two cups in a blender they don't emulsify properly.

If you are making toiletries for several people, it is very important that you have all of your ingredients assembled and at room temperature. This includes pots and pans, mixing bowls, spoons, measuring utensils, a blender and spice mill, and any other relevant appliances. With soaps, emulsions, and certain other recipes, timing is crucial.

Begin by mixing together all of your dry ingredients, then blend your essential oils. This saves you time and keeps the manufacturing process flowing. If the product contains beeswax, you need to work quickly, before the wax hardens, so have your liquid ingredients in the blender if you are making an emulsion.

Place your products in clean or sterile containers, and store them in a cool, dry place if you don't plan to use them right away.

CONTAINERS

IF YOU KNOW ANYONE WHO HAS A BABY AND BUYS BOTTLED BABY food you have an abundant source of the perfect cosmetic container. The average four-ounce baby food jar is just the right size to hold creams, bath salts, and dusting powders; the same size bottle holds a half cup of lotion or shampoo. The two-ounce size works well for lip balm and deodorant. Sterilizing the sturdy, heat-proof glass is no problem; the rubber-lined caps give you a good seal. Although glass is not the ideal material for shipping, baby food jars are durable and should arrive intact if you pack them with lots of cushioning such as crushed paper, bubble wrap, Styrofoam beads, or popcorn. These plain, wide-mouthed jars also lend themselves to decoration. You may want to paint the caps or make decorative round labels that cover the lid, or cover the jar top with appealing fabric and tie with a ribbon or raffia.

Light-sensitive ingredients do best in dark containers. Light-blocking jars of colored glass are lovely, elegant, and expensive. You can get the same effect by painting the jar or covering it with foil or decorative paper.

If you are producing a quantity and want to make a more upscale presentation, check out a container clearinghouse. These are warehouses that carry odd lots of all sorts of containers. Often you can buy them in relatively small amounts. See the appendix for details.

Most of the cosmetics in this book are made from edible ingredients. Like food, they are vulnerable to bacterial contamination. Therefore, the containers in which you store them should be scrupulously clean. Cracked or chipped glass and crockery, which can harbor bacteria, should be discarded. Wash your containers in hot, soapy water—a dishwasher, if possible—and rinse them thoroughly. Scald plastic containers by rinsing them with boiling water. If your glass containers are heat-proof, sterilize them by placing them upside down on a rack inserted in a large kettle. Pour an inch or two of water in the bottom of the kettle, bring to a boil, and simmer for ten minutes.

Let the jars air-dry completely before you use them. To avoid an unwitting recipient's possible allergic reaction, list your ingredients on the label. You might also want to add a note about handling instructions. Creams, lotions, and shampoos, for example, should be refrigerated. Only a finger that has been thoroughly and freshly washed should be inserted into a jar of cream or lotion; otherwise, a clean cosmetic spatula should be used to scoop material out of the jar.

RECIPES AND SUGGESTIONS FOR GIFTS

FOUR-FLOWER FACIAL STEAM MIX

For dry, sensitive, or normal skin:

> 1 part each:
> dried calendula
> rose petals with the white heel removed
> chamomile petals
> lavender petals

PACKAGE your mix in a box or envelope with these instructions:

ADD ¼ cup mix to 1 quart water. Bring the herbs and water to a boil in a facial sauna or saucepan. If a saucepan is to be your sauna, remove it from the heat, drape a towel over your head, and lean over the pot for ten minutes, keeping a comfortable distance from the hot water.

FACIAL STEAM MIX FOR OILY SKIN

> 1 part lavender
> 1 part elder flowers
> 1 part witch hazel bark
> 1 part yarrow
> 1 teaspoon powdered myrrh to each cup of mix

INSTRUCTIONS are similar to those for Four-Flower Steam Mix above.

FOUR-GRAIN COMPLEXION SCRUB MIX

> 2 parts each:
> ground barley
> coarsely ground oats
> 1 part each:
> elder blossoms, coarsely
> pulverized
>
> crumbled rose petals, white
> heels removed
> crumbled mint leaves
> powdered brown rice
> cornmeal

½ part ground almonds or
   sunflower seeds

⅛ part ground apricot seeds (optional)

INSTRUCTIONS should state: Moisten about a tablespoon of the dry ingredients with about ½ tablespoon honey and 1 teaspoon milk, or enough to make a loose paste. The paste should be applied with a gentle, circular motion and rinsed off with tepid water.

SHAVING SOAP

An effective shaving soap softens the hair and makes the skin smooth and slick so the razor glides easily. This one is creamy. The scent is very light, pleasing to both genders. For more information about making soaps, see pages 124 to 129 in Chapter 4.

¼ cup herbal infusion:
   ½ cup distilled water
   1 tablespoon elder flowers
   1 tablespoon shredded marshmallow root
¾ cup grated castile soap
1 teaspoon castor oil
1 teaspoon glycerin
8 drops essential oil of bergamot
2 drops essential oil of grapefruit

BRING water to the boil. Pour over elder flowers and marshmallow root. Cover and steep thirty minutes, then strain through a coffee filter to remove all the solid matter. Measure out ¼ cup. Place the soap and infusion in the top of a double boiler. Simmer very, very slowly until the soap melts, stirring frequently. Remove from the fire. Stir in the castor oil and glycerin, let the mixture cool slightly, then stir in the essential oils, whipping until the soap is clear and smooth. Pour into a small mug, or a mold that would fit into a shaving mug. An eight-ounce yogurt carton dusted inside with cornstarch works well. Leave the soap in the refrigerator overnight to set. Either wrap the soap in pretty paper or present it with the mug and shaving brush.

ORANGE-ELDER AFTER-SHAVE LOTION

Orange water is used in Middle Eastern cooking. It is sold in grocery stores that cater to this trade. Distilled from orange blossoms, the water moisturizes and soothes the skin. The scent is light and refreshing, not "girly," despite the orange water. The feel is refreshing, not harsh and stinging like most commercial lotions.

- ½ teaspoon honey
- ½ cup orange water
- ½ cup vodka
- 1 teaspoon coriander
- 1 teaspoon elder blossoms
- 2 bay leaves
- 2 tablespoons aloe vera gel

DISSOLVE the honey in the orange water. Place all of the ingredients in a glass container with a screw-top lid. Allow the mixture to steep for at least two weeks, shaking daily. Strain and store in a dark glass bottle.

FOREST-BLEND AFTER-SHAVE LOTION

- 2 teaspoons witch hazel
- 2 teaspoons crushed juniper berries
- 2 teaspoons dried, crushed yarrow leaves and flowers
- 2 teaspoons dried, shredded marshmallow root
- 4 tablespoons aloe vera gel
- 1 cup vodka

FOLLOW instructions for Orange-Elder After-Shave.

CITRUS-SPICE AFTER-SHAVE LOTION

The lemon balm and calendula heal and soothe sensitive skin.

- 1 cup vodka
- 2½ tablespoons crushed, dried lemon balm leaves

2 teaspoons linden leaves and flowers, crushed and dried (optional)

2½ tablespoons dried, shredded calendula petals

10 drops essential oil of grapefruit skin

2 teaspoons ground allspice

FOLLOW instructions for Orange-Elder After-Shave above.

YUCCA ROOT SHAMPOO MIX (FOR DARK HAIR)

You might want to include a note about yucca on your label. You will find this information on page 101. Yucca root contains saponins (soaping agents), which cleanse and soften the hair, but unlike the chemicals in commercial shampoo, they do not produce a rich lather. Hence the castile soap. It is an optional ingredient; in fact, the shampoo does a better job without it.

½ cup dried, shredded yucca root

¼ cup grated castile soap (optional)

4 tablespoons dried rosemary leaves

PACKAGE each ingredient separately. Include a label with these instructions: Place the yucca in an enamel or glass saucepan. Add 1 quart distilled water. After simmering over low heat for ten minutes, strain the boiling water over the soap and rosemary. Stir with a wooden spoon until the soap dissolves. Cover and steep for thirty minutes. Strain, bottle and store in the refrigerator. Note: It is better to prepare only a cup of shampoo at one time so it will remain fresh. You might want to divide your mix into four portions and adjust your recipe accordingly.

SOAPWORT-CALENDULA SHAMPOO

Like the mix above, this one is special because it includes an unusual ingredient. It does wonders for blond hair. In this recipe the castile soap is not only optional, but it interferes somewhat with the conditioning effects of the soapwort.

1 cup dried soapwort

½ cup dried calendula petals

¼ cup grated castile soap (optional)

INCLUDE these instructions: Simmer the soapwort in 2 cups distilled water over low heat for ten minutes. Strain and pour over calendula and soap. Stir until soap dissolves, then steep for thirty minutes. Strain, bottle, and use immediately or store in the refrigerator. Note: You might want to divide this mix into four parts also.

SOAPWORT CALENDULA
SHAMPOO
1 c. dried soapwort   ½ c. dried calendula petals   ¼ c. grated castile soap

Simmer the soapwort in 2 c. distilled water over low heat for
10 minutes. Strain and pour over chamomile and soap. Stir until soap dissolves, then
steep for 30 minutes. Strain, bottle, and use immediately or store in the refrigerator.

EFFERVESCING BATH POWDER

This recipe is adapted from George William Askinson's recipe in Perfumes and Cosmetics: Their Preparation and Manufacture. *The first three are the active ingredients; the oils are for scent. If you don't have the ones called for in the recipe, you can substitute others.*

- ½ cup bicarbonate of soda
- 7 tablespoons tartaric acid (a by-product of wine making, provides effervescence)
- ³/₄ cup cornstarch
- 9 drops essential oil of lemon
- 3 drops essential oil of orrisroot (you could substitute 2 tablespoons powdered root)
- 3 drops oil of cananga (you could substitute ylang-ylang)

Follow dusting powder instructions (pps. 167–171).

Dusting Powder

You can assemble large amounts of fragrant after-bath powder in less time than it takes to tell about it. This toiletry is long-lasting and easy to ship. You need to start this a couple of weeks ahead. Below are recipes for the basic powder that you can use for the two powder recipes here, or for your own original blend. If you are a gardener or forager, your recipe may vary with the season. For more detailed instructions on making dusting powder, see pages 167–171.

BASIC DUSTING POWDER MIX

This recipe makes ten ¹/₂-cup servings.

- 2 cups cornstarch
- 1 cup oat flour
- 1 cup kaolin or other white clay
- ³/₄ cup powdered rose petals
- ¹/₂ cup powdered corn silk

LAVENDER-ROSE DUSTING POWDER

- 2¹/₂ cups Basic Dusting Powder Mix
- 3 tablespoons powdered dried lavender petals
- 1 tablespoon powdered orrisroot
- ¹/₄ teaspoon essential oil of rose

MIX dry ingredients by shaking them in a closed container. Sprinkle the oil over the powder, then work it with your fingers until the mixture is smooth and no lumps of scent remain. Cover the mix and let it sit for two weeks. Shake daily.

EASTERN MYSTERY DUSTING POWDER

- 2 cups Basic Dusting Powder Mix
- 3 tablespoons powdered patchouli leaves
- ¹/₄ cup powdered rose petals
- 1 tablespoon powdered sandalwood
- 1 tablespoon powdered orrisroot
- 1 tablespoon ground dried jasmine petals
- 15 drops essential oil of patchouli
- 6 drops essential oil of ylang-ylang

MIX dry ingredients thoroughly with a wooden spoon. Put mixture in a closed container and shake until thoroughly mixed. Sprinkle essential oils over the powder; work them in with your fingers until no lumps of scent remain. Let the mix sit in a closed container for a week. Shake daily.

VIOLET POWDER

Adapted from The Art of Perfumery *by George William Septimus Piesse. Orris, from the root of Florentine iris, has a violet scent and is used in perfumery as a fixative and a substitute for the more expensive flower.*

12 pounds wheat starch [you could substitute cornstarch]

2 pounds orrisroot powder

½ ounce lemon otto [essential oil]

¼ ounce bergamot otto

2 drams ground cloves [about 2 teaspoons]

MIX dry ingredients by shaking them in a closed container. Sprinkle the oils over the powder, then work them in with your fingers until the mixture is smooth and no lumps of scent remain. Cover the mix and let it sit for two weeks. Shake daily.

Floral Toilette Water Mix

Fragrant dried flowers from your garden or surrounding fields or woodlands are a welcome reminder of summer, especially when winter winds are howling. Package a quantity of dried, fragrant blossoms such as rose or lavender. Instruct the recipient to steep the petals in vodka—2 parts alcohol to 1 part flowers—for at least two weeks. The mixture should be infused in a glass bottle with a tight lid and shaken daily, then strained and stored in dark glass or a dark cupboard.

Love Oil

Made in seconds and enjoyed at leisure are oils that stimulate sexual desire. Essential oils of musk, cedar, jasmine, and ylang-ylang are considered very arousing to women. Add ¼ teaspoon of cedar oil or a blend of the other three to ½ cup of almond oil. Warm slightly before using for a sensual massage. A concoction of almond oil with two or three drops of essential oil of peppermint, when applied directly to the genitals, produces a warm, tingling sensation that can be very erotic. Test first, though—peppermint oil can irritate.

Sleep Masks and Pillows

The aroma of certain flowers and herbs is very relaxing and conducive to sleep. Hops pillows have been escorting insomniacs to dreamland for centuries. Lavender, rose, violet, and lilac petals are also good choices. To make one of these items, trace a mask or pillow on a sheet of paper, then transfer the pattern to sheets of satin or muslin and sew them together. A simple Halloween half-mask is a perfect pattern for the former. You can either make the pillow from scratch, or stuff an old pillow with the herbs and cover with a pillow slip.

CALENDULA BABY LOTION

You don't have to be a baby to enjoy this lotion. Calendula petals are very soothing and healing, excellent for softening and easing the soreness of chapped hands and faces. Oatmeal also soothes sensitive and irritated skin. This lotion should be refrigerated and warmed slightly before applying.

1   cup herbal infusion:
   1¼ cups distilled water
   3   tablespoons dried calendula
½ cup olive oil
½ cup safflower, almond, or canola oil
¼ teaspoon powdered gum benzoin
2   teaspoons grated or finely chopped beeswax
2   teaspoons oat flour

BRING water to the boil, remove from fire, add calendula, cover, and steep for thirty minutes. Meanwhile, place the oils, benzoin, and wax in the top of a double boiler. Glass is preferable, but enamel will do.

HEAT gently until the wax melts. Remove from the fire and quickly mix a tablespoon or two of the wax mixture into the oat flour. Stir until you have a smooth paste, then blend the paste into the wax mixture. Strain the herbal infusion, measure out 1 cup and pour it into the jar of an electric blender. When the wax is thick and opaque, but not hardened, add it slowly and gradually to the infusion. Blend at highest speed until the mixture is glossy and thoroughly emulsified. For more information about making emulsions, see chapter one, pages 8 to 10.

BABY POWDER

You can buy the oat flour at a health food store or reduce oatmeal to a powder in your blender or spice mill.

- 2 tablespoons dried lavender
- 2 tablespoons calendula petals
- 1 tablespoon chamomile
- 1 tablespoon lemon balm leaves
- 2 tablespoons corn silk
- 1/2 cup powdered oats
- 3/4 cup cornstarch
- 1/4 cup French white clay

REDUCE the first five ingredients to a fine powder in a blender or spice mill. Put into a closed container with rest of ingredients and shake until well blended. If the baby has diaper rash, add 1 teaspoon powdered myrrh to the mixture. Store in a container with a perforated lid.

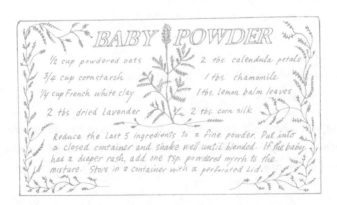

BABY POWDER

1/2 cup powdered oats   2 tbs. calendula petals
3/4 cup cornstarch   1 tbs. chamomile
1/4 cup French white clay   1 tbs. lemon balm leaves
2 tbs. dried lavender   2 tbs. corn silk

Reduce the last 5 ingredients to a fine powder. Put into a closed container and shake well until blended. If the baby has a diaper rash, add one tsp. powdered myrrh to the mixture. Store in a container with a perforated lid.

SPA DAY

mimosa sipped in a Jacuzzi, or perhaps a sunken tub airy with fragrant bubbles—in any case, the ultimate in pampering. So, if you are wondering why a spa day is mentioned only in a chapter about gifts, the answer is: it's better to either give or receive than to try to do it for yourself. When was the last time you tried to wrap yourself in a tea-drenched, full-length bedsheet, or slathered your body with seaweed or wet herbs, then tried to fold yourself like a pork chop into a plastic sheet (easy for butchers, maybe), or tried to plaster sliced fruit on your chin while lying on your back so the fruit wouldn't slide off?

A spa day is a great gift to give a friend, especially one who is stressed, overworked, and maybe needs to tone up, slim down, detox, and mellow out.

You don't need fancy equipment to transform your home temporarily into a spa, nor do you need exotic supplies. You probably have most of what you need in your kitchen or bathroom: plenty of clean towels, soap, vegetable oil and shampoo, manicure and pedicure supplies, and relaxing music.

Many treatments are dehydrating; some encourage your body to get rid of toxins, so it's essential to have plenty of drinking water on hand. The room temperature should be comfortable, your time there uninterrupted. Allow for a ten- or fifteen-minute break between

ADVICE FROM

Sidney Briscese, leading aesthetician at The Beach, an elegant spa in Manhattan's Greenwich Village:

A large part of the spa experience is to relax. Candles, music, and soft lighting help create that kind of atmosphere. When I'm at home, I fill a Crock-Pot with water and add a few drops of essential oil. When I'm giving aromatherapy here at the spa, I'll try several fragrances on a client to find out which essential oil will work best.

It's good to have some sort of table to use for giving your massage. A kitchen or dining-room table is fine. Use an exercise mat, blankets, or some other sort of padding. Over that put a fitted sheet. Apply a generous amount of oil and do a light massage using long, strong strokes. Work on the hands and feet. Everyone likes to have their hands and feet rubbed.

Next, you want to exfoliate with salt before giving any kind of treatment. Your skin is a barrier. If you want the benefits of the herbs or essential oils or seaweed to penetrate the skin, you need to get rid of the dead skin cells on the surface. (See pages 118–119 for details.)

treatments for your "client" to relax, rehydrate, and rest. Ask her to wear loose, comfortable clothing.

Basically, the spa experience includes various cleansing rituals and massage. The full treatment takes all day, but you can do an abbreviated version. Beginning with some exercise may inspire your client to incorporate it into her daily schedule if she doesn't already. Some things to keep in mind when scheduling various activities is to exercise and bathe before rather than after a meal and plan a bath or shower immediately after exercise. Here is a sample game plan. For more details, read advice from The Beach in the box on page 189.

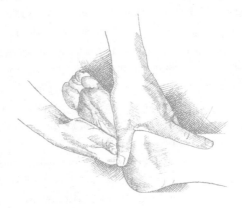

Creating a Spa in Your Home

8 to 8:25 A.M.: Yoga.

To provide cushioning, work on an exercise mat, thick carpet, or several layers of blankets. If one or both of you is a novice, choose a few basic postures such as the cobra, the lion, the lotus, and the spinal twist.

8:30 to 9 A.M.: A brisk walk.

Preferably amid some greenery, followed by five minutes of stretching exercises to cool down.

9:15 to 9:45: Breakfast.

Serve a meal that is low in fat, high in energy, and a cinch to prepare, such as fresh fruit or juice, hot oatmeal, and a hot beverage.

9:45 to 10:45 A.M.:

A ten-minute **scalp massage** followed by a **citrus** or **hot-oil pack**. These treatments are described on pages 95–96, and 84. Meanwhile, give a **manicure** and **pedicure** (see pages 135–137).

11 to 12 NOON: Massage.

Any refined oil will do for a massage, but cold-pressed, simple oils such as olive, sesame, coconut, grapeseed, sunflower, canola, or safflower are preferable to oils that may have been processed with chemical solvents. Almond oil is most commonly used because its light density allows the masseuse's hands to glide at a comfortable speed. You will find recipes for massage oil below.

You don't need to be an expert to give a massage. Apply firm pressure and work with long, fluid, sweeping movements. Work toward the heart, stroking up the arms and legs rather than out toward the fingers and toes. When massaging the abdomen to relieve indigestion or stress, proceed in the direction of digestion, circling around the navel from right to left.

MASSAGE OIL

1 part dried arnica
1 part dried rosemary
Oil to cover
1 vitamin E capsule
A pinch of cayenne pepper

FILL a sterile, clear glass jar or wide-mouthed bottle almost to the top with dried herbs and cayenne. Cover with oil. To prevent moldering, be sure that the herbs are completely submerged in oil. Leave enough space for the solution to move about when the jar is shaken. Seal the container and place it in a sunny window for two weeks, shaking daily. The solution should be kept warm. In winter you could set the container on an old-fashioned radiator or the upper shelf of woodstove, if you have one. After steeping, strain the mixture through a sterile cheesecloth into a dark glass bottle, add vitamin E and seal.

This oil is excellent for muscle strains and sprains. Rosemary stimulates circulation. In Europe, arnica is widely used to treat sports injuries.

Using this same formula, you can easily create a sensual massage oil by substituting rose or jasmine petals for the rosemary and arnica. For a soothing massage oil to relieve stress, use one or more sedative herbs such as St. John's wort, hops, skullcap, catnip, chamomile, passionflower, lemon balm, lavender, or orange blossoms. California herbalist Diane de Luca recommends rose geranium for its uplifting and calming effect. Aches, pains, and stiffness are wondrously relieved by adding a little ginger or cayenne pepper to the oil. Yarrow, pansy, St. John's wort, lavender, nutmeg, and eucalyptus are also recommended for muscle aches and pains. You can buy essential oils of many of the herbs listed above. For a quick massage oil, aromatherapist Mindy Green recommends about ¼ teaspoon essential oil to ½ cup of carrier oil. For muscle aches, Green recommends essential oils of bay leaf, camphor, chamomile, eucalyptus, ginger, juniper, lavender, marjoram, peppermint, rosemary, and thyme.

12 to 12:30 P.M.: Exfoliate

with a salt glow, dry brushing, or complexion grains. See pages 115 to 120 in the Your Body chapter for details. Follow with a warm shower and shampoo.

CONSIDER THE AVOCADO

According to the California Avocado Commission, avocado seeds have been found buried with Peruvian mummies dating back to 750 B.C. The first person known to eat the alligator pear was a Mayan Mexican princess around the tenth century. Not only is this glorious vegetable packed with vitamins A and E and monounsaturated oil, it is one of the most beneficial skin foods you can find. For a treat, buy a couple of avocadoes when you shop for spa day. Slice a little into a salad. The remainder provides you with a cleansing lotion, an exfoliant, a skin mask, and a moisturizer. Indeed, if you have two avocadoes, that's all you need for a complete facial and body scrub.

12:45 to 1:15 P.M.: Steam.

After showering, your "client" can have a treatment with hot towels. This is done by applying damp, heated towels, then covering the towels with a blanket to seal in the warmth.

Sidney Briscoe, who gives this treatment at The Beach spa, has this advice: Steaming has incredible benefits: It increases cellular metabolism and removes toxins. Be sure to serve lots of water along with the steam treatment so the person won't become dehydrated.

Soak towels in water to which you have added a few drops of essential oil. Eucalyptus is very good; peppermint lifts the spirits, but you can use whatever the person likes. Heat the towels in a microwave for a few seconds, then shake them out so they won't be too hot. Limit the steam treatment to twenty minutes maximum.

1:30 to 2:00 P.M.: Lunch.

Like breakfast, this meal should be low in fat, high in vitamins and minerals, and simple to prepare. A veggie burger crowned with sliced tomato and onions and accompanied by a green salad; a yogurt "sundae" with sliced banana, walnut chunks, and whole-grain bread; or a chef's salad with chicken, fish, tofu, or hard-boiled egg, served with tomato and mixed greens, are some possibilities.

2:15 to 3:15 P.M.: Facial Cleansing and Toning.

Cleansing, exfoliation, face mask, and facial. (See Chapter 2 for recipes.) To give a facial, apply a light film of almond or other low-density oil to the face and neck. Starting at the base of the throat, stroke upward and out with gentle finger pressure for about ten minutes. Remove the oil with skin freshener (page 61) followed by a moisturizer if the skin is dry.

Here are three recipes from the California Avocado Commission:

AVOCADO FACIAL CLEANSER

One egg yolk, beaten until light and frothy
½ cup milk
½ avocado, peeled and mashed

BEAT the mixture with a fork until you have a thin cream or lotion consistency. Apply with cotton balls as you would any cleanser.

SANTA BARBARA'S DRY SKIN MASK

1 egg yolk beaten until light and frothy
½ avocado, peeled and mashed

MIX well with a fork or blender. After cleansing, spread the mixture over the face and throat. Leave on for twenty minutes, then rinse with tepid water.

SANTA MONICA'S OILY SKIN MASK

1 egg white
1 teaspoon lemon juice
½ avocado pulp, peeled and mashed

MIX in a blender, apply to skin after cleansing. Leave on for twenty minutes. Follow with cold astringent or skin tonic.

CALIFORNIA AVOCADO MOISTURIZER

THE precious oil hidden away in the peel of an avocado is a wonderful facial moisturizer. To be technical, the oil contains a humectant, a substance that holds moisture. Using gentle upward strokes, lightly massage your face with the inside of the peel. Let the oil residue remain on your skin for about fifteen minutes. At that time you may either leave the oil on your skin and go to sleep, or, if you intend to put on makeup, wash your face gently with three or four rinses of tepid water, and pat dry. The oil will be invisible, but it is there, ready to hold your foundation or powder in place for hours.

AVOCADO FACE AND BODY SCRUB

FINALLY, herbalist Greta Breedlove came up with this wonderful idea for utilizing the seed of the avocado. It makes a moisturizing face and body scrub, especially for dry skin. Let an avocado seed dry for a few days until you can remove the skin easily. Chop, then pulverize in a blender or food mill. Moisten with a little milk and smooth over your face, throat, and body.

3:30 to 4:00 P.M.: Taking the Waters.

Sea plants are rich in minerals; they moisturize and rejuvenate the skin. A soak in a hot tub filled with seaweed is not quite as good as a dip in the ocean, but it comes close. Warning: Long soaks in hot water are not advised for women who are pregnant or have a heart condition, diabetes, or high blood pressure.

Fill the bathtub with hot water until the bather is immersed up to her chin. Add 2 cups of seaweed gathered from a clean, unpolluted shore, or ½ cup of Sea Breeze Therapeutic Bath Salts (see page 123 in the Your Body chapter). Have the bather soak for twenty minutes to a half hour. To prevent overheating, Sidney Briscese recommends a refrigerated cold pack on the face and a serving of the bather's favorite drink. In twenty minutes have the bather ease herself from the tub slowly. Follow with a quick, cool shower.

4 P.M.

Celebrate! Relax with a glass of champagne, iced herbal tea, or fruit juice. You have just given your friend one of the most loving gifts—one of touch, nurturing, and attention.

A FEW LAST WORDS

IT SEEMS FITTING TO END THIS BOOK WITH A CHAPTER ON GIFTS. The ingredients themselves are nature's gifts to us. Transforming these fragrant offerings into beauty products is a joyous experience. In fact, of all the books I have published so far, this one has been the most fun to create.

In these pages I have shared with you some of my experiments and discoveries in making cosmetics. You no doubt will make many others. For possible future editions of this book, I would be grateful to learn of your own discoveries, home remedies, and experiences using these recipes. You can reach me at this E-mail address: sally_Freeman@bigfoot.com. May the spirit of fragrance linger in your home like a cherished and delightful guest.

APPENDIX

BUYING, GROWING, AND GATHERING NATURAL INGREDIENTS

Resources

Later in this chapter you'll find advice on the satisfying hobby of grow-ing your own natural ingredients or gathering them in the wild. Most people however, are busy and prefer to buy the supplies they need to make cosmetics. Shopping in person rather than on-line gives you an opportunity to sample the wares before you buy them. Your local food and herb-buying co-operative or herb dealer can sell you not only the herbs you need but the waxes, oils, and equipment, too. Since many co-ops and herbal outlets buy from local growers whenever possible, you are also supporting local agriculture.

More time-consuming, but usually more fun and certainly more economical, is to buy directly from the grower. Those of you who live in a rural area may find this the most practical way to purchase the herbs you use. Herb growers who produce enough to market are likely to ad-vertise, so you shouldn't have any trouble finding one. Farmer's mar-kets are another excellent source of high quality, organically grown plants. The larger markets frequently offer flowers and essential oils as well.

Herbs, Oils, and Other Supplies

Enfleurage

321 Bleeker Street
New York, NY 10014
Phone: (212) 691–1610
Website: www.aromata.com
High-quality imports. They will sell you single essential oils or custom blends.

Kiehl's

109 Third Avenue
New York, NY 10003
Phone: (800) 543–4571 or (800) 543–4572
Fax: (212) 505–1023
Formerly a homeopathic pharmacy, now a purveyor of fine, supposedly natural toiletries and essential oils. They have been in business since 1851.

Atlantic Spice Co.

Route 6 @ Rt. 6A
North Truro, MA 02652
Phone: (800) 316–7965
http://www.atlanticspice.com
They guarantee the quality of their botanicals and essential oils. They do not sell irradiated herbs.

San Francisco Herb Co.

250 14th Street
San Francisco, CA 94103
Website: http://www.sfherb.com
Phone: (800) 227–4530
West-coast arm of Atlantic Spice.

The Herb Corner

104 North Ramona Avenue
Indialantic, FL 32903
Phone: (407) 768–1551
Website: http://www.herbcorner.net
Many of their herbs are wildcrafted and organically grown. They sell vegetable and essential oils, supplies, and containers.

SAG Brothers, Inc.

P.O. Box 17080
Ft. Lauderdale, FL 33318
Phone: Dr. Sam Hunter (954) 718–1944
Fax: (954) 724–1071
Website: http://www.webspawner.com/users/sheabutter
E-mail: sheabutter@hotmail.com
They sell Omololu natural shea butter from West Africa.

Kremer Pigments, Inc.

228 Elizabeth Street
New York, NY 10012
Phone: (212) 219–2394
Fax: (212) 219–2395
Website: http://www.kremer-pigmente.de/
E-mail: kremer-Inc@aol.com
Mainly a high-quality art supply outlet, they sell indigo, alkanet, Brazilwood, and other natural organic dyes and pigments as well as gum benzoin and other natural resins.

Liberty Natural Products

8120 SE Stark
Portland, OR 97215
Phone: (800) 289–8427
They sell shea butter, and a wide range of vegetable oils .

Trinity Herb

P.O. Box 1001
Graton, CA 95444
Phone: (707) 824–2040
Fax: (707) 824–2050
Website: http://www.trinityherb.com
High-quality herb supplier. Organic and wildcrafted herbs. Wholesale only, but they will direct you to a retailer who sells their products.

Seeds

Johnny's Selected Seeds

203 Foss Hill Road
Albion, ME 04910
Customer service: (207) 437–4357
Website: http://www.johnnyseeds.com
Grow their own seeds or contract from small farmers. They offer organic gardening supplies and an informative catalog.

Burpee Seeds & Plants

Warminster, PA 18974
Customer Service: (800) 333–5808
Fax: (888) 333–1447
Website: http://www.burpeegoshoppingonline.com
A household name for 124 years. All kinds of seeds, including herbs and flowers. Reliable.

Caprilands Herb Farm

534 Silver Street
Coventry, CT 06238
Website: http://caprilands.com
Seeds, live plants, dried herbs. Extensive herb gardens. A lovely place to visit.

The Herb Garden

14 Pleasant Street
Portland, ME 04101
(207) 771–0333
Excellent quality and service. They take mail orders. A nice place to visit.

Containers

House of Cans

7060 N. Lawndale Avenue
Lincolnwood, IL 60712
Phone: (847) 677–2100
Fax: (847) 677–2103
Website: http://www.houseofcans.com
All kinds of containers in different sizes and materials. Small orders okay.

Websites

Miller's Homemade Soap Page, part of the Miller Garden Page

http://www.silverlink.net/'timer
A wealth of excellent information about soap making from Kathy Miller and her correspondents.

Herb Research Foundation

http://www.herbs.org
They publish an on-line newsletter, mostly about medicinal herbs, but well worth reading.

Organizations

American Botanical Council

P.O. Box 144345
Austin, TX 78714–4345
Phone: (512) 926–4900
Fax: (512) 926–2345
Website: http://www.herbalgram.org
The source of information about herbs. In conjunction with the Herb Research Foundation, they publish the quarterly journal *Herbalgram*.

The Herb Society of America

9019 Kirtland Chardon Road
Kirtland, OH 44094
Phone: (440) 256–0514
Fax: (440) 256–0541
Website: http://www.herbsociety.org
They support the national herb garden in D.C., maintain a library at their national headquarters where they answer phone queries, fund research, do seed exchange. Publications include *The Herbarist*, an annual journal.

Publications

See journals listed under Organizations and Websites.

DCI: Drug and Cosmetic Industry

Subscriber Customer Service: (800) 346–0085 ext. 477
Fax: (218) 723–9437

Gathering Herbs

For many people, the most satisfying way to obtain cosmetic ingredients is to grow them at home or gather them in the wild. The more prolific herbs may grow in your backyard. For example, the sturdy, spade-shaped leaves of plantain can be found poking up out of sidewalk cracks in the busiest urban streets. Plantain contains allantoin, a remarkably healing substance that is used in commercial face creams. Red clover, which also heals and soothes the skin and often finds its way into salves and shampoos, can probably be found in your backyard or a nearby vacant lot.

Other herbal treasures can be found on a stroll through woods and fields or along a beach. Depending on where you live, the list could include wild berries of every sort, soapwort or bouncing bet, aloe vera, seaweed, wild roses and their hips, yarrow, horsetail, white pond lily, mint, St. John's wort, iris, comfrey, white oak bark, self-heal, daisy, fig, loosestrife, apple, angelica, echinacea, rosemary, marjoram, and witch hazel. When you sally forth in search of the wild whatevers, take along a field guide to help you identify the plants. The most helpful guides are those featuring your local geographical area.

The best time to harvest plants is in the morning, after the dew has dried. Forage in a place that is well removed from traffic and its consequent automobile exhaust and road dust. Be sure the area hasn't been sprayed with a pesticide or herbicide. If the herb grows on public land, be sure that harvesting is permitted. If it is private property, get permission from the owner.

Some herbs should not be harvested because they are endangered species. You can get a list of these plants from your state department of agriculture or conservation. Learn what they look like, and if you see them in the wild, don't pick them. Plants that grow sparsely, even if they are not endangered, should also be left alone.

Choose plants that are healthy and at their peak. Even when a certain plant does grow in abundance, don't pick every one you see. A traditional Native American practice is to refrain from picking the plant that is closest, and harvesting only one in seven plants, leaving the rest to go to seed so a new crop will grow the following year.

Growing Herbs

Growing your own cosmetic ingredients is for some people the most satisfying method of all. As Linda Buck, a master gardener, herb grower, and massage therapist in Maine points out, growing the herbs you will use in cosmetics is part of a holistic process: You start with a seed and end with a final product. When you plant perennials, you extend that process into years of harvest.

Most herbs are easy to grow, requiring only lots of sunshine, well-drained soil, and occasional watering. For your first herb garden, Linda recommends these plants:

PEPPERMINT

(Mentha piperita) If you plant it near your doorstep, it keeps ants from crawling into your house. Mint is a perennial. If you plant just one seed you could end up with a lot because mint propagates by runners, and one plant produces many of them. Unlike most herbs, mint flourishes near water and prefers a damp soil. To keep it from taking over your garden, plant mint in a large saucer rather than directly in the ground, or be vigilant about cutting back the runners so they won't take root. To encourage mint to keep producing leaves, cut the leaves frequently. This is true of any plant.

CHAMOMILE

There are two kinds: Roman chamomile *(Anthemis nobilis)* is a perennial; German, or wild chamomile *(Matricaria chamomilla)* is an annual. Both are good to plant around your house because the blossoms give out a sweet aroma when you walk on them. Roman chamomile is the kind that you are most likely to see in gardens. Before grass lawns became fashionable, it was planted as a ground cover. German chamomile will reseed itself, but you won't find the second-year plants growing in the same place. You will get a few years out of a plant.

CALENDULA

(Calendula officinalis) The same is true of calendula, another bienniel. The plant will reseed, but not in the same place. As with other flowering herbs, if you keep cutting calendula flowers, the plant will keep producing them.

ROSES

(Rosa spp.) I grow *Rosa rugosa,* a nonhybrid, heirloom plant with red-dish pink, open blossoms like a wild rose. It is known for its rose hips production—the fruit is as big as a cherry. *Rosa rugosa* is very fragrant, requires little care, and it is hardy to northern climates, so you don't need to worry about protecting it in winter. You need a space four- to six-feet square to grow it. Clean out the dead branches in the spring.

ROSEMARY

(Rosmarinus officinalis) can come back for two or three years. Since it doesn't require much light, you could plant it in a container and bring it indoors during the winter.

LEMON BALM

(Melissa officinalis) A member of the mint family, lemon balm has fra-grant, lemon-scented leaves that have a number of cosmetic uses. The herb is a perennial and easy to grow.

COMFREY

(Symphytum officinale) is also a perennial, but be careful—it is invasive!

OTHER PLANTS THAT ARE EASY

for a novice gardener to grow are marjoram, basil, thyme, and violets.

When I am growing plants from seed, I start them in February or March, depending on how long it takes to germinate. This varies from plant to plant, but in general, annuals have a shorter germination pe-riod. Perennial seeds may require chilling, cracking, or other special treatment. You might find it easier to start with a plant rather than the seed. This is true of geranium, lavender, and tarragon. It is advisable to get your seeds and plants from an organic grower.

Mint, chamomile, and soapwort are easily grown from seed, and they tend to spread. If the plant is a biennial, don't expect flowers un-til the second year.

Start with a sterile growing mix that does not have added nutri-ents. Some seeds need darkness in order to germinate, but not the ones I have mentioned here.

For containers, my favorites are recycled plastic foam drinking cups and aluminum foil food containers with a clear plastic lid. Your containers must be clean; a dirty container with trapped moisture fosters mold that can kill your seedlings.

Punch holes in the bottoms of your containers and set them on a plate or a cookie sheet. You don't need big containers. Plants that grow close together must compete for space. The strongest ones survive and ensure that you will have strong plants in your garden. Put masking tape on the cookie sheet with a list of herbs, and mark off each plant with a toothpick bearing a label. What you end up with will look like a miniature garden.

The most important thing to do for germinating plants is to keep them moist. That's where those aluminum containers with tight plastic lids come in handy. Otherwise, cover your plants with a plastic bag to keep in the moisture.

Let your plants germinate in a warm place like the top of a refrigerator or near a radiator. When they pop up, they need a good light source, or they'll be weak and spindly. Transplant them to the same type of soil that you used for germination. Plant them outdoors after the last frost. Here in Maine, Memorial Day weekend is the beginning of the traditional planting season.

Herbs don't require additional nutrients, but they do need sun; otherwise they will be weak and spindly. Mint can do well in either sun or shade. Weed your plants periodically and cultivate them after it rains.

Helen M. Fox, in *Gardening with Herbs for Flavor and Fragrance*, a gardening classic first published in 1933, advises against planting herbs in soil that is too rich. Because most are native to the Mediterranean, they do best in dry, poor, and often rocky ground; otherwise, they tend to be leggy and produce inferior essential oil. If you are a novice, plant your herbs in beds separated by walks. Later you might like to experiment with more intricate gardening designs.

Fox recommends turning the soil two or three times to a depth of eighteen inches to two feet. The seeds should be sowed thinly, then covered with a light layer of sifted soil. Damp down the soil firmly, then water if the soil is dry. Thin the plants when they are two to three inches tall.

At what stage of growth you will harvest depends on what part of the plant you intend to use. If it is the leaves, harvest before the plant flowers, while the strength of the plant is still concentrated in the leaves. Otherwise most of the strength of the plant will go into the flower. If you intend to use the flower, gather it just after it opens. Roots are harvested in autumn after the plant has gone to seed.

If you plan to use the plant while it is fresh, allow it to wilt for a day or so. It will give up its properties more readily then. Otherwise, spread your harvest on an old sheet or some newspapers or paper bags, or on a window screen, and let it dry in a warm, dark place—an attic is perfect. You could tie the plants in loose bunches and hang them up-side down. To protect them from dust or soot, cover them with a large paper bag. In damp weather it's a good idea to dry your herbs in the oven rather than let them hang around and get moldy. Spread them out on a cookie sheet and place them in the oven at its lowest setting. If your oven setting doesn't low enough (i.e., 170 degrees), turn the oven on, let it heat up slightly, then turn it off and put your plants in. They are "done" when they feel brittle.

As soon as the plants are dry, put them in airtight containers, preferably made of glass. They will retain the color and fragrance better if you protect them from the light by storing them in a light-proof container or a dark cupboard. Write on the label the name of the plant, where and when you gathered it, and any other pertinent details.

In the fall, when all of your herbs die down, it is fun to save the seeds. Judy Dunning, writing in *The Herbalist* magazine, has this advice: Choose healthy plants that propagate easily by seed. Snip off the seed heads, spread them out on a cloth, and dry them in the sun for a few days. Finish the drying process by placing the seeds in a paper bag with holes punched in the top for air circulation. Label each bag with the name of the plant and the date it was harvested. Leave the bags for at least a week in a warm place with good air circulation. When the seeds are thoroughly dry, clean away the chaff and other debris and seal them in zipper plastic bags or other airtight containers. Include planting information on the label.

To make sure that your seeds are viable, before planting a batch, test some by sprinkling a few on a damp paper towel. Roll up the towel, place it in a plastic bag, and leave it in a warm dark place for a couple of weeks to see if they germinate.

KITCHEN CURES FOR COMMON SKIN PROBLEMS

If you suddenly run out of a beauty essential, don't despair. You probably have one just as good or better on your pantry shelves. This chart is intended to serve as a reminder of solutions offered elsewhere in this book. For more information, consult the index.

AGE SPOTS
Fresh pineapple
Fresh lemon juice

BAGS UNDER THE EYES
Cucumber slices
Cold tea bags
Cold-water compress
Crescents of sliced avocado

BATH ADDITIVES
Milk
Vinegar
Raspberries
Strawberries
Oatmeal
Barley
Rosemary
Mint
Chamomile
Sage
Coconut

Salt
Seaweed
Marjoram
Basil
Thyme
Wine

CELLULITE—EXTERNAL APPLICATIONS
Ginger
Peppermint
Kiwi

CHAPPED OR ROUGHENED HANDS, FACE, OR LIPS
Glycerin
Sugar dissolved in
   lemon juice
Egg white
Barley
Honey
Salt
Bran

CUTICLE AND NAIL SOFTENERS

Olive oil
Warm milk
Mashed kiwi
Green papaya
Pineapple juice

DANDRUFF

Ripe avocado and olive oil hair
    pack
Aloe vera gel applied to scalp
Strong rosemary or thyme tea
    added to shampoo

DEODORANT

Lemon or orange peel
Aloe
Baking soda
Witch hazel

DRY HAIR

Egg yolk shampoo
Avocado or mayonnaise hair
    pack
Olive or corn hot-oil treatment
Oily fish as regular part of your
    diet

DRY SKIN

Avocado flesh, seed, and inner
    skin
Aloe vera gel
Coco butter
Fruit face mask with
    one or several of these
    fresh ingredients: apple,
    apricot, banana, cherry,
    cranberry, papaya, peach, or
    watermelon
Egg yolk, mayonnaise, cream,
    carrot, artichoke, or raw
    potato face mask

Honey
Milk or cream
Olive, sesame, canola,
    coconut, sunflower,
    almond, or other
    unadulterated
    vegetable oil
Rice water
Vegetable shortening
Vinegar face rinse
Water—as beverage and
    facial spray and room
    humidifier

DULL HAIR

Shampoo with egg white,
    strong black coffee, clove,
    turmeric, or crushed
    raspberries or blackberries
    added
Red wine
Red onions
Green, black, or orange pekoe
    tea
Chamomile tea
Beer

DUSTING POWDER

Cornstarch
Barley flour
Baking soda
Wheat flour
Powdered clove, allspice,
    marjoram, or vanilla bean

ECZEMA

Vegetable shortening
Compresses of strong black
    tea
Beet, celery, and tomato juice
    cocktail

ENVIRONMENTAL FRAGRANCE—
SIMMERING HERBS

Lemon or orange peel
Rosemary
Marjoram
Clove
Cinnamon
Bay leaf

EXFOLIANTS

Green papaya
Pineapple
Kiwi
Raw strawberry
Barley, corn, or oat meal
Powdered rice
Ground almonds
Ground apricot, peach, or
    avocado seeds
Fresh or sour milk or cream,
    buttermilk
Fruit juice
Red or white wine
Dry sugar or salt
Powdered seaweed
Brewer's yeast
Bran
Dried pumpkin or cucumber
    seeds
Lemon juice in a seashell
Facial steam with chamomile,
    mint, green, or black tea
    leaves

EYEBROW DARKENER

Powdered coffee

FACIAL CLEANSERS

Water—on a washcloth, as facial
    steam
Raw oatmeal

Barley
Beer foam
Fresh strawberry
Papaya
Cucumber, carrot, pineapple,
    or tomato juice
Chamomile tea
Green or black tea
Avocado and milk

FINGERNAIL STRENGTHENER

Garlic

GRAY HAIR

Sage, rosemary, or honey, in a
    hair darkening rinse

HAIR CONDITIONERS

Eggs
Milk
Beer
Cider vinegar
Lemon juice
Milk added to shampoo
Avocado, banana, melon,
    kiwi, cooked squash,
    carrots, or potato hair pack
Preshampoo orange and
    grapefruit juice

HAIR DYE

Green, black, or pekoe tea
Coffee
Clove
Honey
Turmeric
Red wine
Red onion
Sage
Cider and malt vinegars
Walnut shells or skins

OILY-HAIR RINSES

Lemon juice
Vinegar
Sage
Rosemary
Green, black, or pekoe tea
Seaweed

OILY SKIN

Red or white wine facial
   splash
Cucumber or lemon
   juice
Spinach water
Egg white mask

PERFUME OR COLOGNE

Almond, vanilla, orange, or
   lemon extract

PIMPLES

Yellow laundry soap
Garlic
Tomato face pack
Raw, bruised cabbage
   leaves
Salt dissolved in lemon
   juice
Onion cooked in lard
Turmeric added to diet

SCARS

Castile soap and honey
Aloe vera
Coco butter

SUNBURN

Applications of strong black
   tea, aloe gel, yogurt, cold
   milk, vinegar
Sliced cucumber, raw tomato
   or potato
A cup of oats or baking soda
   added to bathwater

SUNSCREEN

Aloe vera
Green tea
Sesame, olive, or coconut oil

THINNING HAIR

Rosemary
Peppermint
Basil
Cayenne pepper
Raw onion
Ginger
Chamomile

WARTS

Raw potato
Radish sprinkled with salt
Aloe vera gel
Garlic

WRINKLES

Caviar
Avocado mask
Yogurt
Calcium powder
Seaweed
Egg white

BIBLIOGRAPHY

Askinson, George William. *Perfumes and Cosmetics: Their Preparation and Manufacture.* New York: NW Henley Publishing Co., 1915

Avery, Susanna. *A Plain Plantain: A Stillroom Book.* Taken from a 1688 manuscript. Falls Village, Conn.:Herb Grower Press, 1950

Bailes, Edith. *An Album of Fragrance.* Richmond, Maine: Cardamon Press, 1983

Bernstein, Robert and Michele. *Honey, Mud, Maggots and Other Medical Marvels.* New York: Houghton Mifflin, 1997

Bethel, May. *The Healing Power of Herbs.* London: Thorsons Publishers Limited, 1968

Harding, Anne, with Janice Biehn. *Home Spa.* Buffalo, N.Y.: Firefly Books, 1997

Breedlove, Greta. *The Herbal Home Spa.* Pownal, Vt.: Storey Communications, 1998

Bremnes, Lesley. *The Complete Book of Herbs.* New York: Viking, 1988

Buc'hoz, Pierre-Joseph. *The Toilet of Flora.* Printed for J. Murray and W. Nicoll, London, 1784

Cavitch, Susan Miller. *The Natural Soap Book: Making Herbal and Vegetable-Based Soaps.* Pownal, Vt.: Storey Publishing, 1995

Chase, Deborah. *The New Medically-Based No-Nonsense Beauty Book.* New York: Henry Holt & Sons, 1989

Crisp, Dorothy, "Making Simple Herbal Cosmetics," *The Herbarist,* vol. 2, no. 8, and vol. 2, no. 9, 1983

Drug and Cosmetic Industry magazine, published by Advanstar Communications, Inc., Cleveland, Ohio, 1994–1995, vol. 154, no. 1 to vol. 156, no. 6

Duke, James A. *The Green Pharmacy.* Emmaus, Pa.: Rodale Press, 1997

Dunning, Judy, "Harvesting Your Herb Seeds," *The Herbarist,* no. 65, 1999

Flanders, Angela. *Aromatics.* New York: Clarkson Potter, 1995

Fox, Helen M. *Gardening with Herbs for Flavor and Fragrance.* New York: Dover Publications, Inc. 1970. Reprint from the 1933 Macmillan edition.

Frawley, Dr. David and Dr. Vasant Lad. *The Yoga of Herbs.* Santa Fe, N.M.: Lotus Press, 1986

Freeman, Sally. *Everywoman's Guide to Natural Home Remedies.* New York: Doubleday Direct/Henry Holt & Sons, 1996

Herbs for All Seasons. New York: Plume, 1991

Genders, Roy. *Natural Beauty: The Practical Guide to Wildflower Cosmetics.* Exeter, England: Webb & Bower, 1986

Gerard, John. *Leaves from Gerard's Herbal,* 1597. Arranged by Marcus Woodward. New York: Dover Publications, 1969

Grae, Ida. *Nature's Colors—Dyes from Plants.* New York: Macmillan, 1974

Gunn, Fenja. *The Artificial Face: A History of Cosmetics in England.* Australia: Newton Abbot, David and Charles, 1973

Hamel, Paul B. and Mary Chiltoskey. *Cherokee Plants and Their Uses—A 400 Year History,* printed in 1975.

Idena. "Dietary Antioxidants and Human Health." Highlights of the 1998 conference at Jean Mayer/USDA Center for Human Nutrition Research.

Keville, Kathy and Mindy Green. *Aromatherapy. A Complete Guide to the Healing Art.* Freedom, Calif.: The Crossing Press, 1995

Krochmal, Connie. *Natural Cosmetics from Beehive to Garden.* Ashville, N.C.

Lad, Vasant. *The Complete Book of Ayurvedic Home Remedies.* New York: Harmony Books, 1998

Leyel, Mrs. C. F. *Herbal Delights.* Reprint [1938], New York: Gramercy Publishing Co., 1986

Lupton, Thomas. *A Thousand Notable Things on Various Subjects.* Printed for G. and T. Wilkie and E. Easton, Salisbury, 1785

Lust, John. *The Herb Book.* New York: Benedict Lust Publications, 1974

Mabberley, D. J. *The Plant Book, A Portable Dictionary of the Vascular Plants.* Cambridge, U.K.: Cambridge University Press, 1997

Majeed, Muhammed, PhD, Vladimir Badmaev, M.D., and Frank Murray. *Turmeric and the Healing Curcuminoids.* New Caanan, Conn.: Keates Publishing, 1996

Der Marderosian, Ara Harold. *Natural Product Medicine: A Scientific Guide to Foods, Drugs, Cosmetics.* Philadelphia: G. F. Stickley, 1988

Miller, Jean, Francie Owens, and Rachel Doggett. *The Housewife's Rich Cabinet.* Washington, D.C.: The Folger Shakespeare Library, 1997

Pallingston, Jessica. *Lipstick.* New York: St. Martin's Press, 1999

Piesse, George William Septimus. *The Art of Perfumery and the Methods of Ob-*

taining the Odors of Plants. London: Longmans, Brown, Green and Longmans, 1855

Plat, Sir Hugh. *Delights for Ladies.* London: Lockwood, 1955
Reprint of the 1609 edition published by H. Lownes, London.

——. *The Jewell House of Art and Nature.* Printed in London by Bernard Alsop, 1653

Quasha, Jennifer, "25 Reasons to Love Lemons," *Energy Times,* October 1996

Queen Henrietta Maria. *The Queen's Closet Opened.* Cornhill: Nathaniel Brook, 1655. New York Public Library Rare Books Collection

Ronzio, Robert A. *The Encyclopedia of Nutrition and Good Health.* New York: Facts on File, 1997

Rubenstein, Mala. From a talk on Helena Rubenstein presented at the symposeum on herbs presented by the Herb Society of America in March 1962

Rutledge, Deborah. *Natural Beauty Secrets.* New York: Hawthorn Books, 1967

Sanderson, Liz. *How to Make Your Own Herbal Cosmetics: The Natural Way to Beauty.* New Caanan, Conn.: Keates Publishing, 1979

Scully, Virginia. *A Treasury of American Indian Herbs.* New York: Crown Publishers, 1970

Simmonite, Dr. W. J. and Nicholas Culpepper. *The Simmonite-Culpepper Herbal Remedies.* London: W. Foulsham & Co., 1957

Spiers, Katie. *Recipes for Natural Beauty.* New York: Facts on File, 1998

Spillane, Mary and Victoria McKee. Ultra Age, *Everywoman's Guide to Facing the Future.* London: Macmillan Publishers, 1999

Stoller, Leonard, "Beauty Recipes of Yesteryear," *The Givaudanian,* July/August, 1960

Thompson, Dorothy Hay. "Herbs and the Woman," *Harper's Bazaar,* August 1946

Tourles, Stephanie. *Naturally Healthy Skin.* Pownal, Vt.: Storey Books, 1999

Tovar with Lydia P. Encinas. *Tovar's Classic Beauty.* New York: Contemporary Books, 1986

Trovillion, Violet. *Recipes and Remedies of Early England.* Herrin, Ill.: Trovillion Private Press, 1946

Twigg, Phyllis Margaret. *A Little Book of Conceited Secrets and Delights for Ladies.* Based on sixteenth- to eighteenth-century stillroom or receipt books. London: The Medici Society, 1928

Valmey, Christine. *Christine Valmey's Skin Care and Makeup Book*. New York: Crown Publishers, 1982

Winter, Ruth. *A Consumer's Dictionary of Cosmetic Ingredients*. New York: Three Rivers Press, 1994

Wykes-Joyce, Max. *Cosmetics and Adornment: Ancient and Contemporary Usage*. New York: New York Philosophical Library, 1961

MEASUREMENTS

The chart below was compiled from various sources; not all of them agree.

1 minim = 1 drop = 1 grain

1 milliliter = 15 to 20 drops

1 scruple = 20 grains

1 pennyweight = 24 grains

1 teaspoon = 1 fluid dram = 4.9 milliliters = approximately 5 cc = 60 grains for weight or 60 drops for liquid (Note: other measurement charts define 1 teaspoon as 100 drops. It depends on what dropper you use: I counted 120 drops to the teaspoon. If in doubt, measure the drops yourself.)

1 fluid ounce = 8 drams (drachms) = 29.57 milliliters

1 dry ounce = 28.35 grams

1 cup = 236.6 milliliters

0.9 dry quart = 1 liter

1.06 liquid quarts = 1 liter

1 pound = 454 grams

1000 micrograms = 1 milligram

1000 milligrams = 1 gram

1000 grams = 1 kilogram

INDEX

Acacia, 156, 163, 164
Acid Rinse, 93
Acne, 28, 39, 42, 43, 45, 54, 56,
　60–64, 108
Adder's tongue, 54
After-shave lotions, 182–83
Age spots, 38, 39–40, 57, 107–8,
　209
Aging, premature, 27, 29, 34, 37–38,
　72, 109, 142
Aging skin, 34, 36, 40, 45, 56–57
Alcohol, 131–32, 155, 176
　hair care, 79, 89, 90
　shelf life, 5
　skin care, 32, 40, 47
Algae, 54
Alkanet, 10, 11, 65, 66, 67–68, 103,
　105, 137, 150–52, 153
Alkanet Lip Balm, 67–68
Alkanet Rose Lip Gloss, 152–53
Allergies, 147, 149, 157
Allspice, 11, 100, 105, 162–63, 168,
　169, 183, 210
Almonds/almond oil, 11
　aroma classifications, 162–63,
　　164
　baths/showers, 116
　cellulite, 110
　contrasting or compatible scents,
　　162–63, 166
　fragrances, 154, 162–63, 164, 166,
　　168, 173, 212
　lip gloss, 151, 152–53
　lotions, 139–40, 187–88
　Love Oil, 187

making cosmetics, 6
massage, 191
pedicures, 137
skin care, 34, 37, 38, 40, 46, 47,
　52, 56, 65, 66, 67, 181, 193–94,
　210, 211
Aloe vera, 11
　deodorants, 130, 134–35
　gathering, 203
　hair care, 81, 82, 91, 93, 94–95,
　　210
　lotions, 141
　making cosmetics, 10
　pedicures, 137
　shelf-life, 5, 6
　skin care, 34, 36–37, 38, 39,
　　41–42, 54, 61, 67, 69, 70–71,
　　72, 73–74, 76, 182, 210, 212
　soaps, 129
　sunscreens/sunburns, 142, 143,
　　212
Alpha hydroxy acids. *See* Milk;
　Vinegar; Wine
Alum, 40, 59
Ambergris, 116, 156, 164
American Cancer Society, 30,
　108
Ancient Airs Dusting Powder, 168
Angelica, 11, 90, 203
Anise, 154, 164
Annatto, 11, 150, 151, 153
Annatto-Alkanet Lip Gloss, 153
Antiaging Cream, 41–42
Antibacterial Liquid Soap, 128–29
Anticellulite Massage Oil, 110

Bay leaves, 61, 158, 161, 162–63, 182, 192, 211
Bearberry, 49, 65
Beauty, historical perspective about, 1–4
Bedtime Nail Ointment, 135
Bee pollen, 12, 39, 40, 41–42, 54
Beer, 49, 86, 93, 210, 211
Beer Rinse, 93
Beeswax, 12–13
    deodorants, 132–35
    gifts, 177
    lip gloss, 151, 152, 153
    lotions, 138–39, 140–42, 187–88
    making cosmetics, 6, 9, 10
    manicures, 137
    skin care, 36–37, 38, 41–42, 43, 52, 56, 65, 66, 67, 68, 70–71, 73–74
    source for, 5
Beets, 49, 150, 210
Before-Dinner Face Masks, 60
Bentonite, 52, 54, 120, 122, 123, 169
Benzoin/gum benzoin, 13
    aroma classifications, 163, 164
    baths/showers, 113–14
    combinations with, 164
    deodorants, 132–33, 134–35
    fragrances, 156, 158, 164, 170, 172
    lotions, 139–42, 187–88
    making cosmetics, 10
    mixtures, 177
    shelf-life, 6
    skin care, 36–38, 41–42, 43, 50, 70–71, 73–74
Bergamot, 13
    aroma classification, 162–63, 164
    contrasting or compatible scents, 162–63, 164

deodorants, 131, 132, 133
dusting powders, 186
fragrances, 156, 162–63, 164, 166, 167
manicures, 135
skin care, 29, 47
soaps, 181
Berries, 94, 150, 203
Beta-carotene, 30, 51, 58, 68, 108
Bethel, May, 159
Bicarbonate of soda, 123, 184
Birch/birch bark, 63, 81, 88, 91, 93, 162–63
Bittersweet berries, 88
Black tea
    hair care, 86, 91, 93, 99, 105, 106, 210, 211, 212
    skin care, 49, 69, 74, 75, 210, 211
    sunscreens/sunburns, 143, 212
Blackberry, 54, 85, 91, 93, 210
Blackheads, 42, 50, 60–62
Bladder wrack, 41–42, 123, 127
Blemishes, 50, 53, 60–62, 63
Blond hair, 82, 85, 86, 87, 96, 99, 105–6, 183–84
Blond Hair Dye, 105–6
Body lotions. *See* Hand and body lotions
Body paint, 146
Body scrubs, 116–18, 195
Body wraps, 120
Borage, 28, 34
Borax, 13, 59, 66, 123–24, 177
Boric acid, 134–35, 141–42
    skin care, 36–37, 38, 41–42, 43, 52, 71
Bouncing bet. *See* Soapwort
Boxwood, 13, 88
Bran, 10, 46, 115–16, 117, 209, 211

Brandy, 49, 114, 138, 155, 160
Breedlove, Greta, 195
Brewer's yeast, 39, 46, 54, 117, 211
Briscese, Sidney, 52, 54, 112–13, 118, 123, 189, 193
Broken capillaries, 49
Bromelain, 40
Bronze powder, 103
Brown clay, 52, 55, 58
Brown Eye Shadow, 148
Brunettes. *See* Dark hair
Brushing hair, 83, 96
Buc'Hoz, Pierre-Joseph, 47, 49, 172
Buck, Linda, 123–24, 170, 204
Burdock, 64, 68, 81, 83, 88, 91, 93, 99
Buttermilk, 45, 46, 49, 54, 117, 120, 211

Cabbage, 54, 63, 212
Caffeine, 32
    See also Coffee
Cajeput, 39, 54, 154
Calamus, 127–28, 155, 170
Calcium, 40, 136, 212
Calcium carbonate, 40, 54
Calendula, 13
    baby powders/lotions, 187–88
    growing, 204
    hair care, 83, 87, 88, 99, 100, 103, 105–6, 183–84
    lotions, 140–42, 187–88
    making cosmetics, 10
    shampoo, 183–84
    skin care, 49, 67, 71, 76, 180, 182–83
Calendula Baby Lotion, 187–88
California Avocado Commission, 65, 193
California Avocado Moisturizer, 195

Camphor, 39, 64, 114, 138, 155, 164, 192
Camphor Ice for Rough Skin, 138
Cananga, 184
Cancer, 27, 72, 102, 108, 142
Canola oil, 38, 160, 187–88, 191, 210
Caraway, 13, 73–74, 164
Carnation, 164
Carrot, 13, 50, 54, 59, 94, 210, 211
Cassia ligna, 172
Cassolette, 172
Castile Shampoo, 98
Castile soap, 13
    hair care, 82, 85, 97, 100, 101
    making cosmetics, 10
    manicures, 135
    shampoo, 183–84
    skin disorders, 212
    soaps, 125, 126, 127, 128, 129, 181
Castor oil, 13–14
    hair care, 84
    lip gloss, 150, 151–52, 153
    skin care, 54, 64, 69
    soaps, 126, 127, 181
Catnip, 81, 192
Caviar, 40, 54, 212
Cavitch, Susan, 125
Cayenne pepper, 89, 191–92, 212
Cedar, 81, 88, 93, 163, 164, 171, 172, 186–87
Celandine, 76
Celery, 54, 210
Cellulite, 109–11, 209
Center for Science in the Public Interest, 30
Centuary, 54
Chamomile, 14
    aroma classification of, 162–63
    baby powders, 188
    baths/showers, 122, 209
    contrasting or compatible scents, 162–63

spas, 190, 193, 196
sun, 29
Tal's views about, 107–8
See also Fruits; Vegetables
Dill, 164
Diuretics, 28, 29
Dogberrie, 106
Dogwood, 64
Dominican Scar Remedy, 72
Dr. Zhao Zhangguang's 101 Hair
    Regeneration Liniment, 89–90
Dry Brushing, 118, 192
Dry hair, 79, 80, 82–86, 93, 94, 96,
    97, 99, 210
Dry Hair Shampoo, 85
Dry Shampoo, 101–2, 176
Dry skin, 32–38
    baths/showers, 117, 120
    creams for, 39
    facial cleansers for, 44, 45, 46
    facial masks, 52, 54, 55–57,
        194
    facial steam for, 180
    fluids, 27
    getting clean, 113
    kitchen cures for, 210
    lotions for, 139
    mature skin, 38
    moisturizers for, 33–38, 55–56,
        139, 194
    skin problems and disorders,
        61
    soaps for, 113, 126
    wrinkles, 40
Dull hair, 85–86, 91, 93, 98, 210
Dunning, Judy, 206
Dusting powders, 6, 137, 167–71,
    176, 178, 184–86, 210
Dyes, 102, 104–5

Eastern Mystery Dusting Powder,
    185–86
Echinacea, 38, 64, 203

Eczema, 68–69, 210
Effervescing Bath Powder, 184
Egg, 15
    baths/showers, 116
    hair care, 83, 84, 86, 92, 94–95,
        96, 99, 210, 211
    lotions, 140
    skin care, 41, 51, 54, 57, 62, 194,
        210
    See also Egg white; Eggshells
Egg and Lemon Moisturizer, 57
Egg white
    hair care, 85, 95, 210
    skin care, 40, 44, 54, 56, 60, 75,
        194, 209, 212
Egg White Mask, 56
Eggshells, 59
Elastin, 40
Elder, 15
    hair care, 88, 91, 93, 99, 103
    skin care, 35, 37, 50, 54, 56, 61,
        62, 75, 180–81, 182
    soaps, 127, 181
Emulsions, 8–10
Enfleurage, 159–60
Environmental perfumes, 171–78,
    211
Epsom salts, 112, 121–22, 123
Equipment/supplies, 4–5, 7, 10,
    103, 135, 178, 189
Essential fatty acids, 34, 68
Essential oils
    baths/showers, 112, 113, 115, 116,
        121, 122, 123–24
    cellulite, 110
    deodorants, 131
    fragrances, 154, 156, 157, 160–61,
        164–65, 167, 171, 176
    gifts, 176, 177, 178
    hair care, 81, 88, 93, 98, 102
    lip gloss, 151–52, 153
    lotions, 138
    making cosmetics, 6, 10

Melon, 49, 54, 60, 94, 108, 211
Mignonette, 164
Milk Bath, 115
Milk vetch, 90
Milk/cream, 19
    baths/showers, 45, 111, 113, 115,
       209
    hair care, 86, 92, 96, 101, 211
    manicures/pedicures, 136, 137,
       210
    skin care, 45, 46, 48, 49, 50, 51,
       54, 55, 74, 180–81, 194, 210,
       211
    soaps, 125, 126
    sunburn remedy, 212
    See also Buttermilk; Sour
      milk/cream
Milkweed, 76
Miller, Kathy, 126
Mint, 19
    aroma classifications, 162–63,
      164
    baths/showers, 114, 122, 209
    cellulite, 110, 209
    contrasting or compatible scents,
      162–63, 164
    deodorants, 131
    fragrances, 154, 155, 159
    gathering, 203
    growing, 204, 205, 206
    hair care, 88, 100, 212
    Love Oil, 187
    making cosmetics, 10
    massage, 192
    skin care, 39, 49, 54, 55, 57, 67,
      180–81, 211
    soaps, 127, 129
    spas, 192, 193
Mirbane, 164
Moisturizers
    baths/showers, 113, 115, 117,
      121
    dry hair, 93

lotions, 139
    skin care, 32, 33–38, 60, 113, 194,
      195
    wrinkles, 40
Molasses, 63
Monkshood, 149
Mud, 119–20
Mullein, 86, 88, 93, 102, 103, 105
Musk, 48, 156, 161, 162–63, 164,
      166, 171, 173, 186–87
Mustard, 62, 70
Myrrh, 19, 93, 134
    lotions, 138–39, 141
    skin care, 40, 41, 43, 49, 70–71,
      180

Nail-Strengthening Polish, 137
Narcissus, 164
Nectarine, 53
Neem, 54, 64
Neroli/neroli oil, 19, 47, 163
Nettles, 19, 89, 148
    See also Stinging nettles
Neutrogena, 113
Nut ash, 146
Nutmeg, 51, 114, 121, 155, 164,
      192

Oak bark, 39, 49, 69, 203
Oak moss, 164
Oat flour, in lotions, 187–88
Oats/oatmeal, 19
    baby powders, 188
    baths/showers, 117, 209
    fragrances, 168
    lotions, 140–42, 187–88
    making cosmetics, 10
    skin care, 39, 45, 46, 52, 53, 54,
      59, 60, 75, 180–81, 211
    sun, 73–74, 212
Oils
    hair care, 86
    medicated, 81

skin care, 47
soaps, 127–28

Palm oil, 35–36, 81
Palmarosa, 162–63
Pansy, 49, 54, 149, 192
Papaya, 20, 44, 54, 58, 80, 108, 135,
 143, 210, 211
Papaya Rejuvenating Skin Mask,
 58
Paraffin, 40, 55–56, 65, 66, 67, 68,
 138, 151
Paraffin Mask, 40, 55–56
Parkinson, John, 64
Parsley, 88
Partridge, John, 158
Passionflower, 192
Paste, for skin care, 47
Patchouli, 20
 aroma classifications, 163,
 164
 baths/showers, 122
 contrasting or compatible scents,
 161, 162–63, 164
 deodorants, 131, 132–33,
 134–35
 dusting powders, 185–86
 fragrances, 161, 164, 167, 171
 hair care, 81, 82, 83, 91, 93, 99
 lip gloss, 152, 153
 lotions, 141
 skin care, 39, 53, 54,
 73–74
 soaps, 126, 128
Peach, 20, 54, 60, 164, 210, 211
Peanut oil, 28, 34, 54
Pear, 164
Pedicures, 137, 147, 190
Pekoe tea, 211, 212
Pepper, cayenne, 89, 191–92, 212
Peppermint, 19, 204
 See also Mint
A Perfume for a Chamber, 158

Perfumes, 2–3, 5, 165–67, 176, 212
 environmental, 171–78, 211
 See also Fragrances
Permanents, 79, 83, 87, 96, 97, 103
Peroxide, 135
Petroleum jelly, 20, 34, 35–36, 103,
 135, 138
Piesse, George William Septimus,
 50, 103, 113, 138, 150, 153, 154,
 155, 161, 164, 165, 166, 173, 186
Pimento, 164
Pimple Cream, 64
Pimples, 42, 61, 62–64, 212
Pine, 39, 54, 167, 168
Pineapple, 20, 40, 44, 49, 54, 57,
 135, 164, 209, 210, 211
Pinks, 164
Pistachios, 47
Plantain, 20–21, 64, 83, 86, 93,
 203
Platt, Hugh, 63, 106, 121, 140, 170
Poppy seeds, 59
Potato, 54, 60, 74, 76, 94, 210, 211,
 212
Pouliot, Linda, 67, 76
Powdered glass, 103
Powders
 baby, 178, 188
 dusting, 6, 137, 167–71, 176, 178,
 184–86, 210
 face, 6
 hair, 103
 shelf-life, 6
Premature aging, 27, 29, 34, 37–38,
 72, 109, 142
Preservatives, 147
Primrose, 28, 34, 64, 68
Privet, 102
Propolis, 39
Protein Conditioning Shampoo, 101
Protein Nail Treatment, 136
Psoralea, 90
Psoriasis, 69–71, 80, 87

massage oil, 109, 191–92
   skin care, 38, 42–43, 54
Rosemary Cologne, 159
Rosewood, 93, 162–63, 164, 171
Rue, 155, 164
Rum, 90, 95
Rutledge, Deborah, 50, 64

Sachets, 172–73, 176
Safflower/safflower oil
   deodorants, 132–35
   fragrances, 160
   hair care, 90
   lip gloss, 153
   lotions, 139–40, 141–42,
     187–88
   making cosmetics, 6
   massage, 191
   skin care, 67–68
Saffron, 103
Sage, 21
   aroma classifications, 162–63,
     164
   baths/showers, 114, 120, 209
   contrasting or compatible scents,
     162–63
   deodorants, 131, 132–33
   fragrances, 155
   hair care, 81, 86, 87, 88, 91, 93,
     103, 105, 211, 212
   skin care, 39, 53, 54, 61, 65, 67,
     74
   soaps, 126
Sage Soap for Oily Skin, 126
Sagging skin, 38, 65
St. John's wort, 29, 103, 192, 203
Salad oil, 103, 138
Salicyclic acid, 39
Salt, 10
   baths/showers, 117, 118–19, 120,
     121, 124, 209
   as enemy of beauty, 109
   hair care, 79, 83, 88, 104

   skin care, 63, 75, 118–19, 189,
     192, 209, 211, 212
   spas, 189
   sunscreens/sunburns, 143
Salt Glow, 118–19
Salvia, 90
Sanchez, Martha, 85, 94, 137
Sandalwood, 21
   aroma classifications, 163,
     164
   baths/showers, 122
   contrasting or compatible scents,
     161, 162–63, 164
   dusting powders, 185–86
   fragrances, 161, 162–63, 164, 171
   hair care, 83, 93, 98–99, 100
   skin care, 51, 64
   soaps, 128
Santa Barbara's Dry Skin Mask,
   194
Santa Monica's Oily Skin Mask,
   194
Sarsaparilla, 64
Sassafras, 172
Savory, 172
Scars/scarring, 2, 34, 61, 72, 146,
   147, 212
Scented oils, 159–65
Sea Breeze Therapeutic Bath Salts,
   123, 195
Sea salt, 118–19, 122, 123, 124
Seashell Paste, 48
Seaweed, 21
   baths/showers, 117, 123, 195, 209
   cellulite, 111
   gathering, 203
   hair care, 88, 91, 93
   skin care, 40, 41–42, 54, 211,
    212
   soaps, 127
   See also Kelp
Seaweed Soap, 127
Seeds, 200

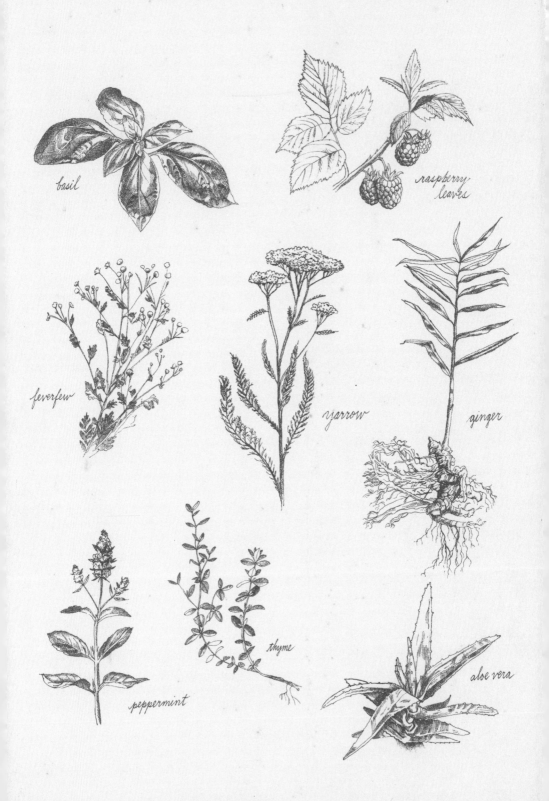

basil

raspberry
leaves

feverfew

yarrow

ginger

peppermint

thyme

aloe vera